WITTGENSTEIN, FRAZER AND RELIGION

Wittgenstein, Frazer and Religion

Brian R. Clack
Tutor in Philosophy
St Clare's International College
Oxford

Published by
PALGRAVE
Houndmills, Basingstoke, Hampshire RG21 6XS and
175 Fifth Avenue, New York, N. Y. 10010
Companies and representatives throughout the world

PALGRAVE is the new global academic imprint of
St. Martin's Press LLC Scholarly and Reference Division and
Palgrave Publishers Ltd (formerly Macmillan Press Ltd).

Outside North America
ISBN 0–333–68240–8

Inside North America
ISBN 0–312–21642–4

This book is printed on paper suitable for recycling and made from fully managed and sustained forest sources.

A catalogue record for this book is available from the British Library.

Library of Congress Cataloging-in-Publication Data
Clack, Brian R.
Wittgenstein, Frazer, and religion / Brian R. Clack
p. cm
Includes bibliographical references and index.
ISBN 0–312–21642–4
1. Wittgenstein, Ludwig, 1889–1951—Religion. 2. Frazer, James George, Sir, 1854–1941. Golden bough. 3. Wittgenstein, Ludwig, 1889–1951. Bemerkugen über Frazers Golden bough. 4. Magic. 5. Religion. 6. Mythology. 7. Superstition. I. Title
B3376.W564C57   1998
200'.92—dc21   98–21471
                                                              CIP

10   9   8   7   6   5   4   3   2
09   08   07   06   05   04   03   02   01

Printed and bound in Great Britain by
Antony Rowe Ltd, Chippenham, Wiltshire

For Celia

Contents

Preface

This book is born out of the conviction both that Wittgenstein's writing on magic has been sadly neglected by philosophers of religion, and that, even where it is discussed, the conclusions drawn about his views are not faithful to what he has written. *Wittgenstein, Frazer and Religion* is my attempt to correct this neglect and these misunderstandings.

Some of the material included in this book has previously appeared in article form. A version of Chapter 3 was first published as 'Wittgenstein and Expressive Theories of Religion' in *International Journal for Philosophy of Religion* (vol. 40 no.1, pp. 47–61), and this is reproduced with kind permission from Kluwer Academic Publishers. Again, elements of Chapter 7 first appeared as 'D. Z. Phillips, Wittgenstein and Religion' in *Religious Studies* (vol. 31 no. 1, pp. 111–20), and I am grateful to the editors and to Cambridge University Press for granting me permission to reproduce that material here.

I have quoted from three published versions of Wittgenstein's *Remarks on Frazer's Golden Bough*: the original German text (published in *Synthese* in 1967); the A. C. Miles translation (published originally in *The Human World* in 1971, and subsequently by the Brynmill Press in 1979); and John Beversluis' translation (published in *Wittgenstein: Sources and Perspectives* (Harvester Press, 1979)). References to these, as to all other works, are within the text, citing author's name and date of edition used. This information is amplified in the bibliography. Notes can be found at the end of the book.

At numerous places in this book, reference is made to Paul Ernst's 'Nachwort' to his 1910 edition of Grimm's *Kinder-und Hausnärchen*. Ernst's essay influenced Wittgenstein greatly, yet it is notoriously inaccessible. (Hence Rush Rhees' remark in the introduction to the first English translation of the *Remarks on Frazer*: 'I have not found a copy of that preface or that edition of the

Märchen'.) Forunately, I managed to track down a copy of Ernst's essay, the significance of which is attested to in the pages of this book. All quotations from this essay are from the translation which was expertly prepared for me by Dr Vanessa Davies of King's College, London. Page references refer to the original German edition. I would like to acknowledge my great debt to Vanessa for her patient work in preparing the translation and for her many interesting reflections on Ernst's argument. In this connection I would also like to thank Dr Peter Hacker, Mr Igor Kuusik and Mr Brian McGuinness for their helpful contributions.

Of those who read or commented on various parts of this book, I would like to thank Dr Beverley Clack, Dr Grace Jantzen, Dr Felicity McCutcheon and Professor Drago Ocvirk, while Professor Paul Helm and Fergus Kerr OP made invaluable comments during their examination of the PhD thesis on which this book is based. Special thanks go to Professor Frank Cioffi for his countless enlightening remarks and encouragement, and, particularly, to Mr Peter Byrne, who supervised the research which ultimately became this book. I owe Peter an enormous debt for his patience, his characteristically astute criticisms, and his friendship. My interest in the subject was sustained by teaching courses on Wittgenstein at Heythrop College London, Westminster College Oxford, and St Clare's Oxford. Thanks go to the following students both for their willingness to discuss at length Wittgenstein's thoughts on magic, and for the subsequent much-cherished gift of their friendship: Jonathan Herapath, Patrycja Kaszynska, Carol Lewis, Sam Norton, Helen O'Sullivan and Ciran Stapleton. For their precious moral support I would like to thank my parents, Alan and Ann Clack, my grandfather Ron Denman, my great-aunt Win Moxham, and many friends, in particular, Phil Baston, Felix and Emma Clayton, Leonardo Dasso, Steve Eyre, Claire Fitzpatrick, Helen Gresty, Robert Lindsey, Michael Mosley, David Parry, Bryan and Margaret Stringer, Pete Thompson, Ed White and Rainy Whiting. Highest thanks to Adam Clayton for being a port in a heavy storm. Finally, for her support, advice, criticisms and much else, more than gratitude is due to Celia, to whom this book is dedicated.

B.R.C.
Oxford

Introduction

1

Wittgenstein, Frazer and Religion

1.1 WITTGENSTEIN AND RELIGION

It is now almost platitudinous to state that there is a profound religious dimension to the work of Ludwig Wittgenstein. Nevertheless, this attribution of a religious quality may seem bizarre when one is confronted with his two masterpieces – *Tractatus Logico-Philosophicus* and *Philosophical Investigations* – which seem to have little application to life, let alone to affairs of the spirit. Yet Wittgenstein's work became associated with religion when sympathetic philosophers applied his notions of 'language-games' and 'forms of life' to religious belief and practice. Closer attention to Wittgenstein's philosophy (and how he perceived it) then revealed that much of his writing was conditioned by religious considerations. For instance, his correspondence with Paul Engelmann and Ludwig von Ficker regarding the contents of the *Tractatus* reveal his conviction that 'the point of the book is ethical' (Wittgenstein 1979a: 94). And there is good reason to think that he regarded his other works as such: for example, the foreword to the *Philosophical Remarks* states 'This book is written to the glory of God' (Wittgenstein 1975: 7).

In his major works, the absence of any sustained treatment of religious questions may be due to his desire to 'cut out the transcendental twaddle' (Engelmann 1968: 11) and remain silent about such matters. In his notebooks and in some lectures, however, Wittgenstein broke this silence and spoke lucidly. For example, in the 'Lectures on Religious Belief' he considers at length fundamental features of Christianity, such as the Last Judgement, the historical basis of the faith, the logic of the word 'God', along with some aspects of spiritualism. Moreover, in the collection of remarks published as *Culture and Value* one finds a number of remarkable (and indeed surprising) comments which centre on beliefs of the Christian religion. Here, he makes comments on the Gospels, on what he perceives to be the 'hierarchical' and unappealing nature of Paul's Epistles, and on such Christian writers as Barth, Bunyan, St John of the Cross and, perhaps most tellingly, Kierkegaard. In addition, there is more than one passage exhibiting the flavour of something like a confession of faith. One of the most remarkable is the following:

> What inclines even me to believe in Christ's Resurrection? It is as though I play with the thought. – If he did not rise from the dead, then he is decomposed in the grave like any other man. *He is dead and decomposed.* In that case he is a teacher like any other and can no longer *help*; and once more we are orphaned and alone. So we have to content ourselves with wisdom and speculation. We are in a sort of hell where we can do nothing but dream, roofed in, as it were, and cut off from heaven. But if I am to be REALLY saved, – what I need is *certainty* – not wisdom, dreams or speculation – and this certainty is faith. And faith is faith in what is needed by my *heart*, my *soul*, not my speculative intelligence. For it is my soul with its passions, as it were with its flesh and blood, that has to be saved, not my abstract mind. Perhaps we can say: Only *love* can believe the Resurrection. (Wittgenstein 1980a: 33)

With such a remark, one can easily move from the idea that Wittgenstein was interested in religious matters to the more contentious claim that he was a Christian, concerned with the salvation of his soul.

Whether or not this was the case has been the subject of much speculation. Many examples spring to mind, one of which is Dallas High's biographical article in which he maintains that 'theistic faith' was the centre of Wittgenstein's values, and that this faith was 'thoroughly Judaic, invoking the God of Abraham, Isaac, and Jacob' (High 1990: 111). Wilhelm Baum pursues a similar line, contending that Wittgenstein's religious life was of the 'twice-born' type, as documented by William James in *The Varieties of Religious Experience*. Accordingly, Baum sees Wittgenstein's life as exhibiting features reminiscent of other 'twice-born' personalities, such as Tolstoy and Augustine, and he maintains that Wittgenstein decided to become a primary school teacher because 'he believed that this ... gave him the opportunity to teach children the Word of Jesus' (Baum 1980: 67). In such a manner it is contended that 'for the whole of his life he would be engaging in an imitation of Christ' (Baum 1980: 68).

The discovery that Wittgenstein was not an atheistic positivist of the Vienna Circle variety, but rather had a profound religious – and apparently Christian – sensibility has not failed to impress itself on the minds of those taking it upon themselves to write about the aspects of his philosophy which impinge upon religion. The upshot of this is that Wittgenstein's thought is often treated as though it were simply an addendum to, or at the very least in the tradition of, Christian theology. The most remarkable of these treatments is that provided by Cyril Barrett.

In *Wittgenstein on Ethics and Religious Belief*, Barrett wants to maintain that 'however unorthodox Wittgenstein's views may seem, they are firmly rooted in a traditional theology and philosophy of religion' (Barrett 1991: vii). Throughout the work, Barrett constantly compares Wittgenstein's musings with those of Anselm, Aquinas, Duns Scotus and William of Ockham, to name but a few, with the explicitly stated intention of showing how his ideas 'can be reconciled with Christian doctrine' (Barrett 1991: 95). Indeed, it is the problems of Christianity *alone* which occupy Barrett, and he often appears to equate the religion of the Bible with religion *per se*. The following remark exemplifies this rather narrow approach:

> Assent to religious beliefs is an ascent or an elevation rather than the result of an upward climb. The driving force that impels this upward thrust is love of Christ and trust in his redemptive power. (Barrett 1991: 181)

An exploration of what Wittgenstein says about the Christian religion and about the person of Jesus is certainly warranted. Some words of reproach, however, are needed if it is being contended that Wittgenstein's thoughts on religion *only* extend this far, or are important only inasmuch as they do. For this really does appear to be Barrett's position. As soon as Wittgenstein's attention turns from theistic concerns to primal ones, Barrett shies away.

Now it is certainly not to be denied that Wittgenstein treats at length certain features of Christianity and aspects of the thought of central figures standing in that tradition. There is, however, a not insignificant set of notes which constitute perhaps his most incisive thoughts on religion. These notes are his *Remarks on Frazer's Golden Bough* and they deal, not with the beliefs of Christians, but with the ritual practices of primitive peoples the world over. These reflections on magic and primitive religion stand in stark contrast to the portrait Barrett paints of an unorthodox yet traditional Christian believer. In these remarks, Wittgenstein speaks of the profundity of magical practices, of the impressive character of a barbarous priest-king as opposed to the 'stupidity and feebleness' of a Christian parson (Wittgenstein 1979b: 5), and he writes – writes as though captivated – about details of human sacrifice. Little wonder then that Barrett is so evidently uneasy in his treatment of these remarks. He refuses to discuss the set of remarks on the Beltane fire-festival (cf. Barrett 1991: 268 n.4), and even maintains that Wittgenstein is wanting to say that such primal religions are inferior to theism (Barrett 1991: 258). Barrett's (often selective) reading of Wittgenstein's thought on religion thus seems to be informed by his desire to 'Christianize' him, and it is this which leads to the *Remarks on Frazer* being given such scant treatment in Barrett's lengthy work.[1]

Barrett's interpretation is no isolated instance, and the very preponderance of Christian readings of Wittgenstein requires some sort of corrective. A sustained examination of the *Remarks on Frazer* can be seen as just such a corrective, counterbalancing the rather parochial tendencies of Wittgenstein's theological commentators. Such an examination can illustrate that Wittgenstein's contribution to the philosophical study of religion extends far beyond the fideistic apologetics so habitually attributed to him. This book will thus expound and analyse the insights contained in that most neglected of Wittgenstein's works, and we will begin in this chapter by looking at the most conspicuous features of the *Remarks*. First, however, it is necessary to understand what Wittgenstein was writing against, and this requires us to examine some elements of the work of a man described by T. S. Eliot as 'the master'. Hence, let us take a glance at Sir James George Frazer and his *chef-d'oeuvre*: *The Golden Bough*.

1.2 THE GOLDEN BOUGH

James Frazer was one of the principal anthropologists of the Victorian era. Of his many works, *The Golden Bough* is the one for which he is most famous. This breathtaking piece of scholarship first appeared in 1890 in two fat volumes. It had swollen to three volumes by the time of the second edition of 1900, and ultimately to a massive thirteen by 1936.[2] An abridged edition appeared in 1922. It is a work which transcends the bounds of anthropology and has helped to shape the cultural climate of the twentieth century, profoundly affecting the work of such writers as W. B. Yeats, D. H. Lawrence and J. M. Synge. While it is generally acknowledged that Frazer's influence within the discipline of anthropology is now minimal, *The Golden Bough* still casts impressive shadows over the arts (witness its impact on Jim Morrison). This artistic influence is due partly to the sheer mass of bizarre and often shocking rituals described within its covers, but also to the evocative style of Frazer's writing and to the dramatic nature of his theme.

The primary aim of *The Golden Bough* is to explain a peculiar ritual of classical antiquity, that of the rule which regulated the succession to the priesthood of Diana at Aricia. The scene of this succession is majestically described, Frazer painting a picture of the allure and tranquillity of the woodland lake of Nemi in the Alban Hills, before moving darkly into an account of the 'strange and recurring tragedy' which occurred there. Guarding an oak tree in the sacred grove of Diana of the Wood, there prowled the grim, sword-carrying figure of a murderous priest-king, warily looking about for an expected assailant who would sooner or later murder him and take up the priesthood himself. 'Such was the rule of the sanctuary. A candidate for the priesthood could only succeed to office by slaying the priest, and having slain him, he retained office till he was himself slain by a stronger or a craftier' (Frazer 1922: 1). Frazer's desire is to explain why the priesthood had this brutal rule of succession, but noting that it has no parallel in classical antiquity, he employs 'the comparative method', casting his net far and wide in order to find practices comparable to the Nemi rite. The purpose of this exercise is explained thus:

> Recent researches into the early history of man have revealed the essential similarity with which, under many superficial differences, the human mind has elaborated its first crude philosophy of life. Accordingly, if we can show that a barbarous custom, like that of the priesthood of Nemi, has existed elsewhere; if we can detect the motives which led to its institution; if we can prove that these motives have operated widely, perhaps universally, in

human society, producing in varied circumstances a variety of institutions specifically different but generically alike; if we can show, lastly, that these very motives ... were actually at work in classical antiquity; then we may fairly infer that at a remoter age the same motives gave birth to the priesthood of Nemi. (Frazer 1922: 2)

Hence, Frazer embarks upon a survey of a broad range of magical and religious practices the world over, particularly as they bear upon the subject of the ritual murder of priests, kings, pretenders to divinity, and other individuals. These researches enable Frazer to formulate a multifaceted explanation of the rule at Nemi. *Rex Nemorensis* – the priestly King of the Wood at Nemi – was believed to be a divine king, an embodiment of the oak-god Jupiter, and in him dwelt the spirit of the tree which he so attentively guarded. The motive for slaying the divine king is traced by Frazer to a belief that the gods are mortal. If a man-god, such as *Rex Nemorensis*, should become diseased or aged, then the primitive fears that the god who inheres in him will suffer a corresponding decay, thus imperiling the general course of nature. So the king must be killed in his prime, and the god's spirit transferred to his successor. The death of the king may also have been combined with a custom of driving out evils, transferring the sins of the community to one individual who would take those sins away to the world beyond the grave. So, in the course of *The Golden Bough*, Frazer establishes the status of *Rex Nemorensis* as both man-god and scapegoat, explaining thus the reasons for his violent death, while at the same time implicitly elaborating a scandalous interpretation of the basis of Christianity.[3]

Frazer (1936j: vi) describes the King of the Wood as 'the nominal hero' of *The Golden Bough*, preferring to let the reputation of his book rest, not on his explanation of Nemi, but on the broader sweep of his reflections on magic and religion. These reflections are placed in an evolutionary schema which Frazer adopted from such thinkers as Turgot, Condorcet and Comte. The last of these had propounded a three-stage philosophy of history, whereby the human mind was seen to have progressed through the phases of theology and metaphysics to the triumphant scientific (or 'positive') stage. Likewise, Frazer posits a universal threefold progression of the human mind from systems of thought which are magical, to those which are religious, and finally to the scientific stage which the West has reached. Progressive and optimistic to the core, Frazer sees the history of culture as the story of humankind's scientific liberation from superstitious ignorance. Frazer holds, then, that the earliest of humankind's philosophies of life is *magic*. The practice of magic is, he contends, grounded in a theoretical framework – a system of natural law. He traces the principles on which this system is based to the three kinds of association of ideas isolated by David Hume, '*viz.* RESEMBLANCE, CONTIGUITY in time or place, and CAUSE and EFFECT' (Hume 1987: 58). Magical thought neglects the third variety, and instead employs the other two:

> If we analyse the principles of thought on which magic is based, they will probably be found to resolve themselves into two: first, that like produces like, or that an effect resembles its cause; and, second, that things which have once been in contact with each other continue to act on each other at a distance after the physical contact has been severed. The former principle may be called the Law of Similarity, the latter the Law of Contact or Contagion. (Frazer 1922: 11)

Features of these theoretical laws can be illustrated by noting their application in practical magic. The Law of Similarity gives rise to Homoeopathic or Imitative Magic. On the principles of homoeopathic magic, a magician wishing to harm his enemy may fashion a small model of that person and then proceed to damage that model by running a needle through it, or by burning it, or by breaking it into pieces. Because 'like produces like', destroying the image will have the same effect as destroying the real man; the needle pushed into the head of the effigy will produce a corresponding pain in the man represented by the effigy. In a like fashion, the Law of Contagion underlies Contagious Magic. Here, the magician wishing to harm his enemy will gather together the nail pairings, hair, spittle or clothing of that person, and set about burning them, believing that they maintain a sympathetic relation to the man with whom they were once in contact.

In both of these examples, the total futility of magic is demonstrated: no amount of effigy-burning can produce the desired result of the enemy's death. Savages fail to recognize that the only way in which to achieve the ends they desire is to employ the law of cause and effect, namely that form of the association of ideas which they neglect. As it stands, then, the logical basis of magic 'is a *mistaken* association of ideas' (Frazer 1922: 37–8, emphasis added). Note that Frazer does not hold magic irrational, for 'its fundamental conception is identical with that of modern science; underlying the whole system is a faith, implicit but real and firm, in the order and uniformity of nature' (Frazer 1922: 49). For the magician as for the scientist, there is an unerring and regular system of laws of nature which can be understood and subsequently used to one's advantage. The defect of magic must therefore be located in something other than irrationality:

> The fatal flaw of magic lies not in its general assumption of a sequence of events determined by law, but in its total misconception of the nature of the particular laws which govern that sequence. (Frazer 1922: 49)

This is due to an illegitimate application of the association of ideas:

> Legitimately applied they yield science; illegitimately applied they yield magic, the bastard sister of science. It is therefore a truism, almost a tautology, to say that all magic is necessarily false and barren; for were it ever to become true and fruitful, it would no longer be magic but science. (Frazer 1922: 49–50)

Here we come up against one of the distinctive features of Frazer's theory: that magic is *defined* in terms of error.

That magic is not more speedily discarded is put down to the existence of certain 'blocks to falsifiability' within the system. So, for example, a rain-making ceremony may appear successful just because rain does tend quite naturally to fall anyway, and the unavoidable death of a man can always be attributed to a previous spell. Nevertheless, despite such blocks, it is inevitable that the inherent futility of magic is eventually discovered by those sagacious enough to perceive that their cherished incantations and rites do not achieve their desired results, and that man does not have the ability to manipulate at pleasure those natural forces previously considered to be within his control. Frazer stresses that what results from this is not just a change of theory, but a change of *attitude*, involving the abandonment of hubris; a confession of human weakness, which R. R. Marett would later describe as 'the birth of humility' (Marett 1914: 169). In this act of humility, savages give up their claim to power and instead bow down to powerful spirits and gods who, it is believed, control the course of nature: religion is born. This successor to magic must suffer the same fate when it, too, is recognized to be wanting. Writing to Baldwin Spencer in 1898, Frazer summarizes neatly the drift from magic through to the eventual victor, science:

> I am coming more and more to the conclusion that if we define religion as the propitiation of natural and supernatural powers, and magic as the coercion of them, magic has everywhere preceded religion. It is only when men find by experience that they cannot *compel* the higher powers to comply with their wishes, that they condescend to *entreat* them. In time, after long ages, they begin to realize that entreaty is also vain, and then they try compulsion again; but this time the compulsion is applied within narrower limits and in a different way from the old magical method. In short, religion is displaced by science. (Frazer to Spencer, quoted in Ackermann 1990: 157)[4]

In this passage the central tenet of Frazer's account is clear: both magic and religion are elementary and erroneous theories of the nature of the universe, pathfinders for science.

Frazer's approach is nothing idiosyncratic, for the contention that magical and religious beliefs are in the nature of explanatory hypotheses marks his theory off as a species of *intellectualism*. A dominant strand of anthropological thinking about religion, intellectualism contends that magic and religion arise and function as explanations of the world and of natural phenomena. What is essential about religion is its theoretical foundation; ritual actions are therefore secondary, and are practical applications of theory. The function of ritual is instrumental, focused on the achieving of concrete, empirical ends. All of these factors are present within *The Golden Bough*: ritual practices (such as the rule at Nemi) are to be understood by uncovering the underlying motives and beliefs of the ritualists; the motive of any ritual is generally seen to be the achievement of a desired end; and the underlying beliefs are fundamentally theoretical, the speculations of primitive men characterized as rudimentary philosophers. And all of these intellectualist themes are combined with the characteristically Frazerian contention that magical and religious beliefs are in the nature of vulgar errors.

1.3 WITTGENSTEIN AND *THE GOLDEN BOUGH*

The intellectual confrontation which takes place in Wittgenstein's notes on *The Golden Bough* is remarkable. Wittgenstein and Frazer were, contemporaneously, Fellows of Trinity College, Cambridge, although there is no evidence to suggest that they ever met.[5] This (accidental) link is, however, as far as any likeness can be pressed. The two men held radically divergent views about the nature of religion, and their overall world-views differed profoundly, the Scots anthropologist's confidence in the march of human progress contrasting sharply with the cultural pessimism of the Austrian philosopher. And it is this latter difference, as much as any other factor, which causes the antagonism so evident in the *Remarks on Frazer*.

M. O'C. Drury (1984: 119) relates that it was in 1931 that Wittgenstein first expressed his desire to read *The Golden Bough*. Drury borrowed from the Cambridge Union library the first volume of the full edition and read it aloud to Wittgenstein for some weeks. This first volume is entitled *The Magic Art and the Evolution of Kings* and treats of the character of the rule at Nemi, the principles of magic, the magical control of the weather, and the idea of incarnate human gods. Wittgenstein was sufficiently stimulated by his reading of *The Golden Bough* to write a set of notes on what he saw as the weaknesses of Frazer's theory. These notes appear in a manuscript, catalogued by G. H. von Wright as MS 110, entitled '*Philosophische Bemerkungen*', and were composed in June and July 1931. Although the composition of this set of notes ceased in 1931, this was only a temporary break, for in 1936 Raymond Townsend gave Wittgenstein a copy of the abridged edition, and this once again prompted thought and composition. This second set of notes appears as MS 143, and is described as: 'Notes on Frazer's *The Golden Bough*. Loose sheets of varying size. 1936 or later' (Wright 1982a: 45). Rhees suggests that they were written 'probably after 1948' (Rhees 1979: vi). The content of this later set is concerned almost exclusively with Frazer's account of the fire-festivals of Europe, particularly the Beltane festival in Scotland.

Wittgenstein's reaction to the argument of *The Golden Bough* is one of disapproval, and he is of the opinion that Frazer has misrepresented the character of magical practices in his desire to show them to be erroneous:

Frazer's account of the magical and religious notions of men is unsatisfactory: it makes these notions appear as *mistakes*.

Was Augustine mistaken, then, when he called on God on every page of the *Confessions?*

Well – one might say – if he was not mistaken, then the Buddhist holy-man, or some other, whose religion expresses quite different notions, surely was. But *none* of them was making a mistake except where he was putting forward a theory. (Wittgenstein 1979b: 1)

When we survey the content of these notes we can detect a three-fold criticism of Frazer. Wittgenstein appears to attacking Frazer in the following areas:

(i) as a scholar and a thinker;
(ii) as a representative of his age; and
(iii) as a proponent of a false theory of magic and religion, namely intellectualism, and an inadequate historical-genetic method of understanding and explaining such customs as the Beltane festival.

To take the first of these, a great deal of Wittgenstein's ire is directed against Frazer as a thinker and as an unspiritual individual, who misinterprets the nature of – indeed, fails to grasp the *significance* of – magical rites in his attempt to make such practices 'plausible to people who think as he does' (Wittgenstein 1979b: 1). The attitude taken is certainly one of derision:

What narrowness of spiritual life we find in Frazer! And as a result: how impossible for him to understand a different way of life from the English one of his time!

Frazer cannot imagine a priest who is not basically an English parson of our times with all his stupidity and feebleness. (Wittgenstein 1979b: 5)

Wittgenstein notes an irony in Frazer's treatment of magic:

Frazer is much more savage than most of his savages, for these savages will not be so far from any understanding of spiritual matters as an Englishman of the twentieth century. His explanations of the primitive observances are much cruder than the sense of the observances themselves. (Wittgenstein 1979b: 8)

It is by no means obvious that these criticisms of Frazer are justified. The principal charge is that Frazer fails to understand the nature of ritual because he lacks poetic imagination and is closed to the life of the spirit. This is not altogether correct. If we allow Frazer to speak for himself, we can certainly detect in his words a level of romantic imagination and, indeed, an implied criticism of over-rationalistic approaches to myth and ritual. For example, in *Folk-lore in the Old Testament* we read:

> The folk-lore of scents has yet to be studied. In investigating it, as every other branch of folk-lore, the student may learn much from the poets, who perceive by intuition what most of us have to learn by a laborious collection of facts. Indeed, without some touch of poetic fancy, it is hardly possible to enter into the heart of the people. A frigid rationalist will knock in vain at the rose-wreathed portal of fairyland. The porter will not open to Mr. Gradgrind. (Frazer 1923: 291)

Frazer can indeed be seen as something of a romantic poet himself, and this would in part explain his great influence on creative artists.

So Wittgenstein's attack on Frazer's lack of imagination and spirituality may not be wholly sound, but nor is it of any abiding interest. Frazer is now habitually ridiculed: Mary Douglas (1978: 152) has noted that he is attacked as a thinker, a theorist and a stylist; and even his biographer begins his account by saying that Frazer is 'an embarrassment' (Ackerman 1990: 1). So Wittgenstein's critique will be of little significance if it simply reinforces what are now standard (and somewhat ungracious) criticisms. Moreover, Frazer's more recent critics have taken him to task for more professionally serious matters than simply a blindness to the life of the spirit. Take just two examples. Firstly, Sir Edmund Leach, in a damning article in which he claims that Frazer's early success was due to the fact that he 'was well in on the Establishment' (Leach 1961: 372), contends that the author of *The Golden Bough* 'was not an accurate scholar or an original thinker' (Leach 1961: 377). Using illustrative examples, Leach shows how Frazer, in taking his information about primitive rituals from missionaries and other writers, amended it, twisting the evidence to suit his own theories.

Jonathan Z. Smith also has shattering words to say about Frazer's enterprise. Among other criticisms, notably that the title of the book is a misnomer, having no connection with the golden bough of Virgil's *Aeneid*, he contends that the description of the King of the Wood is simply 'a masterful example of Victorian purple prose', more than half of which is 'derived entirely from Frazer's fancy' (Smith 1973: 347–8). There is no 'textual or historical warrant' (1973: 348) for the questions which Frazer sets himself or the answers which he provides. So one cannot maintain (as Wittgensteinians often do) that the most direct criticisms of Frazer in the *Remarks* are exceptional. If anything, they are now rather ordinary.

Reflect on another feature of Wittgenstein's personal critique: the claim that Frazer is radically ethnocentric and by virtue of his Englishness incapable of understanding ritual. Once again, one should not be stunned or overly impressed by this, for it too is a commonplace. Anthropologists frequently criticize their Victorian counterparts for possessing a patronizing attitude towards the peoples they studied and having an overly optimistic view of their own status in the scheme of things. Leach remarks:

All anthropologists operated within a schematic framework which placed themselves, as representatives of White, European, usually Protestant, culture, at the summit of a mountain called Civilisation, while the rest of mankind, in varying degrees of moral and intellectual inferiority wandered as barbarians in the forests far below. (Leach 1985: 221)

Consequently, then, what is of abiding interest in the *Remarks* cannot simply be the personal attack on Frazer, as it is by no means clear that this assault is not wholly hackneyed and even unfounded. However, the question of ethnocentricity *does* raise another aspect of Wittgenstein's analysis, for, as the quotation from Leach indicates, the attitude taken by Frazer is not idiosyncratic, but part of the far wider intellectual climate in which he worked. As such, this leads into the second, and far more interesting, dimension of the critical element of the *Remarks*: that Frazer is being criticized as a representative of the culture of which he is a part.

For Wittgenstein, it is unsurprising that Frazer should have misconstrued the nature of magic and religion for he proudly represents features of our age: optimistic, forward-looking, confident in the progress of science and, Wittgenstein says, *petty*.

Consequently, Frazer's verdict on a different culture and a different age is predictable, for 'one age misunderstands another; and a *petty* age misunderstands all the others in its own nasty way' (Wittgenstein 1980a: 86). The charge that Frazer is superficial in his treatment of magic can thus be seen as a swipe at a whole series of thinkers reflecting the dominant concerns of our civilization and who are characterized by Wittgenstein as 'shallow' thinkers.[6] Some illumination can be thrown upon the nature of Wittgenstein's attack on Frazer's superficiality by seeing this criticism as emerging from his struggle with specifically Viennese problems, 'not least of which was the tendency to distort the beautiful and trivialize the profound' (Janik 1979: 162). Hence, Wittgenstein, sensing the profundity of magic, was appalled by Frazer's characterization of it as a farrago, as 'false physics' (Wittgenstein 1979b: 7). The source of Frazer's error is thus attributed to his obsession with *science*. When Frazer makes magical practices plausible 'to people who think as he does', these acts are presented as a form of proto-science (and thus *mis*represented). Frazer seems to see every human endeavour as scientific in character, and to divide everything into either 'good science' or 'bad science' (magic). Such a trait is characteristic of our age, in which science – near-divinized – flourishes and in terms of which everything is interpreted and evaluated. That Wittgenstein laments the dawn of this ubiquitous scientific understanding can be seen in his remarks on Renan's view that it was natural phenomena which were the cause of religious belief, primitive man misunderstanding the nature of these forces. Although rejecting this view (a theory described in the Remarks as 'the stupid superstition of our time' (Wittgenstein 1979b: 6)), Wittgenstein does, however, concede that natural phenomena *are* a cause of wonder. Indeed, he states that it is primitive *not* to feel awe over these things: 'Man has to awaken to wonder – and so perhaps do peoples. Science is a way of sending him to sleep again' (Wittgenstein 1980a: 5). The scientific mind is thus seen as the primitive, dehumanizing one, and hence Frazer is not the only 'civilized savage': in this attack, Wittgenstein appears to betoken *all* thinkers exhibiting the same kind of scientific pretensions typical of 'the darkness of this time' (Wittgenstein 1958: vii). As will be demonstrated in the final chapter, it is this hatred for the present age which constitutes the unifying theme of the *Remarks on Frazer's Golden Bough*. Though Wittgenstein's notes are certainly an important contribution to debates in the philosophy of religion, it is as a critique of a particular phase of our culture's development that the *Remarks* gain their ultimate significance.

It is, however, the third area of Wittgenstein's critique which has received most attention. When addressing the *theories* of *The Golden Bough*, Wittgenstein attacks Frazer's most basic contentions: that magic is essentially erroneous; that it has a proto-scientific character; and that therefore magical and religious beliefs arise and function as (mistaken) hypotheses. Wittgenstein is also critical of Frazer's intention to *explain* ritual actions, an intention which, perhaps bizarrely, Wittgenstein says is illegitimate ('the attempt to find an explanation is wrong'). Frazer's attempt to explain the nature of age-old rituals (such as the Scottish Beltane festival) by historical methods is also criticized.

There is no need at this stage to dwell on the nature of Wittgenstein's critique of Frazer's approach, for this book as a whole is an explication of that critique. The book falls broadly into three parts. In the first part, I consider the reasons for Wittgenstein's rejection of intellectualism, and whether this rejection is, as commonly thought, accompanied by the recommendation that magic should be viewed as an *expressive*, rather than an *instrumental*, activity. The second part of the book considers matters of methodology, focusing on why Wittgenstein is contemptuous of Frazer's explanatory aims, and expounding what he means by a 'perspicuous representation' of ritual phenomena. I deal with this in some detail, because Wittgensteinian philosophers of religion tend baldly to proclaim the need both for such a representation and for a 'non-explanatory' approach. That proclamation has something of the air of a mantra, and the content and implications of that methodology are rarely if ever explained. The second part of this book thus goes some way to correct that failure.

In the final part of the book, the core elements of Wittgenstein's analysis are isolated and examined. Having eschewed the habitual expressivist interpretation, I locate Wittgenstein's central thesis in his Müller-like contention that magico-religious beliefs emerge – like metaphysics – from a 'misunderstanding of the logic of language'. The problem then becomes one of how the perceived profundity of religion can be preserved, and this Wittgenstein does by linking it to perennial elements of human nature, and specifically to the darker elements of that nature. With this latter point in mind, the penultimate chapter is devoted to an examination of his thoughts on human sacrifice. The concluding chapter returns us to a theme already trumpeted, namely that the *Remarks on Frazer* gain their coherence and ultimate significance when set against the backdrop of Wittgenstein's conviction, absorbed from Spengler, that our age is one of decline. This pessimistic conviction underlies both his distaste for Frazer's progressive optimism, and his nostalgic yearning for the passionate beliefs and practices of a bygone age.

To begin with, though, I want to address that most common perception of Wittgenstein's writing on ritual; namely, that he offers us a version of expressivism.

Part I
Expressivism

2
Wittgenstein's 'Expressivism'

There is a broad consensus among commentators, both sympathetic and hostile, that the fundamental idea of the *Remarks on Frazer* is that magic and religion are essentially *expressive* activities. Illustrative of this is, first, a passage from *The Danger of Words*, where M. O'C. Drury writes:

> Frazer thinks he can make *clear* the origin of the rites and ceremonies he describes by regarding them as primitive and erroneous scientific beliefs ... Now Wittgenstein made it clear to me that on the contrary the people who practised these rites already possessed a considerable scientific achievement: agriculture, metalworking, building, etc., etc.; and the ceremonies existed alongside these sober techniques. They were not mistaken beliefs that produced the rites but the need to *express* something. (Drury 1973: x)

Similarly, though at the other end of the critical spectrum, Rudich and Stassen, who dismiss Wittgenstein's anthropology as 'contentless', summarize his stance thus:

> For Wittgenstein, those customs are instinctual responses to an inner need for release and satisfaction, unconscious and with no other purpose. (Rudich and Stassen 1971: 86)

The very fact of the preponderance of such readings should by itself serve to suggest that these interpretations are not groundless, and part of the purpose of this chapter is to show how they are consistent with a large number of Wittgenstein's comments. In what follows, the seeds of this expressivism will be surveyed, and the elevation of those remarks into an 'expressive theory' by the likes of Michael Banner and John Cook will be examined.

2.1 THE SEEDS OF 'WITTGENSTEIN'S EXPRESSIVISM'

Wittgenstein's positive remarks regarding the nature of ritual belief and practice can be seen as arising from his negative or critical comments. That is, that he rejects one interpretation of magic and religion and, consequently, opts for another, competing interpretation. What this suggests is that the religious practices of primitive peoples (and indeed religion *per se*) can be understood in two different and mutually exclusive ways. And indeed, this *is* the idea which is propounded by many of those who commentate on the *Remarks on Frazer*. Time and again one sees the contrast drawn between intellectualist/instrumental vs. expressive (Banner), objectivist vs. emotivist (Cook), effective vs. expressive (Redding), and so on, with Frazer said to be exemplifying the former approach and Wittgenstein the latter. *The Golden Bough* does indeed manifest the properties of an intellectualist approach to religious and magical phenomena. The major features of the intellectualist account of ritual were presented in Chapter 1, but the important point to be reminded of here is that an interpretation such as that provided by Frazer conceives magical practices as misinformed effective or instrumental actions based upon erroneous proto-scientific theories. Such intellectualist interpretations give explanatory primacy to the beliefs underlying ritual acts and, as we shall see, Wittgenstein denies that this approach has legitimacy. The crucial question of whether a straightforward denial of Frazer's tenets entails not just the rejection of intellectualism but the embracing of expressivism needs to be addressed, but first we must note the factors which seem to show just this: that the *Remarks on Frazer* constitute an expressive thesis. The drift towards expressivism could be said to take the following stages:

(a) Belief as Hypothesis and Mistake

As noted in Chapter 1, the object of the most vociferous of Wittgenstein's criticisms is Frazer's view that religious beliefs are erroneous hypotheses, i.e. *mistakes*. He notes that 'it is very queer that all these practices are finally presented, so to speak, as stupid actions' and proceeds to muse on the implausibility of such an idea. Wittgenstein is maintaining that it is bizarre to suppose that the fascinating (and often terrifying) phenomena collected by Frazer, illustrative of the ritual life of mankind, could all have been the product of error. That Frazer's verdict is perverse is said to be shown by an observation of the numerous practical skills that members of primitive societies possess:

> The same savage who, apparently in order to kill his enemy, sticks his knife through a picture of him, really does build his hut of wood and cuts his arrow with skill and not in effigy. (Wittgenstein 1979b: 4).

If this is the case, then it is surely wrong to suggest that 'a savage hardly conceives the distinction commonly drawn by more advanced peoples between the natural and the supernatural' (Frazer 1922: 10). Paradoxically, Frazer recognizes the considerable scientific and practical achievements of less advanced peoples. For example, in his researches into the Osiris cult, Frazer writes at considerable length about the Egyptian farmers' knowledge of the rise and fall of the Nile, commenting on the 'elaborate system of dams and canals' which distributed the flooding Nile's waters over the almost rainless land, producing thus its great fertility (cf. Frazer 1936f: 30–48). Wittgenstein believes that such facts give the lie to Frazer's view that savages perform rituals because they lack practical knowledge, saying:

> The nonsense here is that Frazer represents these people as if they had a completely false (even insane) idea of the course of nature, whereas they only possess a peculiar *interpretation* of the phenomena. That is, if they were to write it down, their knowledge of nature would not differ *fundamentally* from ours. Only their *magic* is different. (Wittgenstein 1979c: 73–4)

In the place of Frazer's model he presents to us the idea that ritual activities are not of a kind with scientific ones; that there are two kinds of human activity which one sees manifested in a culture. Hence:

> One might begin a book on anthropology in this way: When we watch the life and behaviour of men all over the earth we see that apart from what we call animal activities, taking food &c., &c., men also carry out actions that bear a peculiar character and might be called ritualistic.
> But then it is nonsense if we go on to say that the characteris-

tic feature of *these* actions is that they spring from wrong ideas about the physics of things. (This is what Frazer does when he says magic is really false physics, or as the case may be, false medicine, technology, &c.) (Wittgenstein 1979b: 7)

If we construe magical and religious actions as being analogous to scientific ones, or as arising from the same motives, then we do seem to be left with the conclusion that these ritual actions are mistaken, that such goals cannot be obtained by *these* methods. But as Wittgenstein stresses, this is purely a matter of presentation, for 'there is a mistake only if magic is presented as science' (1979b: 4). In rejecting the contention that magic is a species of science, Wittgenstein calls into doubt the universal applicability of a model of the nature of human action which Frazer applies wholesale in *The Golden Bough,* and as a result the idea of ritual as effective action is spurned and the possibility of an expressive interpretation opened up.

(b) The Nature of Ritual Actions

Following his draft for a hypothetical book on anthropology, Wittgenstein remarks: 'What makes the character of ritual action is not any view or opinion, either right or wrong' (1979b: 7). And again he says:

The characteristic feature of primitive man, I believe, is that he does not act from *opinions* he holds about things (as Frazer thinks). (Wittgenstein 1979b: 12)

One should not interpret this remark as the drawing of a Lévy-Bruhlian-type distinction between the respective minds of the primitive and the civilized. In certain circumstances the primitive obviously *does* act from opinions he holds about things (he builds his hut out of this material rather than that because he regards one as being sturdier than the other, and so on). Rather, if one substitutes the phrase 'man in his ritual mode' for 'primitive man', there emerges the elements of a differentiation between scientific and religious action. Such a differentiation of action is not present in Frazer's work, for he attempts an explanation of the rule at Nemi by an uncovering of 'the motives which led to its institution' (Frazer 1922: 2); that is, he contends that – as with effective action – in the religious realm beliefs have explanatory primacy over actions. This whole framework of understanding human action is of the familiar teleological type. Such an explanation treats an action as being the result of certain beliefs and desires. For example, say we see a man sitting in a room; he is shivering, rises and closes the window. On the teleological method of explanation, we produce the following schema for the understanding of this man's action:

Desire – to be warmer
Belief – an open window allows cool air to enter a room
Action – close the window

This seems perfectly reasonable when applied to normal human behaviour, though we would, of course, want a different explanation for the compulsive window-shutting of a neurotic. However, the issue at stake between Frazer and Wittgenstein is whether the teleological method is a helpful one when dealing with ritual, and it comes to a head when Frazer speaks of the killing of the divine king. Wittgenstein responds:

> When he explains to us, for example, that the king must be killed in his prime because, according to the notions of savages, his soul would not be kept fresh otherwise, we can only say: where that practice and these views go together, the practice does not spring from the view, but both of them are there. (Wittgenstein 1979b: 2)

This severing of the explanatory link between belief and action is made explicit in a number of Wittgenstein's comments, of which the following two are representative:

> Burning in effigy. Kissing the picture of a loved one. This is obviously *not* based on a belief that it will have a definite effect on the object which the picture represents. It aims at some satisfaction and it achieves it. Or rather, it does not *aim* at anything; we act in this way and then feel satisfied. (Wittgenstein 1979b: 4)

> When I am furious about something, I sometimes beat the ground or a tree with my walking stick. But I certainly do not believe that the ground is to blame or that my beating can help anything. 'I am venting my anger.' And all rites are of this kind.

Such actions may be called Instinct-actions. (Wittgenstein 1979c: 72)

With these two remarks we have moved from the idea that ritual actions do not rest on *opinions* to the more explicitly expressivist ideas in the *Remarks on Frazer.* These must now be surveyed.

(c) Magic as Expressive

Wittgenstein is scornful of Frazer's presentation of certain adoption ceremonies in primitive societies. Consider the following passage from *The Golden Bough* in which Frazer attempts to show how the law of similarity and 'the principle of make believe' brings about a ritual by means of which unsophisticated people view a simulated birth as a real one.

If you pretend to give birth to a boy, or even to a great bearded man who has not a drop of your blood in his veins, then, in the eyes of primitive law and philosophy, that boy or man is really your son to all intents and purposes ... Among the Berawans of Sarawak, when a woman desires to adopt a grown-up man or woman, a great many people assemble and have a feast. The adopting mother, seated in public on a raised and covered seat, allows the adopted person to crawl from behind between her legs. As soon as he appears in front he is stroked with the sweet-scented blossoms of the areca palm, and tied to the woman. Then the adopting mother and the adopted son or daughter, thus bound together, waddle to the end of the house and back again in front of all the spectators. (Frazer 1922: 14–15)

Wittgenstein chides Frazer for imagining 'there is an error in this' (1979b: 4). All we need to understand is that the ceremony expresses the love of the mother for her adopted son or daughter; that these feelings are made public and thus understood by the whole community. To claim that such rites occur because primitives do not understand the nature of childbirth is, Wittgenstein claims, evidence of misunderstanding.

Much of Wittgenstein's thinking on the unsatisfactory nature of Frazer's account is consonant with his reflections on what it is to be misled by 'surface grammar' (cf. Wittgenstein 1958: §664). In other words, Frazer appears to think that all human action, all human questioning, is fundamentally *the same*: when human beings act, they are trying to achieve ends; when they ask 'Why?' they are asking for the causes of events; and so on. Wittgenstein contends, on the other hand, that there is no such uniformity to human action and utterance, and that if one looks to the 'depth grammar' of *religious* utterance, one finds, not the logic of scientific enquiry, but something altogether different. Two examples will serve to illustrate how, contrary to surface appearance, the depth grammar of religious utterance is said by Wittgenstein to reveal its expressive nature:

> When it is said in a funeral oration 'We mourn our...' this is surely supposed to be an expression of mourning; not to tell anything to those who are present. (Wittgenstein 1958: 189)

> If someone who believes in God looks round and asks 'Where does everything I see come from?', 'Where does all this come from?', he is *not* craving for a (causal) explanation; and his question gets its point from being the expression of a certain craving. He is, namely, expressing an attitude to all explanations. (Wittgenstein 1980a: 85; cf. Wittgenstein 1977b: 58)

In magic and religion, then, we have utterances which look like enquiries and explanations, but which a fuller analysis reveals to have an expressive character. Thus, Frazer's error is that he occupies himself purely with the surface grammar of magic and religion, and as a result can only see them as misguided attempts to explain and control the course of nature.

Rejecting intellectualism, Wittgenstein appears to be saying that rituals are essentially expressive acts with no effective intention. They are seen by him to be expressive of desires, feelings and values. Of the first of these expressions he writes:

> The description of a wish is, *eo ipso*, the description of its fulfilment.
> And magic does give representation to a wish; it expresses a wish. (Wittgenstein 1979b: 4)

Of the second:

> If I, who do not believe that somewhere or other there are
> human-superhuman beings which we might call gods – if I say 'I
> fear the wrath of the gods', then this shows that with these words
> I can mean something or express a feeling that need not be
> connected with that belief. (Wittgenstein 1979b: 8)

This presents the idea once again that ritual activities are not
underpinned by beliefs (or more specifically, that the beliefs
involved in ritual are also expressive and do not take the form of
hypotheses or opinions). The view that magic expresses feelings
can also be seen in the conception of it as a *celebratory* activity. This
idea shows itself in Wittgenstein's observation that 'towards
morning, when the sun is about to rise, people celebrate rites of the
coming of day, but not at night, for then they simply burn lamps'
(Wittgenstein 1979b: 12). And thirdly, Wittgenstein's observation
that the priest-king's life makes manifest a concern for 'the majesty
of death' (1979b: 3) puts forward the notion that the rites of magic
and religion give expression to particular values and ideas.

2.2 THE BLOSSOMING OF THE EXPRESSIVE THEORY

Both Michael Banner and John Cook see the distinctive feature of
Wittgenstein's approach to religious phenomena as being the idea
that such rites 'express attitudes' towards things: towards the
world, one's own life and death, and so on. Cook summarizes
Wittgenstein's position thus:

> He is suggesting that the man who makes magic over his newly
> planted garden is not to be thought of as taking one more tech-
> nological step after selecting his tubers and preparing the soil but
> is to be thought of, rather, as expressing something in regard to
> his crop, the wish that it be abundant, the hope that it has not
> become infested, or whatever. (Cook 1983: 4)

Similarly, Banner says that on Wittgenstein's account, religion is
'primarily concerned with expressing and commending a particular attitude towards the world' (Banner 1990: 69), and is not a
species of explanation. Believers do not appear to treat their beliefs

as though they were hypotheses, and as such, it is best to see such beliefs as manifestations or expressions of what goes deep in their lives. Thus, Banner says that the essence of Wittgenstein's view is that the sense of the rituals and beliefs spoken of by Frazer 'will be found to lie in the nature of human life and the emotions, rather than in speculative, explanatory theories' (1990: 70).

For Banner, Wittgenstein's notes constitute an 'expressive theory' consisting of four separate arguments designed to show the erroneous nature of an instrumentalist account of ritual, and to illustrate the plausibility of an expressive interpretation. These four arguments are:

(1) the immunity to criticism argument
(2) the technical competence argument
(3) the due season argument
(4) the obviousness of error argument

It will be helpful to take each of these in turn, for each illustrates an aspect of the *Remarks*, while Banner's criticisms highlight the weaknesses which are said to inhere in an expressive interpretation of religion.

Throughout his presentation of Wittgenstein's alternative to intellectualism, Banner makes much of the first argument, concerning immunity to criticism, although the evidence taken from the *Remarks* to support the presence there of this idea is rather poor, relying solely on the following passage:

> It may happen, as it often does today, that someone will give up a practice when he has seen that something on which it depended is an error. But this happens only in cases where you can make a man change his way of doing things simply by calling his attention to his error. This is not how it is in connexion with the religious practices of a people; and what we have here is *not* an error. (Wittgenstein 1979b: 2)

Yet this remark does not have the import which Banner thinks it has. Rather than it saying that religious beliefs are immune to criticism, its actual purpose is as a comment on the logical status of belief and, specifically, on what Wittgenstein sees as Frazer's confused notion of that status. Wittgenstein is indeed maintaining that a magical or religious rite is not given up because of a recognition that it is based on a false belief, but this only serves to reinforce the point he makes earlier, namely:

> A religious symbol does not rest on any *opinion*.
> And error belongs only with opinion. (Wittgenstein 1979b: 3)

The meaning, therefore, of the passage used by Banner is a straightforward criticism of the basic tenet of intellectualism: that religious actions are grounded in false beliefs and will be abandoned when the error is recognized. Now if Wittgenstein is correct, then while it might indeed be true that religious actions will not be affected by criticisms of *beliefs*, the actions *themselves* might be criticized and possibly given up as a result (for example, a missionary might convince a tribe that, say, cannibalism is immoral). But that is certainly not to say that such actions are erroneous from a theoretical point of view. And certainly, aside from these speculations, Wittgenstein's comments on this do not amount to the claim that religious beliefs could never be affected by outside influences or relinquished at all, for they plainly *are*.

Banner's appeal to the idea of criticism immunity must therefore be put down to a source other than the *Remarks on Frazer*. That source is not hard to find, for it is a sad fact that Wittgenstein's major legacy for the philosophy of religion is the concept of the language-game and its application to belief. The idea that religion constitutes a distinctive language-game with its own internal criteria of meaning, rationality and truth has been propounded by a number of Wittgenstein's followers. One of them writes:

> Religion is a form of life; it is language embedded in action –
> what Wittgenstein calls a 'language-game'. Science is another.
> Neither stands in need of justification, the one no more than the
> other. (Malcolm 1977: 212)

One aspect of such a characterization is the notion that one language-game cannot be judged by the standards of another; so, for example, scientists cannot criticize what is held to be true by the religious. Consequently, religion is regarded as being sealed off from other forms of human life, invulnerable to outside attack, and hence immune to criticism. This notion of 'Wittgensteinian Fideism' has been the subject of much controversy and, without wishing to rehearse the details of that debate, it is enough to say that it has not been established that Wittgenstein intended to widen the scope of the concept of a language-game so as to include such large-scale activities as 'science' or 'religion'. Indeed, if one turns to the *Philosophical Investigations,* a language-game appears to be something far less ambitious, characterizing such actions as telling jokes, play-acting, cursing and greeting, and so on (Wittgenstein 1958: §23).

What import, then, does this have for the expressive theory? Very little, in fact. Neither criticism immunity nor 'the religious language-game' are ideas present in the *Remarks on Frazer,* and even if they were, this would not by itself show that Wittgenstein was advocating an expressive interpretation. For it would not be at all obvious that 'the language-game of religion' would have an exclusively expressive character.

Turning now to the second point, the 'technical competence argument', Wittgenstein tells us not to think of magic and religion as poor substitutes for science. Rather, these practices exist alongside the practical activities of the community. It therefore seems reasonable to say that someone familiar with practical skills will not resort to magic and religion to achieve the same technical ends. This being so, we are urged to see ritual practices as having a different character than scientific activity: rather than viewing a religious act as instrumental, more sense is made of the practice if we see it as expressive of something. Yet that argument is fairly weak, for ritual often concerns those areas of human life over which technology is itself futile, areas such as personal frustration and death. Where technology will not help, perhaps the gods will. Hence Malinowski's observation concerning the magic of the Trobriand islanders:

It is most significant that in the lagoon fishing, where man can rely completely on his knowledge and skill, magic does not exist, while in the open-sea fishing, full of danger and uncertainty, there is extensive magic ritual to secure safety and good results. (Malinowski 1948: 31, cited in Cook 1983: 22)

One could, of course, imagine an expressive theorist providing this rejoinder: why should the expression of things which go deep in a man's life not be directed precisely at those things which most endanger his existence, and that these expressions should be less concerned with the mundane? There is an impasse here. Both instrumental and expressive accounts are plausible and neither interpretation succeeds in refuting the other. Let us move to fresh ground.

The 'due season argument' contends that if rituals were performed in order to achieve observable ends then they would be performed *whenever* there was a need for the required effect. Yet, Wittgenstein maintains, this is not what happens:

> I read, amongst many similar examples, of a rain-king in Africa to whom the people appeal for rain *when the rainy season comes*. But surely this means that they do not actually think he can make rain, otherwise they would do it in the dry periods in which the land is 'a parched and arid desert'. (Wittgenstein 1979b: 12)

This opens up the possibility of such a ritualized appeal being part of a celebratory activity, rather than a form of genuine request based on the model of asking and receiving. So, echoing Wittgenstein, Phillips (1976: 35) writes:

> The greeting of the sun at the coming of day can be seen as a celebration of its coming. It is not that people who, say, raise their arms at the dawning of day think that unless they raise their hands, the dawn will not break, but, rather, knowing that the dawning of the day is at hand, they want to express a greeting to it in this way.

But such apparently celebratory rites can be explained just as well by an instrumental account. To this end, Banner presents the idea of a rich uncle who gives presents to his nieces and nephews solely on the occasion of their birthdays, but will do so only when asked.

> A similar thing may be true in the case of aptly timed ceremonies for rain or harvest. The Christian might say that God will provide a plentiful harvest at the ordained and fitting time, but only when prayers are made. Hence though prayers for harvest should not be addressed to God in December, let us say, it is still the case that the request is, in the spring, instrumental. (Banner 1990: 83–4)

Once again, the instrumental and expressive accounts have equal plausibility. The balance may, however, be tipped in favour of the instrumentalist option by further consideration of the case of the rain-king. An Abyssinian king, the Alfai, is held to be able to cast down rain, and:

> if he disappoints the people's expectation and a great drought arises in the land, the Alfai is stoned to death, and his nearest relations are obliged to cast the first stone at him. (Frazer 1922: 107)

The tension between a case such as this and the expressive theory is clear, for it appears that in this instance there is undeniably a sense in which the rain-king is regarded as responsible for the coming of the rains. Now, there may indeed be cases where Wittgenstein's interpretation fits and the appeal to a rain-maker is an act of a purely celebratory nature. The case of the Alfai, however, suffices to show that the expressive theory cannot be universally applied, and that some ritualists really do think that the rain-king can make the heavens open.[1]

The final argument concerns 'obviousness of error'. If magic and religion really are based on a mistake, then how come it is not perceived? Wittgenstein remarks:

> Frazer says it is very difficult to discover the error in magic and this is why it persists for so long – because, for example, a ceremony which is supposed to bring rain is sure to appear effective sooner or later.
>
> But then it is queer that people do not notice sooner that it does rain sooner or later anyway. (Wittgenstein 1979b: 2)

This is, in fact, a rather weak argument, for the intellectualist can, by recourse to the notion of blocks to falsifiability, produce a whole host of reasons why the futility of magic is not noticed 'sooner or later'. And A. J. Ayer makes the telling observation that 'if the believers in the efficacy of the rain dance never omit to perform it, what grounds do they have for concluding that the rain would arrive anyway?' (Ayer 1986: 89). So, as an argument against the notion of blocks to falsifiability, Wittgenstein is plainly wrong.

Having reviewed these four areas of contrast between expressive and intellectualist approaches, it has to be said that, although there are no outright winners and losers from the confrontation, on the level of plausibility the intellectualist does seem to have the upper hand: it is hard to imagine that a ritualist does not seriously expect his actions to have any practical effect. And if Wittgenstein *is* saying that no practical ends are sought in magical activity, then this would appear to be a fatal flaw in his argument. Ethnographic material does clearly show that at least some magic is performed with efficacious intent (cf. Cook 1983: 11–16), and this being so, Wittgenstein is surely wrong in believing magic to be performed with no desired end in mind.

Of course, someone who found Wittgenstein's writings implausible on precisely these grounds need not have to accept the intellectualist claim that ritual is essentially instrumental activity. Cook, for example, contends that a middle way between Frazer and Wittgenstein is possible. This middle way he locates in the writings of John Beattie, who, whilst maintaining that magic is 'essentially expressive' (Beattie 1966: 204), concedes that its practitioners do not see it thus and instead feel they are pursuing some achievable end. Beattie's position does then look like a midway point between Frazer and the expressivist drift of Wittgenstein's *Remarks*, and we will do well to isolate the main elements of this middle position. This will serve two ends: first, it will further sharpen the concept of expressivism; and second, it will begin to illustrate the shortcomings of attributing to Wittgenstein an expressivist position.

2.3 BEATTIE'S FORM OF EXPRESSIVISM

It is hard to read Beattie's *Other Cultures* and not be struck by the similarities between his account of magic and that offered by Wittgenstein. Beattie reinforces a number of the criticisms Wittgenstein makes of Frazer, and, in particular, a version of the technical competence argument is used, it being maintained that 'no community, "savage" or otherwise, could possibly survive if its members were quite unable to distinguish between fancy and experience' (Beattie 1966: 66). And he claims, like Wittgenstein, that Frazer and other intellectualist theorists misunderstand ritual by representing it as a species of scientific activity:

> We do the grossest injustice to the subtle allusive and evocative power of language if we require all meaningful verbal expression to conform to the rules of syllogism and inductive inference. Coherent thinking can be symbolic as well as scientific, and if we are sensible we do not subject the language of poetry to the same

kind of examination that we apply to a scientific hypothesis. (Beattie 1966: 69)

Like Wittgenstein, Beattie feels that a distinction needs to be drawn between two areas of human life, and his opposition of instrumental and expressive would appear roughly to correspond to Wittgenstein's animal/ritual distinction. About these two areas of life Beattie says:

> Instrumental activity is directed to bringing about some desired state of affairs; it is oriented towards an end. Expressive activity is a way of saying or expressing something; usually some idea or state of mind. (Beattie 1966: 71)

Beattie explains that the realm of the expressive is the realm of the symbolic, these symbols providing people with 'a means of representing abstract ideas, often ideas of great practical importance to themselves indirectly, ideas which it would be difficult or even impossible for them to represent to themselves directly' (Beattie 1966: 70).

To take an example, Beattie, like Wittgenstein, considers the case of a rain-making ceremony, and similarly maintains that the essential element of this rite is not an instrumental intention. Rather, 'the man who consults a rain-maker, and the rain-maker who carries out a rain-making ceremony, are stating something; they are asserting symbolically the importance they attach to rain and their earnest desire that it shall fall when it is required' (1966: 203). So, the purpose of religious and magical ceremonies is not the pursuit of some end. Rather, these rites should be seen as 'symbolizing certain important aspects of the physical and socio-cultural environment' (Beattie 1970: 263). In other words, religious rites have as their concern those elements of human life which are of the greatest import: birth, marriage, sex, death, the seasons, the elements, war and so on. In the ceremonies of magic and religion, the significance of these matters is expressed.

It is easy to see affinities between Beattie's approach and the expressivist position commonly attributed to Wittgenstein. However, the interpretations should not be assimilated for, as earlier noted, Beattie maintains that the practitioners of magic really do believe they are engaged in effective action: 'Although magic *is* magic because it is essentially expressive and symbolic, the people who use it think of it as instrumental' (Beattie 1966: 212). The contention that the participants perform magic 'to bring about ends they desire' (1966: 213) certainly appears to go contrary to Wittgenstein's claim that magic 'does not *aim* at anything' (1979b: 4). A second, and crucial, difference concerns the translatability of rituals. Beattie explains the rituals of primitive people by describing them in terms of the concerns and desires they address and to which they give expression (the transitoriness of life, dependence on the natural world and on social relations, and so on), whereas Wittgenstein wants to say that the sentiments of the rites cannot be made known *apart from* the rites or without reference to other comparable ones. Hence his comment to Waismann:

> In religion talking is not *metaphorical* either; for otherwise it would have to be possible to say the same things in prose. (Waismann 1979: 117)[2]

This is connected with certain ideas in the 'Lectures on Religious Belief'. By stressing that 'the whole *weight* may be in the picture' (Wittgenstein 1966: 72), Wittgenstein wishes to say that a religious concept cannot be given a straightforward 'cash-value' and is to that extent non-reducible. Thus:

> Suppose someone, before going to China, when he might never see me again, said to me: 'We might see one another after death' – would I necessarily say that I don't understand him? I might say [want to say] simply, 'Yes. I *understand* him entirely.'
>
> *Lewy*: In this case, you might only mean that he expressed a certain attitude.
>
> I would say 'No, it isn't the same as saying "I'm very fond of you"' – and it may not be the same as saying anything else. It says what it says. Why should you be able to substitute anything else? (Wittgenstein 1966: 70–1)

In this passage we see the roots of dissent from the notion that religious beliefs simply 'express attitudes' – here Wittgenstein clearly eschews such a notion. And this is not just an isolated and accidental remark, an anomaly in an otherwise consistently expressivist approach. As we shall now see, it is in fact a fundamental error to believe that the *Remarks on Frazer* constitute an expressive theory of religion.

3

The Possibility of Expressivism

3.1 THE DYNAMICS OF EXPRESSIVISM

We have hitherto seen that the purpose of the *Remarks on Frazer* has been said to lie in the production of an expressivist account of religion; one, that is, which claims that the point of magical and religious rituals is to express deep human emotions and attitudes about life and the world. It must now be ascertained whether the attribution to Wittgenstein of an expressive theory is satisfactory. More specifically, we must uncover the philosophical roots of the expressive interpretation; such roots as are, it will be contended, so fundamentally at odds with the direction of Wittgenstein's philosophy that his reflections on ritual cannot be as straightforwardly expressivist as most commentators insist.

When we survey what is generally written about Wittgenstein's encounter with Frazer, it is found that the following dichotomy is set up: Frazer, and other thinkers of his ilk, see magical and religious *ritual* as instrumental or effective action, and the *theory* (or world-view) which underlies such action is explanatory or descriptive in character. Contrariwise, Wittgenstein (it is contended) sees ritual as being purely expressive and not at all concerned with getting things done, and sees also the accompanying beliefs as having little or nothing to do with describing or explaining the way the world is. Looked upon in this way, the difference between Frazer and Wittgenstein is over whether religious thought is *cognitive* or *non-cognitive* in character; whether, to use the terminology of C. L. Stevenson, it is to do with either *beliefs* or *attitudes*.[1] Such thoughts are uppermost in Banner's account of the *Remarks on Frazer's Golden Bough*, for he asks:

Is religious discourse concerned primarily with describing and explaining (hence with making statements to be judged true or false), or is it primarily concerned with expressing and commending a particular attitude towards the world? For shorthand, we call these the 'intellectualist' and 'expressive' (or non-cognitive) accounts respectively. (Banner 1990: 69)

We will return shortly to this remark and observe how elements of Wittgenstein's thought question the validity of such neat distinctions, thus disabling the tenacious cognitive/non-cognitive dichotomy. Initially, however, we must achieve greater clarity as to how the belief vs. attitude distinction arises and what it is grounded in.

Its origins may be seen to lie in a particular view of the nature and function of language, such an interpretation as is found in Wittgenstein's own *Tractatus Logico-Philosophicus*. There, Wittgenstein attempted to demarcate the bounds of sense by propounding strict criteria for the meaningfulness (or otherwise) of propositions. As is well known, the theory of meaning contained therein stems in part from Wittgenstein's being struck by an incident in a French court case, where a road accident was reconstructed in the court room by means of model vehicles and figures. It seemed to Wittgenstein that this model threw light on the way in which language related to the world, and in his war notebook he stated: 'In the proposition a world is as it were put together experimentally. (As when in the law court in Paris a motor-car accident is represented by means of dolls, etc.)' (Wittgenstein 1961a: 7). The insight contained here is spelled out in detail in what is known as the 'picture theory' of meaning: the structure of language and of the world exhibits a fundamental isomorphism which permits the picturing or representational relation of the former to the latter. To expand, the world is said to be 'the totality of facts' (Wittgenstein 1961b: 1.1); these facts are compounded out of 'states of affairs' (1961b: 2), which are themselves made up of 'a combination of objects (things)' (1961b: 2.01). This three-stage constitution of the world is mirrored in language, where a proposition is held to be 'a truth-function of elementary propositions' (1961b: 5), which are themselves made up of particular concatenations of names. In the picturing relation, the names, elementary propositions, and propositions of *language* go proxy for, respectively, the objects, states of affairs, and facts which make up the *world*. That language is seen by Wittgenstein to have an essentially pictorial nature is shown when he remarks:

In order to understand the essential nature of a proposition, we should consider hieroglyphic script, which depicts the facts that it describes.

And alphabetic script developed out of it without losing what was essential to depiction. (Wittgenstein 1961b: 4.016)

Whether a proposition is true or not depends on whether it accurately depicts a state of affairs. Thus, the 'one and only ... complete analysis' of a proposition (Wittgenstein 1961b: 3.25) shows how that proposition stands in relation to reality, whether it depicts an existing state of affairs. To understand a proposition, then, is 'to know what is the case if it is true' (Wittgenstein 1961b: 4.024), a knowledge of its truth-conditions being the only way in which one can understand a proposition: 'in order to be able to say, "'p' is true (or false)", I must have determined in what circumstances I call "p" true, and in so doing I determine the sense of the proposition' (1961b: 4.063).

The only meaningful uses of language, apart from tautologies, are those which picture either possible or actual *facts* or states of affairs. As a consequence of this, Wittgenstein claims that 'the totality of true propositions is the whole of natural science' (1961b: 4.11). Any use of language other than that which attempts to depict facts is seen as senseless, so when Wittgenstein states what 'the correct method in philosophy' should be, he describes it in the following way:

To say nothing except what can be said, i.e. propositions of natural science ... and then, whenever someone else wanted to say something metaphysical, to demonstrate to him that he had failed to give a meaning to certain signs in his propositions. (1961b: 6.53)

In such a manner, the respective discourses of aesthetics, ethics, religion and metaphysics are 'passed over in silence'. These uses of language are *unsinnig*, they say nothing and depict nothing. As Hudson elucidates with regard to the language of religion: 'God, as transcendent, is beyond the world, and what is beyond the world is *not* the world. Language is meaningful – on the picture theory – if, and only if, it mirrors the world which *is*' (Hudson 1968: 27). As such, this cognitively meaningless language requires a different analysis from that suitable for the propositions of natural science.

What Wittgenstein says about this is the subject of differing interpretations, and is at any rate notoriously obscure. For a more
straightforward account of how discourse which is cognitively
meaningless should be treated, we can turn to the analysis of
language provided by Logical Positivism.

As with Wittgenstein's treatment of them in the *Tractatus*, A. J.
Ayer considers there to be a simple test of cognitive significance
which the linguistic expressions of religion, ethics and metaphysics
fail. Here the test is the verification principle: 'We say that a
sentence is factually significant to any given person, if, and only if,
he knows how to verify the proposition which it purports to
express' (Ayer 1971: 48). Under this analysis, statements of value
pose a certain difficulty, for though they seem to be 'genuine
synthetic propositions ... they cannot with any show of justice be
represented as hypotheses' (Ayer 1971: 136), and, as a consequence,
cannot be capable of verification. Rather than maintaining that
ethical statements were nonsensical (although he was happy to
dispose of theology and metaphysics by rendering them as such),
Ayer propounded an 'emotive theory of values', the central notion
of this being that 'the presence of an ethical symbol in a proposition
adds nothing to its factual content ... For in saying that a certain
type of action is right or wrong, I am ... merely expressing certain
moral sentiments' (Ayer 1971: 142). Ayer's theory springs entirely
from his strict test of cognitive meaningfulness, which ethical and
theological statements fail. Hence, if these areas of discourse are not
simply to be nonsensical they must have a meaning other than a
cognitive one. The emotive significance of statements of value is,
however, set out in greater detail by Charles Stevenson, whose
working models of ethical statements illustrate precisely how the
utterances of ethics are viewed when their meaning becomes
subject to such strict criteria of meaning as propounded by positivists:

(1) 'This is wrong' means *I disapprove of this; do so as well.*
(2) 'He ought to do this' means *I disapprove of his leaving this
undone; do so as well.*
(3) 'This is good' means *I approve of this; do so as well.* (Stevenson
1944: 21)

Indeed, Stevenson's discussion of emotive meaning provides a
crucial insight into the way in which many theories of religion have

been constructed. Stevenson says that 'emotive meaning is a meaning in which the response (from the hearer's point of view) or the stimulus (from the speaker's point of view) is a range of emotions' (Stevenson 1944: 59). It is the notions of response and stimulus which are of interest here, and the former is applied by R. B. Braithwaite who, in his famous paper 'An Empiricist's View of the Nature of Religious Belief', discusses the implications of an acceptance of the verification principle for one's view of religion. Braithwaite accepts that the principle rules out the possibility of religious utterances having the same descriptive character as the hypotheses and statements of scientific discourse. Instead, he maintains, religion is to do with emotion, and as a consequence of this:

> If religion is essentially concerned with emotion, it is natural to explain the use of religious assertions on the lines of the original emotive theory of ethics and to regard them as primarily evincing feelings or emotions. (Braithwaite 1971: 79)

Braithwaite admits that such an account of religion would generally be unacceptable to religious believers. He maintains, however, that fewer objections can be mounted against an emotive account which treats religious assertions as having a *conative* character. On this view, such statements are to be regarded primarily as 'declarations of adherence to a policy of action, declarations of commitment to a way of life' (Braithwaite 1971: 80). Religious assertions are not to be thought of as statements of fact, and religious *belief* is 'not ordinary belief ... belief in a proposition' (1971: 89). Braithwaite claims instead that 'a religious belief is an intention to behave in a certain way (a moral belief) together with the entertainment of certain stories associated with the intention in the mind of the believer' (1971: 89).

Henceforth, this type of account of religion, which stresses the role of religion as a spur to action, shall be labelled *expressive-conative*. Another example of it can be seen in the theory of magic put forward in R. G. Collingwood's *The Principles of Art*, though this is less explicitly tied to a theory of language than Braithwaite's view is. Collingwood claims that while magical practices are indeed used as means to a preconceived end, these ends are not, *pace* Frazer, the same ones as sought by science or by more practical activities. The end sought is simply the arousing of emotion, and Collingwood points to some features of ritual activity (for example, the use of the bull-roarer, the performance of a war-dance) to support this view. In magical acts, emotions are 'focused and crystallized, consolidated into effective agents in practical life' (Collingwood 1958: 66). As such, magic is not, for Collingwood, a cathartic activity, whereby emotions would be expressively *released* in the rituals: indeed, 'the process is the exact opposite of a catharsis' (1958: 66). Rather, 'the primary function of all magical acts … is to generate in the agent or agents certain emotions that are necessary or useful for the work of the living' (Collingwood 1958: 66). This characterization of magic is said to account for its everyday employment, and the fundamental idea is that magic is good for morale, 'a kind of dynamo supplying the mechanism of practical life with the emotional current which drives it' (Collingwood 1958: 69). Magic used to avert an earthquake or to stop flooding might, by instilling in folk a Job-like acceptance, produce an attitude by means of which such hardship can be countered, but such effects are the real and only products of magic: Collingwood is under no illusion that magic *really* intended to bring about a concrete, physical end is anything other than folly.

Just as the expressive-conative account of magic can be seen to employ something akin to Stevenson's notion of evincing a response, the contrasting idea of the stimulus behind magic being a range of emotions emerges in those accounts which shall be referred to as *expressive-cathartic*. Such cathartic interpretations are numerous, and are familiar within social anthropology: for example, Radcliffe-Brown contends that magical and religious rites are 'the regulated symbolic expressions of certain sentiments' (Radcliffe-Brown 1952: 157). Cathartic accounts often adopt expressive clothing having previously noted the failure of religious discourse to assume a 'literal' character. One such account is provided by George Santayana, who, claiming that religion possesses no 'literal truth' (Santayana 1905: 10), proceeds to illustrate how the essence of certain aspects of religion (such as prayer) is expressive 'rather than calculating' (1905: 36). A religious rite, for Santayana, 'will bring about an emotional catharsis' (1905: 38), and 'therefore calms the passions in expressing them' (1905: 44).

And it is *this* kind of theory which is ascribed to Wittgenstein by many of those commenting on the *Remarks on Frazer*, and is explicitly seen in Rudich and Stassen's comment that for Wittgenstein, magical rites and ceremonies are 'instinctual responses to an inner need for release and satisfaction' (Rudich and Stassen 1971: 86).

Also notable is O'Hear's commentary, which attributes to Wittgenstein a view which is both conative *and* cathartic:

> Ritual itself is fundamentally action 'without purpose' ... symbolizing and expressing our feelings and attitudes ... In Wittgenstein's view, there is in human beings a deep need to symbolize and express what is important to them in their lives ... Primitive rituals and their accompanying beliefs do for those who participate in them what the symbolic acts we have do for us, expressing and evoking deep needs and emotions. (O'Hear 1984: 10–12)

Such readings of the *Remarks on Frazer* are so abundant that, in the face of these exegeses, it appears practically eccentric to want to challenge the consensus. Yet if we are not to misunderstand Wittgenstein's analysis of religious belief, it is precisely this expressivist portrayal which must be jettisoned.

Before this is effected, however, it will be helpful to extract from the above and summarize what it is that underlies the belief/attitude distinction. In all cases, it is considered that the forms which language takes are standard, uniform and unchanging, and that, consequently, a unified account of meaning can be given for all sentences in natural language. There are seen to be, besides tautologies, two forms of language which can be readily recognized: the cognitive or descriptive (consisting of hypotheses) and the emotive (consisting of utterances to do with 'value'), this latter type generally being regarded as a deviation from the primary, fact-stating purpose of language. Descriptive language is thus held to be of an unvarying character, and in the *Tractatus* this is articulated by stating that: 'The general form of the proposition is: This is how things stand' (Wittgenstein 1961b: 4.5). In the theories of language which followed in the wake of Wittgenstein's early work, it was contended that the essential uniformity of language entailed that there could be simple criteria of what was to count as meaningful; indeed, one single criterion of what was to count as *descriptive* of the world. For the positivists, this criterion, as stated earlier, was the verifiability principle, one which spelled disaster for religion when employed to test the significance of its discourse: the 'pseudo-propositions' of religion were 'not even in principle verifiable' (Ayer 1971: 49), and hence cognitively senseless. Thus, if religious utterance has no descriptive content, then (if it is to be anything other than nonsense) its content must be *non-descriptive*. Here we can contrast the expressivism of Braithwaite and Santayana (and, purportedly, of Wittgenstein) with that of Durkheim, for whom religion, although expressive, was not wholly devoid of cognitive content, for it served to represent, albeit in an indirect and symbolic fashion, the reality of social relations (cf. Lukes 1973: 465). For the expressivist writers under consideration here, religion has no cognitive or descriptive function whatsoever. Instead, religion and magic are said to be to do with *attitudes* and feelings, rather than with belief and knowledge, and we see the hard dichotomies emerge between the descriptive and the non-descriptive, and between the articulating of *beliefs* and the expressing of *attitudes*. This is why Richard Swinburne, in characterizing the views of Braithwaite and Phillips as 'attitude theories', says that for these writers, 'religious assertions, including credal sentences, express intentions to live in certain ways, or express attitudes of approval for certain patterns of life or do *something else other than stating how things are*' (Swinburne 1986: 85, emphasis added). These, then, are the dichotomies which provide the environment for the charge that the *Remarks on Frazer* constitute 'an expressive theory'. Let us now turn to Wittgenstein to see if such crucial distinctions are either endorsed or repudiated by him, for on this the whole question of his expressivism turns.

3.2 WITTGENSTEIN'S PHILOSOPHY AND THE POSSIBILITY OF EXPRESSIVISM

One is faced with a certain difficulty when ascertaining whether Wittgenstein's philosophy allows for the possibility that the *Remarks on Frazer* amount to an expressivist understanding of magic and religion. This is due to a number of factors, the predominant one being that the *Tractatus* was, as noted earlier, supremely influential on philosophers concerned with the workings of language, so that it was Wittgenstein's own theories which largely produced the possibility of a non-cognitive understanding of religion. Wittgenstein's later philosophy, however, repudiated many of the central positions of the *Tractatus*, and stands full square against the rather grandiose schemes of semantic theorists. His relation to the kind of linguistic theories which give birth to the cognitive/non-cognitive distinction is thus quite paradoxical: he is both father-creator and enemy. Consequently, one can use the later work of Wittgenstein in order to criticize those trends in philosophy from which the idea of non-cognitivism springs. However, the issue of to which period of his philosophy the *Remarks on Frazer* belong needs to be settled. For if one wished to argue that the account of religion, magic and ritual offered in the *Remarks* was straightforwardly expressivist, it would need to be demonstrated that these notes were consonant with the aims of Wittgenstein's early work. On the other hand, if the *Remarks* are of a piece with those trains of thought which brought about the *Philosophical Investigations*, and if the latter can be shown to rule out a neat descriptive/non-descriptive dichotomy, then it can be said with some safety that Wittgenstein's criticisms of *The Golden Bough* do not extend to the advocacy of an expressive alternative. Where, then, do the *Remarks on Frazer* stand?

It can be said with certainty that the second set of remarks (on the Beltane festival) belong with the later philosophy, for, as Rhees tells us, they were written 'not earlier than 1936 and probably after 1948' (Rhees 1979: vi), a period in which the distinctive character of Wittgenstein's later work was well established. The first set of remarks, however, from which most of the evidence for Wittgenstein's 'expressivism' is plundered, has a more ambiguous context, for these notes were written in 1931. Accordingly, the problem is this: that it is this very period of Wittgenstein's work (from 1929 until about 1934) which constitutes his 'transitional phase', that period of his writing which, whilst conspicuously unlike the position of the *Tractatus*, had yet to resemble his mature view. If one thing could be said to characterize this middle period it would be a concern with *verificationism*. In his conversations with the Vienna Circle (which took place between 1929 and 1932, and were recorded by Friedrich Waismann), and in the text of the *Philosophical Remarks* (written in 1930), Wittgenstein makes some rather absolute claims about the status of verification, which rival those of any logical positivist:

> If I can never verify the sense of a proposition completely, then I cannot have meant anything by the proposition either. Then the proposition signifies nothing whatsoever. (Waismann 1979: 47)

> The verification is not *one* token of the truth, it is *the* sense of the proposition. (Einstein: How a magnitude is measured is what it is.) (Wittgenstein 1975: 200)

It would not, then, be preposterous to assume that the writings of the middle period are congruous with those theories we earlier isolated as the progenitors of non-cognitivism.

When, however, one turns to the first set of *Remarks on Frazer*, we find that, far from reflecting the verificationist concerns exhibited in the discussions with Schlick and Waismann, these notes have more in common with the style of the *Investigations* than their date would suggest. Ideas characteristic of the later period appear in abundance: there is the typical loathing of *explanation*, the stress on the primacy of action and instinct in concept formation, and, most significantly, his ground-breaking thoughts on perspicuous representation – passages which are repeated verbatim in the *Investigations*. Indeed, one can regard the *Remarks on Frazer* as being of fundamental importance for the emergence of Wittgenstein's mature philosophy, and there is, at any rate, certainly enough textual evidence to ally them with the concerns of the later period. Consequently, therefore, our conclusion as to whether the arguments of this period rule out a non-cognitive understanding of magic and religion will be sufficient to decide the question concerning the 'expressivism' of the *Remarks*.

As promised, then, let us return to Banner's question regarding the choice that is said to face us. Either, he says, religion is to do with expressing attitudes, or else it is to do 'with describing and explaining (hence with making statements to be judged true or false)' (Banner 1990: 69). The generality of Banner's remark is not incidental. He shares with many philosophers a belief in the essential uniformity of descriptive language, and, as a result, in the possibility of producing a unified account of meaning and truth for sentences in natural language, invariant of subject matter. In other words, Banner believes that all those elements in the alternative he presents us with – the elements of description, explanation, truth and falsity – are timeless and context-independent; that description is always one thing, that the notion of 'truth' is uniform, and so on. Banner's question, then, implies that 'the descriptive' has a general form, and, as we shall now see, this is firmly repudiated by Wittgenstein.

One fundamental purpose of Wittgenstein's later work is to challenge the view that a unified account of language could be given, that we could in any useful way establish the 'general form' of certain features of language, notably that of the proposition: that part of his earlier work which had given him 'most headache'

(Wittgenstein 1958: §65). Whereas in the *Tractatus* Wittgenstein had searched for the underlying form of the proposition, in the later work such a form is held to be a philosophical illusion. The reason for this is that, rather than being a 'super-concept', the proposition is a family resemblance concept, with no essence and no 'general form'. To say 'This is how things stand' is not to express the essence of the proposition, but just to stipulate what we are going to call 'a proposition': 'One thinks that one is tracing the outline of the thing's nature over and over again, and one is merely tracing round the frame through which we look at it' (Wittgenstein 1958: §114). A belief in the uniformity of the concept of a proposition is, Wittgenstein claims, suggested to us by the written or spoken appearance of words and sentences, by the fact that 'the clothing of our language makes everything alike' (Wittgenstein 1958: 224). Famously, the difference between the appearance and the use of language is put in terms of surface and depth grammar (cf. Wittgenstein 1958: §664), and the lesson to be learned is that if we concern ourselves with the depth grammar of language, researches into such things as 'the general propositional form' will be recognized as futile, corrupting even:

> The basic evil of Russell's logic, as also of mine in the *Tractatus*, is that what a proposition is is illustrated by a few commonplace examples, and then pre-supposed as understood in full generality. (Wittgenstein 1980c: §38)

Thus, the question which Wittgenstein poses himself in the *Philosophical Grammar*, namely 'Do we have a *single* concept of proposition?' (Wittgenstein 1974b: 112), is answered in the negative. The concept can be explained, not in terms of its general form, but, rather, by the presentation of *examples*.

If Wittgenstein says that the concept of 'proposition' has no general form, then it is equally true that he says the same about the idea of 'description', thus countering the very phrasing of Banner's distinction, which, as we have seen, relies on a hard and unvarying category of 'the descriptive'. Rejecting this, Wittgenstein contends that there is not one thing that we can call 'description'; that 'the descriptive', as a family resemblance concept, has no general form:

> Think how many different kinds of thing are called 'description': description of a body's position by means of its co-ordinates;

description of a facial expression; description of a sensation of
touch; of a mood. (Wittgenstein 1958: §24)

Not: 'How can I describe what I see?' – but 'What does one *call*
"description of what is seen"?'
And the answer to *this* question is 'A great variety of thing'.
(Wittgenstein 1980c: §981)

Contrary, then, to Banner's intention to create a clear distinction
between the 'descriptive' and the 'emotive', Wittgenstein would
claim that all that is performed here is an exercise in question-
begging, for one could justifiably ask: 'What does description
amount to in this context?'

To this counter-question it could, however, be objected that what
description 'amounts to' in this, or any, context is simple, for a
descriptive statement is characterized by its possession of *truth-
conditions*. Thus, according to Banner's reading of the *Remarks on
Frazer*, Wittgenstein denies that magical and religious utterances
have truth-conditions, and consequently contends that they constitute non-descriptive, emotive language. It should not, however, be
presumed that in his later work Wittgenstein would have held, as
he had earlier done in the *Tractatus*, that 'a proposition is the
expression of its truth-conditions' (Wittgenstein 1961b: 4.431). One
reason for this is his rejection of the rigid notion of 'truth' involved
in the conception of a 'truth-condition'. This is hinted at in his
lectures in the early 1930s, where, asked to choose between Broad's
three 'theories of truth' (namely the Correspondence Theory, the
Coherence Theory, and the Pragmatic Theory), Wittgenstein,
noting instances of the application of each, remarked that 'it is
nonsense to try to find *a* theory of truth, because we can see that in
everyday life we use the word quite clearly and definitely in these
different senses' (Wittgenstein 1980b: 76). As could be expected,
this theme is amplified in the later work, where the multiplicity of
uses of such words as 'true' is stressed. And if we do not have a
single concept of 'truth', then we cannot have a single concept of a
'truth-condition' which could act as arbiter for what is to count as
the descriptive and the non-descriptive. It is in order to reject the
idea of truth-conditions, in which the notions of truth and falsity
are regarded as capable of explaining the nature of propositions,
that he claims that the word 'true' *'belongs* to our concept "proposition" but does not *fit* it' (Wittgenstein 1958: §136). Instead, then, of

appealing to fixed and unvarying notions, Wittgenstein's suggestion is that whether a sentence is 'true', or 'descriptive', is
dependent on the circumstances in which it is uttered.[2]
Furthermore, far from claiming that religious language is non-
descriptive, and as though to confound Banner's programme
altogether, Wittgenstein actually speaks of religious creeds as
descriptions, for he writes:

> Christianity is not a doctrine, not, I mean, a theory about what
> has happened and will happen to the human soul, but a descrip-
> tion of something that actually takes place in human life. For
> 'consciousness of sin' is a real event and so are despair and salva-
> tion through faith. Those who speak of such things (Bunyan for
> instance) are simply describing what has happened to them,
> whatever gloss anyone may want to put on it. (Wittgenstein
> 1980a: 28)

Here, then, the question is not one of the discourse of religion
being either descriptive or non-descriptive, but of what one *calls*
'description' in the religious context. It is in such a manner that
Wittgenstein's philosophy breaks down the neat contrast which is
so fundamental to the attributing of an expressivist label to the
Remarks on Frazer.

Banner and Swinburne contend also that the expressivist model
rejects the idea that religious discourse articulates beliefs which can
be judged to be true or false. Similar points can be made here.
Belief, for Wittgenstein, is not a unified concept, but rather a polythetic one; like the concept of description, and as he says of the
word 'thinking', the idea of 'belief' 'is simply far more erratic than
it appears at first sight' (Wittgenstein 1980d: §234). Hence, when
faced with Banner's challenge as to whether religious discourse has
to do with beliefs or not, the Wittgensteinian will simply say: 'There
are beliefs and beliefs' (Malcolm 1964b: 110).[3] Wittgenstein certainly
speaks of religious and magical beliefs in the *Remarks on Frazer*, and
while these may not have the same character as scientific beliefs, it
would be contended that these are *beliefs* nonetheless, and not to be
regarded as 'secondary': for there is no 'standard' belief, no 'ordinary belief' (as Braithwaite puts it) from which a *religious* belief
deviates. As with the descriptive/non-descriptive distinction, then,
the belief/attitude dichotomy cannot be the basis for 'Wittgenstein's
expressivism'. To summarize, then, if 'description' may denote 'a

great variety of thing', then there can be no *single* criterion of what is to count as 'the descriptive' as opposed to 'the non-descriptive'. Consequently, this entails that the descriptive/non-descriptive, cognitive/non-cognitive, belief/attitude, and, thus, explanatory/ expressive distinctions are, for Wittgenstein, redundant.

If the foregoing attack on received opinion is correct, then two principal effects follow. First, one will have to surrender the near-habitual characterization of the nature of Wittgenstein's critique of Frazer and his alternative conception of ritual. And second, we are left with an interpretative problem relating to those of the *Remarks* which appear unashamedly expressivist in nature, remarks relating to kissing photographs, beating trees, and the like. If these are not to be treated as simply anomalous or a throwback to Tractarian tendencies, then they will need to be reinterpreted. This will be undertaken in Chapter 7, but our immediate task is to focus upon another conspicuous feature of the *Remarks on Frazer*: the rejection of explanation in anthropology and the advocacy of a superior method in the form of 'perspicuous representation'.

Part II
Methodology: Description and Explanation

4

Perspicuous Representation

The upshot of the previous argument is that Wittgenstein's critique of Frazer cannot be said to involve the advancement of a comprehensive expressive theory of religion. Having thus dispensed with one habitual characterization of the *Remarks on Frazer*, it is now necessary to assess Wittgenstein's methodological suggestions for the study of magic and religion: in brief, the eschewal of explanation and the advocacy of 'perspicuous representation'.

The purpose of this chapter, then, will be the explication of a small number of crucial remarks, from which Wittgenstein's embryonic methodology may be gleaned. First, Wittgenstein, commenting on Frazer's explanation of the rule at Nemi, says:

> I think one reason why the attempt to find an explanation is wrong is that we have only to put together in the right way what we *know*, without adding anything, and the satisfaction we are trying to get from the explanation comes of itself. (Wittgenstein 1979b: 2)

There then follows this remark:

> We can only *describe* and say, human life is like that. (1979b: 3)

And most importantly, there is the following block of comments (Wittgenstein 1979b: 8–9):

> An historical explanation, an explanation as an hypothesis of the development, is only *one* kind of summary of the data – of their synopsis. We can equally well see the data in their relations to one another and make a summary of them in a general picture without putting it in the form of an hypothesis regarding the temporal development.

> Identifying one's own gods with the gods of other peoples. One becomes convinced that the names have the same meaning.

'And all this points to some unknown law' is what we want to say about the material Frazer has collected. I *can* set out this law in an hypothesis of development, or again, in analogy with the schema of a plant I can give it in the schema of a religious ceremony, but I can also do it just by arranging the factual material so that we can easily pass from one part to another and have a clear view of it – showing it in a *'perspicuous'* way.

For us the conception of a perspicuous representation is fundamental. It indicates the form in which we write of things, the way in which we see things. (A kind of *'Weltanschauung'* that seems to be typical of our time. Spengler.)

This perspicuous representation makes possible that understanding which consists just in the fact that we 'see the connections'. Hence the importance of finding *intermediate links*.

But in our case an hypothetical link is not meant to do anything except draw attention to the similarity, the connection, between the *facts*. As one might illustrate the internal relation of a circle to an ellipse by gradually transforming an ellipse into a circle; *but not in order to assert that a given ellipse in fact, historically, came from a circle* (hypothesis of development) but only to sharpen our eye for a formal connection.

But equally I might see the hypothesis of development as nothing but a way of expressing a formal connection.

The resemblance of these remarks to sections 122–33 of the *Investigations* is striking, and it thus seems that Wittgenstein's reading of Frazer led to important insights about what the correct method of philosophy should be. The significance of these comments should not, then, be understated.

In the first part of this chapter, Wittgenstein's conception of the nature of philosophy, of philosophical problems, and their 'cure' by perspicuous representation will be set out. In the second and third parts, I will show how this applies to material such as that collected by Frazer in *The Golden Bough*. In doing so, we will be in a position to assess whether Wittgenstein's alternative to Frazer's explanations of primitive religious phenomena is a valid one: that is, whether the concept of a perspicuous representation is a helpful suggestion for anthropological methodology.

4.1 THE IDEAL OF PERSPICUITY IN WITTGENSTEIN'S LATER PHILOSOPHY

Many philosophers of religion influenced by Wittgenstein lay great stress on the importance of a perspicuous representation of religious phenomena. So, for example, D. Z. Phillips claims that 'philosophy's task is to give a perspicuous representation of religious differences when we are tempted to mischaracterise them' (Phillips 1988: xvi); and Richard Bell similarly stresses the need for 'a more "perspicuous representation" of how things are in the world' (Bell 1984: 299). Yet it is rarely made clear precisely what such a representation involves. One is told that it consists in 'seeing connections' or the like, but this is ambiguous, particularly when there is controversy over what Wittgenstein himself means by a perspicuous representation as the idea is put forward in the *Investigations*. Thus, in order to clarify what a philosopher of religion or writer on anthropological matters would mean by stressing the need for such a concept, and what its effects would be when applied, we must initially establish the content of the idea as Wittgenstein presents it.

If we are to have any success at all in this matter, we must understand something about Wittgenstein's conception of the nature of philosophy and of philosophical problems. It can be said that one of the continuities which runs through Wittgenstein's early and later thought is the act of distancing himself from Bertrand Russell's demand that philosophy should take on the methods of the natural sciences. Russell stressed the 'importance of applying to philosophical problems certain broad principles of method which have been found successful in the study of scientific questions' (Russell 1986: 57). Rejecting Russell's view that philosophy should aim for a general theoretical understanding of the world, Wittgenstein emphasized the discontinuities between philosophy and the sciences, and looking back on the *Tractatus'* stance on this issue, he wrote that 'it was true to say that our considerations could not be scientific ones' (Wittgenstein 1958: §109). Rather than amassing greater knowledge, uncovering hitherto unknown facts, making discoveries or putting forward theories, philosophy's task was the Kantian one, that of adjudicating the bounds of sense. Philosophy, he wrote in the *Tractatus*, aims at the logical clarification of thoughts and propositions (Wittgenstein 1961a: 4.112). This desire for clarity is a constant feature of Wittgenstein's thought. We see it in all periods of his work, from the comments quoted above, through the middle period, in which a 'striving after clarity and perspicuity' (Wittgenstein 1975: 7) is stressed, right up until the *Investigations*, where we find the following remark:

> For the clarity that we are aiming at is indeed *complete* clarity. But this simply means that the philosophical problems should *completely* disappear. (Wittgenstein 1958: §133)

And this takes us to the heart of Wittgenstein's later conception of the nature of a philosophical problem.

Wittgenstein claimed, contrary to Russell and Frege, that ordinary language was in good working order, and that the construction of an ideal language – a 'concept-script' – was unnecessary and could lead to fundamental misunderstandings and confusions. Though ordinary language is in good order it is, however, the source of philosophical problems. It is in order to stress this point that Wittgenstein introduced the distinction between surface and depth grammar. Philosophical problems arise out of the misleading nature of surface grammar, for we tend to overlook the fact that sentences which are structurally similar ('I am in pain', 'He is the owner of this vehicle') may have uses (their depth grammar) which are radically different from each other. It was this observation which led Wittgenstein to bemoan the main mistake made by philosophers: 'that when language is looked at, what is looked at is a form of words and not the use made of the form of words' (Wittgenstein 1966: 2), and to claim that, for a large number of cases, 'the meaning of a word is its use in the language' (Wittgenstein 1958: §43). The superficial structural similarities between various words and sentences is not the only cause of philosophical confusion (cf. Hacker 1986: 168–75), but it is certainly fundamental and enables us to understand Wittgenstein's view of the nature of the problems with which philosophy has been occupied. The essence of his view is that such problems are illusory, and are not so much to be solved as *dissolved*.

It is here that one can detect just how much Wittgenstein was influenced by Heinrich Hertz.[1] In the introduction to *The Principles of Mechanics*, Hertz considers problems concerning the 'mysterious' natures of electricity and force. He wonders why it is that the same 'wearisome' questions are not asked as to the nature of gold or velocity. His answer is remarkable in its similarity to Wittgenstein's treatment of philosophical problems:

> I fancy that the difference must lie in this. With the terms 'velocity' and 'gold' we connect a large number of relations to other terms; and between all these relations we find no contradictions which offend us. We are therefore satisfied and ask no further questions. But we have accumulated around the terms 'force' and 'electricity' more relations than can be completely reconciled amongst themselves. We have an obscure feeling of this and want to have things cleared up. Our confused wish finds expression in the confused question as to the nature of force and electricity. But the answer which we want is not really an answer to this question. It is not by finding out more and fresh relations and connections that it can be answered; but by removing the contradictions existing between those already known, and thus perhaps by reducing their number. When these painful contradictions are removed, the question as to the nature of force will not have been answered; but our minds, no longer vexed, will cease to ask illegitimate questions. (Hertz 1956: 7–8)

Similarly, Ludwig Boltzmann, Hertz's fellow physicist and an equally important influence on Wittgenstein's thought, contended that by acts of pure description one could resolve all metaphysical problems, such as whether other human beings have sensations or thoughts. Such questions are brought to silence by the revelation that 'one sees that one did not know what one was really asking' (Boltzmann 1974: 75). Again:

> My present theory is totally different from the view that certain questions fall outside the boundaries of human cognition. For according to that latter theory this is a defect or imperfection of man's cognitive capacity, whereas I regard the existence of these questions and problems themselves as an illusion. (Boltzmann 1974: 167)

It is in this context that we should understand the comment of *Investigations* §464: 'My aim is: to teach you to pass from a piece of disguised nonsense to something that is patent nonsense'. As Anthony Kenny elaborates, 'when we are suffering from philosophical problems we have a bit of hidden nonsense in our minds, and the only way to cure it is to bring it out into the open' (Kenny

1982: 3). This is very much connected with Wittgenstein's therapeutic – even psychoanalytic – programme for philosophy,
whereby 'the philosopher's treatment of a question is like the treatment of an illness' (Wittgenstein 1958: §255). What is significant
here is the notion that a philosophical question (whether there are
other minds, whether time can be measured, etc.) is not some great
problem in need of a momentous answer, but rather a piece of
nonsense in need of a cure. Philosophical problems are not empirical problems, and they are solved

> by looking into the workings of our language, and that in such a
> way as to make us recognize those workings: *in despite of* an urge
> to misunderstand them. The problems are solved, not by giving
> new information, but by arranging what we have always known.
> Philosophy is a battle against the bewitchment of our intelligence
> by means of language. (Wittgenstein 1958: §109)

In his struggle against this bewitchment, Wittgenstein employs a
number of methods. Supreme among these is the concept of a
perspicuous representation (*übersichtliche Darstellung*, and often
translated as 'synoptic view' (Wittgenstein 1981: §464) or 'bird's-eye
view' (Wittgenstein 1975: 52)), which is introduced in the
Investigations as the means whereby we can combat the greatest
source of philosophical trouble: our failure to see clearly the subtle
differences between forms of language, the uses to which different
language-games are put. He says:

> A main source of our failure to understand is that we do not
> *command a clear view* of the use of our words. – Our grammar is
> lacking in this sort of perspicuity. A perspicuous representation
> produces just that understanding which consists in 'seeing
> connexions'. Hence the importance of finding and inventing
> *intermediate cases.*
>   The concept of a perspicuous representation is of fundamental
> significance for us. It earmarks the form of account we give, the
> way we look at things. (Is this a 'Weltanschauung'?)
> (Wittgenstein 1958: §122)

This is one of the most remarkably pregnant passages of the
Investigations. In it a number of themes are condensed. First, there
is a clear statement of the cause of philosophical puzzlement, the

contention that the form of our language hides from us the actuality of multiple diversities of use; and there follows from this a prescription for our blindness. It is the concept of a perspicuous representation which is to act as a cure for what he calls 'the sickness of the understanding' (Wittgenstein 1956: 157). Yet, even without doubting its 'fundamental significance', it has to be said that the concept itself lacks perspicuity, and Wittgenstein does not follow his selling of the concept with even a single example. If we wish to clarify the idea we will need to turn to sources other than the *Investigations*.

Before embarking on an analysis of this concept, however, we should just briefly return to the writings of Ludwig Boltzmann, where the germ of Wittgenstein's idea can perhaps be seen. In his speeches on both mechanics and theoretical physics, Boltzmann constantly stresses the need for what he sometimes calls 'a perspicuously comprehensive description' (Boltzmann 1974: 161), and at other times, 'the overview of the whole, [which is] required for any mental activity aiming at discovering something new or even just essentially new combinations of old ideas' (Boltzmann 1974: 77). Hence, if we are to accept the idea that an *Übersicht* is fundamentally a bird's-eye view, then we need look no further than the following passage for a formative influence on Wittgenstein's thinking about this matter:

> There is a need for making the utmost use of what powers of perception we possess, and since the eye allows us to take in the greatest store of facts at once (significantly enough we say 'survey'), this gives rise to the need to represent the results of calculations and that not only for the imagination but visibly for the eye and palpably for the hand, with cardboard and plaster. (Boltzmann 1974: 6–7)

There are many points of contact between this and the only illustration of a bird's-eye view in Wittgenstein's writings: the example of the colour-octahedron in *Philosophical Remarks*.

The octahedron is a three-dimensional model (or two-dimensional diagram of the model) which has pure colours at the corner points. It functions as 'a grammatical representation' (Wittgenstein 1975: 51) of colour space, and from such a model we can read off the spectrum of shades between two particular colours: it 'wears the rules of grammar on its face' (Wittgenstein 1975: 278). With this representation we have a model which, it could be said, 'contained the whole of the grammar' (Wittgenstein 1974b: 55); and, moreover, one which is indeed 'capable of being taken in at a glance'. 'Using the octahedron as a representation', writes Wittgenstein, 'gives us a *bird's-eye view* of the grammatical rules' (Wittgenstein 1975: 52). There then follows this comment:

> The chief trouble with our grammar is that we don't have a *bird's-eye view* of it. (Wittgenstein 1975: 52)

The inference is that such a form of representing should be applied to those segments of our language which trouble us and which are the cause of philosophical puzzlement.

If the 'bird's-eye view' motif is taken literally, this suggests that the philosopher should in some way be looking down over the surface of the phenomenon being studied, observing a particular aspect of it, or else seeing it holistically.[2] A bird's-eye view of language is to be attained by the careful description of the uses of ordinary language, by the 'quiet weighing of linguistic facts' (Wittgenstein 1981: §447). When obtained, we will 'be able to "take in at a glance" a segment of grammar, so that one will not be misled by surface grammar, false analogies, or pictures embedded in language which, considered independently of their application, mislead us' (Baker and Hacker 1984b: 306).

So, the construction of a perspicuous representation would appear to be the positive aim of philosophy, contrasting with the negative or therapeutic side of Wittgenstein's method, which highlights pieces of philosophical nonsense with the aim of removing them. However, these positive and negative aspects are not in opposition but rather intimately connected. This is due to Wittgenstein's claim that 'philosophy isn't anything except philosophical problems' (Wittgenstein 1974b: 193). Thus, we wish to remove these problems (negative), and the way in which we do this is by establishing an overview of all uses of language (positive). This positive aspect of Wittgenstein's philosophy, the attainment of surveyability, is perhaps uppermost in his mind when he contends that perspicuous representation might constitute a *world-view*: 'Is this a "Weltanschauung"?' he asks (Wittgenstein 1958: §122). This certainly gives the impression that what is on offer ('the way we look at things') is something rather ambitious, and it leads Kenny to say that one can find in the *übersicht* concept 'a view of philosophy as giving a very general view of the world, an overall understanding' (Kenny 1982: 5). But that interpretation is not unproblematic. It would surely be bizarre if Wittgenstein, having undeviatingly rejected Russell's prescription that philosophy should aim at general theoretical understanding, would then, through the motif of *Übersichtlichkeit*, advocate such a project himself. And one may also have justifiable doubts about the intelligibility of the notion of 'taking in at a glance' a piece of grammar. Worries such as these should lead us to entertain a model of perspicuity divergent from the ubiquitous 'bird's-eye view' model. To this end we may note Gordon Baker's later thinking on the subject, which rejects his analyses both in earlier papers (cf. Baker 1986: 30) and in his collaborative work with Hacker.

Baker's interpretation lays stress on the *function* rather than the features of a perspicuous representation. His claim is that a representation is a perspicuous one if it succeeds in introducing a level of perspicuity to a confusing philosophical matter and thus helps us to 'find our way about'. If this is the case, then 'there is no general restriction on what form a perspicuous representation may take' (Baker 1991: 45–6); it certainly need not take the form of something which is either 'surveyable' or else constitutes a 'bird's-eye view'. Rather, Baker maintains that there is a case for 'linking its content to the idea of exposing new aspects of systems of expression in order to break our bondage to analogies absorbed into the forms of our language' (Baker 1991: 45). Hence, the idea of perspicuity is connected with the discussion of 'seeing-as' in part two of the *Investigations*, and, indeed, Baker compares someone in thrall to a philosophical dogma with the person who can only see one aspect of the duck-rabbit diagram. We remedy such aspect-blindness by bringing 'hitherto unnoticed aspects of things to a person's awareness, that is to get him to *see* things differently' (Baker 1991: 50). The ways of achieving such a 'conversion' are, of course, legion: we may do it by placing the problematic thing alongside an object of comparison, by setting it in different surroundings, and so on. Indeed, Baker maintains that 'perspicuous representations in Wittgenstein's writings have several radically different forms. Their diversity matches the diversity of procedures for bringing somebody to notice a new aspect in a drawing' (Baker 1991: 57). So, we are blind to certain aspects of the grammar of our language due to their familiarity (cf. Wittgenstein

1958: §129) and we need to *remind ourselves* of the ordinary uses to which troubling segments are put. A representation is perspicuous when it succeeds in bringing us to such an understanding. If Baker's interpretation is correct, we can no longer complain that there are no examples of such representations in the *Investigations:* in fact, it is packed full of reminders of the everyday uses of words which philosophers tend to think of as 'super-concepts' – 'being', 'experience', 'proposition', etc. If the representation of these words (the attempt to bring them 'back from their metaphysical to their everyday use' (Wittgenstein 1958: §116)), is successful, then it will be one which is 'perspicuous'.

None of this is particularly different from the thoughts of other commentators. What *is* at variance is the contention that there is no perspicuous representation *over and above* these therapeutic methods; that there is no *positive* goal beyond the negative task of dissolving philosophical confusions.

> Giving a perspicuous representation is essential to a conceptual therapy, not something to be contrasted with particular therapies as an independent project manifesting Wittgenstein's hankering for a more global, positive, or systematic role for philosophy. (Baker 1991: 51)

On this reading, then, the term 'perspicuous representation' designates the family of tools and methods so employed as to yield clarity and dissolve philosophical illusions.

Some evidence for the accuracy of this small-scale model may be gained if we reflect on Wittgenstein's conception of perspicuity in mathematical proof. In his *Remarks on the Foundations of Mathematics*, Wittgenstein lays great stress on the claim that 'a mathematical proof must be perspicuous (*übersichtlich*)' (Wittgenstein 1978: 143). Similarly, he claims that such a proof must be 'capable of being taken in' (Wittgenstein 1978: 143). The word he uses in this instance is '*übersehbare*', which has the connotation of 'an overall view'. Here, then, we patently appear to be concerned with the holistic model of perspicuity. However, when we come to look at what Wittgenstein is really pursuing when he speaks of a perspicuous proof, we find that it is nothing particularly grand or global. Rather, the emphasis is placed on the 'repeatability' or 'reproducibility' of a proof:

The proof must be a configuration whose exact reproduction is certain. Or again: we must be sure we can exactly reproduce what is essential to the proof. It may for example be written down in two different handwritings or colours. (Wittgenstein 1978: 143; cf. Wittgenstein 1989: 37)

Thus, what Wittgenstein means by a perspicuous proof is 'a memorable configuration' (Wittgenstein 1978: 149). Such a proof is contrasted with one which is incapable of being taken in, the example of which Wittgenstein provides is that of the 'proto-thousand': 'a long row of strokes engraved in hard rock which is our paradigm for the number that we call 1000' (Wittgenstein 1978: 150). This is capable neither of easy recognition nor easy reproduction: it has no 'characteristic visual shape' (Wittgenstein 1978: 151), and cannot thus be called 'perspicuous'.

This digression into Wittgenstein's view of perspicuity in mathematics is intended to do nothing other than to show that even where there is talk of overviews and surveyability, what is really being put forward is not an imperialistic conception of philosophy such as that suggested by Kenny – such a conception as seems drastically at odds with the drift of Wittgenstein's mature work. No, there is reason to believe that talk of a 'bird's-eye view' is largely figurative, simply expressive of a desire for clarity, and not committing Wittgenstein to a global or systematic philosophical project. Similarly, the *Weltanschauung* Wittgenstein speaks of constitutes *a way of viewing things* rather than *a particular view of things*. Hence, the *Weltanschauung* 'typical of our time' refers to a striving after clarity, and Wittgenstein is recommending a manner of thought typical among those thinkers who inspired him (Hertz, Boltzmann, Ernst, Spengler) and who share with him a desire for perspicuity. These considerations should lead us to the conclusion that Baker has perhaps provided us with the key to the *übersicht* concept.

Although Baker's interpretation has been seen to be the most plausible, it may be worthwhile to withhold final judgement until we have seen how these opposing accounts of perspicuous representation function when applied to religious phenomena. This exercise should illustrate the greater validity of one of the two rival interpretations by noting their success (or otherwise) when given an application to a concrete matter: namely, the study of the ritual life of mankind.

4.2   PERSPICUOUS REPRESENTATIONS AND MAGICO-RELIGIOUS PHENOMENA

In the *Remarks on Frazer* Wittgenstein introduces the idea of a perspicuous representation as an alternative to Frazer's *explanations* of magical rites and beliefs. Frazer's purpose in writing *The Golden Bough* is to provide a 'fairly probable explanation' for the Arician rule. He does this by uncovering the motives which led to its institution, the beliefs which underlay the ritual. Hence, Frazer claims, the King of the Wood was slain because the participants in the rite believed that the violent succession of the kings secured the plentiful growth of the crops. The same method of explanation is employed for many other rites: the sacrament of first-fruits is explained by attributing to the celebrants the belief that the harvested crops are animated by spiritual beings who must be propitiated; effigy-burning is explained by a more or less tacit belief in the laws of sympathetic magic; the lighting of midsummer fires is explained by positing in the agents the belief that such fires serve to drive away evil powers; and so on. Frazer's explanations do not end here, however, for he needs to explain the existence of the beliefs themselves, and these are accounted for as being rude attempts at scientific thought. The final explanatory move is to place the whole field of magico-religious phenomena in an evolutionary schema, showing its role in the developing intellectual life of mankind.

As noted previously, Wittgenstein appears to wish to discount teleological and intentional explanations from an account of ritual. Yet in the discussion of perspicuous representation in the *Remarks*, it is not the *particular* inadequacy of Frazer's explanations which is stressed. Rather, Wittgenstein appears to be saying that *any* explanation would be out of place in an account of the religious life of mankind. Hence, he says that 'the attempt to find an explanation is wrong', implying that it is not just *Frazer's* explanations which are unwanted. Instead of explaining religious rites and beliefs, here 'we can only *describe* and say, human life is like that' (Wittgenstein 1979b: 3). Similarly, the 'satisfaction' Frazer is trying to achieve by means of his explanations is, rather, brought about by 'putting together in the right way what we *know*' (Wittgenstein 1979b: 2). The outlawing of explanation and the recommending of description is, of course, a familiar theme in Wittgenstein's philosophy (cf. Wittgenstein 1958: §§109, 124), and in the *Remarks on Frazer* it is the idea of a comprehensive description, stripped of all explanatory and historical elements which appears to provide the content of a perspicuous representation of magical and religious phenomena. Wittgenstein states that irrespective of whether or not Frazer's historical explanation of ritual action and belief is correct, it is 'only *one* kind of summary of the data – of their synopsis' (Wittgenstein 1979b: 8), and that 'we can equally well see the data' in other ways. The contention here is that we are presented with a vast amount of data which needs to be ordered before confusions arise or in order to dispel such misunderstandings as may already be rooted. Wittgenstein's idea of clarity is not, however, monolithic: 'we want to establish an order in our knowledge of the use of language: an order with a particular end in view; one out of many possible orders; not *the* order' (Wittgenstein 1958: §132). His examples of bringing order allow for many alternatives: consider the ways in which we may want to arrange books in a library (cf. Wittgenstein 1969: 44); or the various places at which a president may be seated at a banquet so as to mark his position of authority (cf. Kenny 1982: 6).

It is in this open fashion that Wittgenstein presents the concept of a perspicuous representation as one possible ordering of ritual phenomena, and it is in such a context that we should understand this most important of passages, where Wittgenstein muses that all the information contained in *The Golden Bough* seems to be crying out for some kind of interpretation:

> 'And so the chorus points to a secret law' ['*Und so deutet das Chor auf ein geheimes Gesetz*'] one feels like saying to Frazer's collection of facts. I *can* represent this law, this idea, by means of an evolutionary hypothesis, or also, analogously to the schema of a plant, by means of the schema of a religious ceremony, but also by means of the arrangment of its factual content alone, in a '*perspicuous*' representation. (Wittgenstein 1979c: 69)

Here Wittgenstein states that while Frazer's method of ordering may in fact be legitimate, (at least) two other possibilities are conceivable. What should concern us initially is the first of these possibilities mentioned, and the only way to understand this alternative is to appreciate the influence which lies behind it. The influence is Goethe, and Wittgenstein makes this clear by his appeal to the poem 'The Metamorphosis of Plants', quoted below in David Luke's prose translation:

You are confused, beloved, by the thousandfold mingled multi-tude of flowers all over the garden. You listen to their many names which are for ever, one after another, ringing outlandishly in your ears. All their shapes are similar, yet none is the same as the next; and thus the whole chorus of them suggests a secret law, a sacred riddle [*Und so deutet das Chor auf ein geheimes Gesetz*]. Sweet lady, could I but at once convey to you in a word the happy solution! (Goethe 1986: 147–8)

Goethe's scientific method – which Wittgenstein thought was actu-ally a method of conceptual enquiry (cf. Wittgenstein 1980b: §950) – is very much at the core of the discussion about perspicuous representation in the *Remarks on Frazer*. The quest for the *Urpflanze* or 'Primal Plant' is specifically mentioned. Goethe's search for this centres on his concern with the 'hypothesis that it might be possi-ble to derive all plant forms from one original plant' (Goethe 1970: 71), thus providing 'the fundamental principle of metamorphosis' (Goethe 1970: 368). Goethe's (fundamentally Romantic) method appears to be intuitive: the investigator somehow comes to *see* the principle of unity binding together a particular grouping of natural phenomena. Some commentators (notably Rowe 1991: 289–90) have claimed that Wittgenstein's later work amounts to a defence of Goethe's method, but we must be careful not to state this unqual-ifiedly, for elements of Goethe's technique of explanation may appear anathema to Wittgenstein's concerns. For instance, we may note the episode in his *Italian Journey* where Goethe finds himself surrounded by a variety of plants, and muses:

Among this multitude might I not discover the Primal Plant? There certainly must be one. Otherwise, how could I recognize that this or that form *was* a plant if all were not built upon the same basic model? (Goethe 1970: 258–9)

Wittgenstein might very well have regarded this as an example of 'the craving for generality', resulting from 'the tendency to look for something in common to all the entities which we commonly subsume under a general term' (Wittgenstein 1969: 17). Indeed, Wittgenstein's remarks against essentialism could be used to attack Goethe's presuppositions here: the fact that we cannot isolate the essence of a phenomenon does not entail that we are unable to recognize an instance of that phenomenon (cf. Wittgenstein 1958:

§69). Yet not all Goethe's conjectures about the *Urpflanze* are open to such criticisms. As Rowe shows, Goethe seems to have developed more sophisticated forms of these ideas. He moves from the relatively crude idea that the Plant had actually existed at some time, to thinking that the leaf was the Primal Plant with all other plant organs having metamorphosized from it, and finally to the idea that 'the *Urpflanze* was an archetype whose origin lay partly within man's self, and that it was a way of grouping or intellectually grasping the totality of plants' (Rowe 1991: 289).

Thus, when Wittgenstein says that he can set out the 'unknown law' in 'the schema of a religious ceremony' he is saying that we *can* order the material collected by Frazer by applying a principle of unity analogous to Goethe's *Urpflanze*. Wittgenstein does not suggest how such a programme would work in this context, but we would perhaps construct a simple, exact language-game which could act as a religious *Ur-phenomenon* with which we might compare, order and evaluate existing rites and customs. Such a primal religious act might be something like a ceremonial offering at the grave of an ancestor, or perhaps the sacrifice of an animal or man (consider how Girard (1977: 306) saw *an act of violence* as being that which united all rites). The important thing to note here, though, is that such an *Ur-phenomenon* (or proto-phenomenon) would function only as an *ideal* and not as something which could summarize what religion really *is* or what it *evolved from*. Failure to understand this may lead us to search fruitlessly (as Goethe initially did) for that to which the ideal corresponds. Waismann is particularly helpful on this point. He recommends the setting up of lists or rules with which to compare the functions of ordinary language, but warns against taking this ideal as the real form of our language. Rather, he compares this idea with Boltzmann's method of 'describing a physical model ... without making any claim that it conformed to something in the real world' (Waismann 1965: 77):

> We simply place the patterns beside language and let it throw as much light upon its nature as it can. It is as if Boltzmann's model were placed beside the process of electricity and someone said 'Just look at that!' (Waismann 1965: 77)

In this manner, the religious *Ur-phenomenon* would have a purely heuristic function, serving the same purpose as the circle in this example from the *Remarks*:

One might illustrate the internal relation of a circle to an ellipse by gradually transforming the ellipse into a circle; *but not in order to assert that a given ellipse in fact, historically, came from a circle* (hypothesis of development) but only to sharpen our eye for a formal connection. (Wittgenstein 1979b: 9)

And significantly, Wittgenstein states that Frazer's developmental hypothesis might be helpful if it was presented as 'nothing but a way of expressing a formal connection' (Wittgenstein 1979b: 9).

Our understanding of what Wittgenstein means when he speaks of 'the ideal' can perhaps be deepened by reflection on his understanding of Oswald Spengler's conception of the life patterns of cultures. The aim of historical writing, according to Spengler, is to construct 'an ordered presentation of the past' (Spengler 1926: 15), and his particular ordering served to stress how the growth and decline of a culture followed a necessary and hence predictable pattern. By a study of the cultures of the past (the Indian, the Classical, and so on), one could hope to understand the stage one's own culture had reached. Although Wittgenstein was much impressed by Spengler's methods and vision and regarded him as a major influence on his own thought (cf. Wittgenstein 1980a: 19), he did not believe that one could discern, as Spengler had felt possible, the laws which govern the growth and decline of cultures. He maintained, rather, that Spengler's mapping of the life of a culture is best understood as the expression of an ideal, part of a heuristic project by means of which one could understand *particular* cultures. Thus:

How is a view like Spengler's related to mine? Distortion in Spengler: The ideal doesn't lose any of its dignity if it's presented as the principle determining the form of one's reflections. A sound measure. (Wittgenstein 1980a: 27)

Thus, if Goethe employs an ideal *Urpflanze* with which to order flora, then Spengler has his own ideal, that of 'the primitive culture-form, *the* Culture that underlies as ideal all the individual Cultures' (Spengler 1926: 104). Hilmy elaborates on how Spengler's morphology of cultures influenced Wittgenstein's method, stressing how the notion of 'the ideal' enters into the latter's conception of language-games:

Spengler used an epoch (the Roman) as an object of comparison to come to an understanding of our present (West European/American) epoch; analogously Wittgenstein uses language-games (of the hypothetical, exact variety) as objects of comparison to shed light on the facts of our language (our extant 'language-games'). (Hilmy 1987: 262)

Hence, when we wrote earlier that Wittgenstein's analogue in the *Remarks on Frazer* to Goethe's *Urpflanze* was a constructed or exact 'religious' language-game, we were stating something which is a ubiquitous element of Wittgenstein's later philosophy, and thus the Goethean aspect of this first alternative to Frazer's explanatory method is certainly consonant with his later concerns as a whole.

Nevertheless, although there certainly are connections between Goethean morphology and the Wittgensteinian quest for perspicuity, in the *Remarks on Frazer* the perspicuous representation of religious phenomena appears to be clearly differentiated from the morphological one, and its features are spelled out as follows:

This perspicuous presentation makes possible that understanding which consists just in the fact that we 'see the connections'. Hence the importance of finding *intermediate links*. (Wittgenstein 1979b: 9)

What such a representation would appear to be is a highly detailed and comprehensive description of (in this case) religious phenomena so that one could note the similarities and differences between a number of examples. Strangely enough, an example of this phenomenological method comes from Frazer himself in his treatment of the fire-festivals of Europe. There Frazer describes a great mass of customs, and draws connections between, for example, midsummer fires and the fires of Hallowe'en. Commenting on this, Wittgenstein says:

The most noticeable thing seems to me not merely the similarities but also the differences throughout all these rites. It is a wide variety of faces with common features that keep showing in one place and in another. And one would like to draw lines joining the parts that various faces have in common. (Wittgenstein 1979b: 13)

And this seems to be the essence of the idea: a perspicuous representation appears to provide a perspective from which one can see relations between more or less similar or dissimilar rites, and from which a particular rite can be seen against the backcloth of analogous rituals. In such a manner, and particularly in its affinity with his thoughts on 'family resemblance', the idea of perspicuity seems here radically different from the Goethean notion of applying a 'unifying principle', which, in the context of *The Blue Book*, would still smack too much of essentialism. The representation, then, is achieved, not by the application of a unifying principle, but by taking in the field of ritual in its totality. Attainment of this perspective will allow us to see 'a complicated network of similarities overlapping and criss-crossing: sometimes overall similarities, sometimes similarities of detail' (Wittgenstein 1958: §66). What presents itself to us here is a clear statement of the 'bird's-eye view' model of an *Übersicht*, with Wittgenstein recommending that we build up a large-scale description of religious phenomena, and present this picture without offering any causal, evolutionary, or psychological explanation, nor, as appears to be the suggestion, with any historical context in mind. For after maintaining that Frazer's method is only one kind of synopsis, he says:

> We can equally well see the data in their relations to one another and make a summary of them in a general picture without putting it in the form of an hypothesis regarding the temporal development. (Wittgenstein 1979b: 8)[3]

We are urged, then, to construct a map-like, synchronic picture of ritual, a vast, comprehensive description of religious phenomena. Rhees writes in an editorial note to the *Remarks* that the idea constitutes 'a way of setting out the whole field together by making easy the passage from one part of it to another' (Wittgenstein 1979b: 9). Hence, the purpose is to 'see the connections' between different examples. A physiognomy of ritual without suggestions of how such acts arose seems to be what Wittgenstein is offering.

Avishai Margalit elaborates on this, saying that an account of ritual should take the form of:

> a sort of stamp album. The ritual ceremonies should be interpreted as the stamps in an album, enabling the collector to clarify their similarities and differences. Just as the album begins or ends

with the stamps of the interpreter's own country, the act of classification enables the interpreter to understand the content of the ritual. (Margalit 1992: 308)

Rather than putting forward explanations of rituals, Wittgenstein, Margalit maintains, is embarked on the project of 'successful elucidation'. A description of ritual activity is perspicuous when an interpreter can see his way from one rite to the next, and when it 'makes use of the links connecting it to the interpreter's own life and practices' (Margalit 1992: 308).

Margalit's view is shared by Richard Eldridge, who has attempted the most far-reaching application of Wittgenstein's method, one which stems from his expressivist interpretation of the *Remarks*. It is when we sense that religious and magical actions are not the practical applications of mistaken theories about the world that it dawns on us that Frazer's explanations are of little importance:

> When what is wanted is an account of what practices express and how they reflect human being in the world ... then simply setting out the cases and letting the interpretation of human being in the world emerge from the connections and point to new ones, producing a perspicuous representation, is what is most appropriate. Only connections among practices, and not a science of mind and thinking, can lead us to understand, critically and tentatively, how we fit into the world and what our practices reflect about us. (Eldridge 1987: 240–1)

Thus far, this is a standard interpretation. However, Eldridge goes further than most commentators in actually indicating how one would go about constructing such a representation. One would initially group the cases 'according to an inarticulate sense of their likeness, a sense compounded all at once of prior experience ("my experience with people"), of affective response, and of rough and groping discursive formulations, a sense that stems from sensibility' (Eldridge 1987: 242). Presented neither genetically nor schematically, the representation would simply arrange the phenomena 'so that only minor transitions are required in moving from one case to the next' (Eldridge 1987: 242). Arranged in terms of likenesses, the cases would form a family, and thus arranged, the material would provide a detailed picture of the human attitudes and concerns which are expressed in ritual.

Eldridge evidently wishes to recommend perspicuous representation as an ideal anthropological tool, but serious doubts about the notion of a bird's-eye view of ritual can be voiced. For one thing, Eldridge's presentation would surely be no less prejudiced than Frazer's account, the initial grouping being based on 'expressive' significance. Moreover, it is hard to see where the 'stamp album' model differs from Frazer's approach. As Wittgenstein himself recognizes, Frazer's presentation of the European fire-festivals itself constitutes a perspicuous representation. Indeed, the whole of *The Golden Bough* can be seen as a veritable stamp album of exotic and familiar rituals. Frazer entirely follows the pattern suggested by Margalit, noting instances of similar religious rites – say, licentious behaviour preceding the expulsion of evil in a material vehicle – beginning with exotic instances, then exploring similar occurrences in classical antiquity and in contemporary Europe and Britain. Whatever it was that possessed Wittgenstein's followers to presume Frazer was *not* engaged in perspicuously representing magical and religious phenomena, it was certainly not an acquaintance with the arguments and methods of *The Golden Bough*.

Yet, the Wittgensteinian may claim, what distinguishes Wittgenstein's prescription from Frazer's method is the absence of explanations concerned with motives, historical development, and so on. It is, in other words, synchronic and non-explanatory. Frazer's work is indeed not short of explanations, yet it must be noted that he did not view these as the most important aspect of his work, and even contended that they could perhaps be shorn from it. Hence, in the preface to *Balder the Beautiful* he writes about his theories:

> I hold them all very lightly and have used them chiefly as convenient pegs on which to hang my collections of facts. For I believe that, while theories are transitory, a record of facts has a permanent value, and that as a chronicle of ancient customs and beliefs my book may retain its utility when my theories are as obsolete as the customs and beliefs themselves deserve to be. (Frazer 1936j: xi)

Thus, if the Wittgensteinian is so dissatisfied with Frazer's theories, then he may simply strip them from the work and be left with just the comprehensive description that he is looking for.

And the synchronic element? While it is certainly true that one may transform an ellipse into a circle without positing the temporal priority of the one over the other, this need not persuade us that a similar procedure may be applied to the study of humans, who by their very nature are historical beings. Carlo Ginzburg, for example, reveals how he began his study of European witchcraft by employing a similar a-historical method, documenting 'purely formal affinities ... without bothering to insert it into a plausible historical framework' (Ginzburg 1990: 15). But this proved a fruitless course of action, for it failed to do justice to the sufferings endured by the tortured practitioners of witchcraft:

> I was dealing not with circles and ellipses (entities which are by definition divorced from a temporal context), but with men and women ... Human history does not unfold in the world of ideas, but in the sub-lunar world in which individuals are irreversibly born, inflict or endure suffering and die. (Ginzburg 1990: 15–16)

Ginzburg's rejection of perspicuous representation is thus based on the grave charge that it is a purely abstract mechanism, unsuitable for preserving the human dimension of religion.

So there are serious problems with the global, bird's-eye view model of perspicuous representation when applied to religious phenomena. Might Baker's small-scale model fare better?

4.3 PERSPICUOUS REPRESENTATION AS 'MAKING CLEAR'

To a casual reader, it may seem absurd to suggest that when Wittgenstein in the *Remarks on Frazer* talks about perspicuity he is doing anything other than thinking of the bird's-eye view model. Nothing in the sections explicitly concerned with methodology suggests otherwise. Nevertheless, there are scattered throughout the notes a number of comments which exhibit the characteristics of an *Übersicht* as the idea is presented by Baker. Consider Wittgenstein's remark that 'all rites' are akin to beating the ground with a walking stick. A connection having here been made between something 'we' do and something primitives do, Wittgenstein continues:

> Once such a phenomenon is brought into connection with an

instinct which I myself possess, this is precisely the explanation wished for; that is, the explanation which resolves this particular difficulty. (Wittgenstein 1979c: 72)

Here, then, Wittgenstein is attempting to clarify a rite by effecting a change of aspect; and he does this by bringing that rite into connection with something less alien. Looked upon in this fashion, as a species of 'seeing-as', we can begin to see a number of examples of perspicuous representations of ritual phenomena in the pages of the *Remarks on Frazer*. For example, the assimilation of effigy-burning to kissing pictures or names can be seen as nothing other than an attempt at a perspicuous representation. In this manner, Wittgenstein's project of perspicuous representation is at one with his attempt to dispel what he sees as the errors in Frazer's account, for instance the portrayal of certain customs and ceremonies as 'stupid actions'. By placing an alien rite next to a familiar action, Wittgenstein is trying to show that just as *our* ritual practices – say, tossing confetti at a newlywed couple, or (more personal) using a 'lucky' pen – are not informed by false science, so primitive rituals – the slaying of temporary kings, say, or the imposition of taboos – need not be either. Hence, the conceptual reminders Wittgenstein offers are not to be contrasted with the more systematic project of producing a complete description of ritual phenomena. Rather, each specific reminder employed, if successful in its clarification, may legitimately be termed a 'perspicuous representation' of a segment of ritual life.

So whereas Frazer offers explanations of rites, Wittgenstein offers perspicuous representations. Thus:

> The religious actions or the religious life of the priest-king are not different in kind from any genuinely religious action today, say a confession of sins. This also can be 'explained' and cannot be explained. (Wittgenstein 1979b: 4)

The form of 'explanation' favoured by Wittgenstein we may term 'making clear by perspicuous representation'. Frank Cioffi says that 'making clear' is the act of taking us 'from a state in which we find something "difficult to understand" to a state in which we find it less so' (Cioffi 1990b: 49). It is a method which G. K. Chesterton employs also, when he attempts to reveal what he sees as the confusions inherent in certain accounts of funerary practices in exotic lands. An example of the kind of account Chesterton might have in mind is the following passage, taken from Fustel de Coulanges' *The Ancient City*:

> No-one today thinks that an immortal being rests in a tomb. But in those ancient days they believed so firmly that a man lived there that they never failed to bury him with the objects of which they supposed he had need – clothing, utensils, and arms. They poured wine upon his tomb to quench his thirst, and placed food there to satisfy his hunger. (Fustel de Coulanges 1979: 16–17)

Chesterton objects to such speculation, and reminds us of our own practices, thus hoping to suggest a rationale for their exotic equivalents:

> It is like saying, 'The English in the twentieth century believed that a dead man could smell. This is attested by the fact that they always covered his grave with lilies, violets, or other flowers. Some priestly and tribal terrors were evidently attached to the neglect of this action, as we have records of several old ladies who were very much disturbed in mind because their wreaths had not arrived in time for the funeral.' (Chesterton 1905: 145)

Such a remark aims to dispel the confusion contained in the first account. In reminding us of our own customs regarding the dead, Chesterton is claiming that primitive funeral rites need not be generated by beliefs about what a dead man can do, think, feel, or require. Such actions should rather be seen as marks of respect, or expressions of mourning. Note also in this context Drury's juxtaposition of primitive magical acts with the actions of Western males, removing their hats in church (Drury 1973: x).

In these examples, the perspicuous representation is intended to replace an intellectualist rationale (the primitive acts on the basis of some theory in order to achieve some end) with an expressive one (the primitive is giving vent to certain feelings or attitudes). This is achieved by assimilating the exotic rite to a ritual practice or ritual inclination of our own (cf. Cioffi 1990a: 4). Followers of Wittgenstein often stress that it is simply by surveying such inclinations that we can arrive at an understanding of primitive ritual, and that Wittgenstein's rejection of Frazer's methods includes the rejection of empirical enquiry. Witness Rhees:

We need not go in search of new facts, nor conjecture them, to understand how there came to be such forms of magic and of ritual. All that we need for this is with us ... in our ways of thought and feeling. (Rhees 1971: 21)

Richard Bell similarly wants to say that empirical enquiry is unnecessary, and invokes instead 'an analogy of self-understanding' (Bell 1984: 296). We must begin by understanding our own ritual propensities, and then transport ourselves imaginatively into the lives of the exotic ritualists. We will then be in a position to understand their ways of acting and what they hope to achieve by their rituals.

This method relies on the idea of empathic understanding. It is this technique Collingwood employs as his model for historical understanding, contending that in order to understand an historical event it is not enough to confine oneself to an appreciation of its outward form. Collingwood draws a distinction between what he calls the outside and the inside of an event. The outside of the event refers to everything that can be described in terms of physical movement, while the inside of the event refers to that 'which can only be grasped in terms of thought' (Collingwood 1946: 213). The historian's task is to grasp the totality of a particular action (meaning the unity of inner and outer), and thus his work can never end with a description of the outside of the event: 'his main task is to think himself into this action, to discern the thought of the agent' (Collingwood 1946: 213). This pattern of understanding, Bell maintains, is discernible in the *Remarks on Frazer*: Wittgenstein is chastizing Frazer for concerning himself purely with the outside of ritual actions, whereas 'understanding requires that something be seen "from inside"' (Bell 1984: 309).

Leaving aside the inaccuracy of this characterization of Frazer's project, serious doubts can be cast on the possibility of an empathic understanding of ritual of the kind Bell suggests. There are great difficulties involved in re-experiencing someone else's thoughts, and this is sharpened further by the fact that, in this context, we are concerned, not with understanding the actions of historical figures from our own culture, but with the far more difficult enterprise of understanding the actions of members of *other* cultures. The patterns of reasoning of such people may be so different from ours that it will be impossible to imagine ourselves acting as they do. As W. H. Walsh says, while there may be little difficulty in re-experiencing the thoughts of men like Nelson and Julius Caesar, it may be a hazardous exercise to try to recreate for ourselves the thoughts of an African witch-doctor or a Viking chief:

> To make anything of the behaviour of such persons, we should all be inclined to say, we need something more than sympathetic understanding; we need experience, first- or second-hand, of the ways in which they commonly react to the situations in which they find themselves. (Walsh 1967: 57)

Without such fieldwork (that kind of enquiry which the Wittgensteinian seems to think unnecessary), the possibility of *mis*understanding is great. Indeed, it is all too likely that we should simply project ourselves (with our habits and attitudes) into the mind of the primitive ritualist. It should be plain that I cannot, for example, surmise the nature of *dakpa* solely by reflection on the feelings I have when performing my own pseudo-divinatory acts. No, the only way to establish what a member of the Azande expects and believes when he engages in divination is through observation of *his* (and not *my*) behaviour.

What is interesting here is that the error of this empathic approach exactly mirrors the mistake commonly attributed to Frazer himself. Radcliffe-Brown dubbed this the 'if-I-were-a-horse' fallacy, from the tale of a farmer whose horse had strayed from its paddock. Standing in the paddock and adopting the posture of the horse, the farmer mused: 'Now if I were a horse, which way would I go?' Frazer purportedly acts likewise, reconstructing primitive rationales by reasoning: 'If I were a savage, how in my ignorance would I think?' By such a method Frazer transforms the savage into an elementary scientist or philosopher, and has been widely castigated for so doing. But just as Frazer's savage is a (primitive) image of himself, so is Bell's. Though no longer a proto-scientist, Bell's savage is a harmless attitude-expresser. The criticism is perhaps more acute of Bell than it is of Frazer: having eschewed empirical enquiry, the Wittgensteinian has no way of checking whether the motivations for his own ritual impulses match those of the savage.

So what can we ultimately say about all this? The 'making clear' model of perspicuity seems on one level more attractive than the ambitious bird's-eye view type, yet this can only be the case if its purpose is purely negative and critical. That is, it can legitimately be used to illustrate that, on the premise that our own ritual inclinations seem not to be informed by false science, the primitive ritualist's actions *need not be* either. On the other hand, if what is attempted is a positive reconstruction of the primitive's reasons for performing ritual actions, then we have an inadequate method. This conclusion results from the baldly stated intention to avoid all empirical enquiry, and to 'do away with all explanation'. So the question needs to be asked: why prohibit explanation?

5

The Prohibition on Explanation

Wittgenstein is vehement that what is crucially wrong in Frazer's account is his attempt to *explain* rituals, say the killing of *Rex Nemorensis*. This prohibition on explanation requires attention. It is a central feature not only of Wittgenstein's reflections on religion, but also of those of his followers (witness the title of one of D. Z. Phillips' books: *Religion Without Explanation*), and it seems a most bizarre and obscurantist injunction. We should do well, then, to isolate what it is about rituals that render them non-explainable. This will take us right into the heart of the Wittgensteinian interpretation of religion.

5.1 RELIGION 'WITHOUT EXPLANATION'

Wittgenstein's direct influence on the philosophy of religion filtered through rather slowly after his death, and it was not his explicit remarks on religion which were initially the focus of attention. Rather, certain features of his later work were recognized to be of significance to perennial questions concerning the nature of religious belief. In addition to ideas culled from the *Philosophical Investigations*, the blueprint for a specifically Wittgensteinian philosophy of religion was largely provided by Peter Winch's book *The Idea of a Social Science*, the principal theme of which is a thoroughgoing rejection of the methods of natural science in the study of human and social affairs. Thus, Winch firmly opposes the view (found, for example, in Mill) 'that there can be no fundamental logical difference between the principles according to which we explain natural changes and those according to which we explain social changes' (Winch 1958: 71). Instead, he puts forward a conception of understanding human behaviour which 'is more closely analogous to the way in which we understand expressions of ideas than it is to the way we understand physical processes' (Winch

1958: 132). He says that such understanding 'is like applying one's knowledge of a language in order to understand a conversation rather than like applying one's knowledge of the laws of mechanics to understand the workings of a watch' (Winch 1958: 133).

Naturally, this approach has certain consequences for the study of religious life. An investigation of religion must attempt to understand the phenomenon, not as one would attempt to explain the workings of a machine, but rather by describing it as a rule-governed activity in which *ideas* are expressed (cf. Winch 1958: 87; 131–3). Moreover, this understanding must be carried out *on religion's own terms*, and it would thus be illegitimate to portray religion as a bungled or perverted reflection of another form of behaviour. So just as Wittgenstein chastizes Frazer for presenting magic as abortive science, Winch castigates Pareto's view that the actions of a practitioner of magic are akin to the mistakes of a businessman:

> Is the entrepreneur's mistake really comparable at all to the performance of a magical rite? Surely it ought rather to be compared to a *mistake* in the magical rite. The entrepreneur's mistake is a particular act ... within the *category* of business behaviour; but magical operations themselves *constitute* a category of behaviour. Magic, in a society in which it occurs, plays a peculiar role of its own and is conducted according to considerations of its own. (Winch 1958: 99)

This stress on the irreducibility of any one social practice to another leads to the claim that perhaps typifies the standard Wittgensteinian approach to religion more than any other: 'Science is one such mode [of social life] and religion is another; and each has criteria of intelligibility peculiar to itself' (Winch 1958: 100). These 'modes of social life' are often described as 'forms of life' or 'language-games'.

There are two reasons why the denial of explanation flows from the characterization of religion as a distinctive language-game. First, explanation can be seen as paradigmatic of scientific understanding, and if religion is not a species of science, nor to be evaluated by alien (scientific) standards, then it will follow that explanation will be out of place in an account of religion. Secondly, the very notion of a language-game as described by Wittgenstein involves the idea that an explanation of these elemental human practices cannot be effected, that the language-game is, so to speak, a 'given' which may only be described and not further explained. Hence:

> Our mistake is to look for an explanation where we ought to look at what happens as a 'proto-phenomenon'. That is, where we ought to have said: *this language-game is played.* (Wittgenstein 1958: §654)

> You must bear in mind that the language-game is so to say something unpredictable. I mean: it is not based on grounds. It is not reasonable (or unreasonable).
> It is there – like our life. (Wittgenstein 1977a: §559)

If, then, religion is a language-game, it must only be noted and described and the investigator will have to surrender the desire to provide an explanation of it. Of course, we may provide explanations *within* the language-game, explanations of why it is, for example, that bread and wine are consumed during the Eucharist, or why the celebration of Passover is so central to the Jewish religion. What *is* prohibited is the attempt to offer an explanation of the language-game *in toto*; and thus the attempts of Feuerbach, Durkheim and Freud to offer philosophical, sociological and psychoanalytic explanations for *the existence of religion as such* are illegitimate. 'The existence of religious practices can no more be explained than the existence of sports, or of musical composition' (Malcolm 1993: 85).

Yet this cannot be the reason for Wittgenstein's eschewal of Frazer's explanations. In the *Remarks*, as we have earlier seen, he nowhere speaks of religion as a language-game, nor is the idea even implicit there. No, though explanation beyond a certain level is indeed rejected, the terminus of explanation is there located in something other than the language-game.

5.2 THE PRIMITIVE REACTION

A conspicuous aspect of Wittgenstein's later work, and indeed one which is manifest in the *Remarks on Frazer*, is his conception of human beings as instinctive animals, and it may be that it is the religious instinct, the ceremonial impulse, which lies beyond explanation. We need, then, to examine the role of 'primitive reactions' in religion, before considering why these are to be regarded as ur-phenomenal.

To begin with, then, consider the following passage, from *Culture and Value*:

> The origin and the primitive form of the language-game is a reaction; only from this can more complicated forms develop.
>
> Language – I want to say – is a refinement, 'in the beginning was the deed'. (Wittgenstein 1980a: 31; cf. Wittgenstein 1976: 420)

Nowhere is this Goethe-inspired thought made more explicit than in Wittgenstein's notes from 1937 on 'Cause and Effect: Intuitive Awareness'. Here, he rejects rationalistic accounts of causal language (whereby such language originates in observations of constant sequences of events), and proposes in its place an account which is striking in its insistence that our concepts of causation originate in primitive reactions:

> *We react to the cause.*
>
> Calling something 'the cause' is like pointing and saying: '*He's* to blame!' (Wittgenstein 1976: 410)

> There is a reaction which can be called 'reacting to the cause'. – We also speak of 'tracing' the cause; a simple case would be, say, following a string to see who is pulling at it. If I then find him – how do I know that he, his pulling, is the cause of the string's moving? Do I establish this by a series of experiments? (Wittgenstein 1976: 416)

Wittgenstein's purpose in these notes is to claim that our notions of cause and effect emerge not from a process of ratiocination, but are, rather, *instinctive*: 'Don't we recognize immediately that the pain is produced by the blow we have received?' (Wittgenstein 1976: 409). Malcolm elaborates on these points by imagining the case of a child who runs into another, knocking him down. The fallen child may leap up and hit the other one. This we call 'reacting to the cause'. Such an action can be called 'immediate', and this means that there is no uncertainty over, or inferring to, the cause involved here:

The child who retaliates against the one who crashed into him does not act because he 'thinks' that this caused his fall. No! He just acts! It is like brushing away an insect that is tickling one's skin. One does not make experiments to determine whether the tickling sensation is caused by the insect. (Malcolm 1986: 150)

Malcolm's point is that the language of causation is 'grafted on to these immediate reactions' (Malcolm 1986: 150).

Wittgenstein's emphasis on primitive reactions is not peculiar to his treatment of causation. As the passage from *Culture and Value* makes clear, his anti-rationalist critique concerns all areas of discourse.

I really want to say that scruples in thinking begin with (have their roots in) instinct. Or again: a language-game does not have its origin in *consideration*. (Wittgenstein 1981: §391)

I want to regard man here as an animal; as a primitive being to which one grants instinct but not ratiocination. As a creature in a primitive state. Any logic good enough for a primitive means of communication needs no apology from us. Language did not emerge from some kind of ratiocination. (Wittgenstein 1977a: §475)

These themes are prominent in *On Certainty*, where Wittgenstein is at pains to stress that doubt is secondary to a more primitive acceptance: 'The game of doubting itself presupposes certainty' (Wittgenstein 1977a: §115). The certainty that human beings have is 'something animal' (1977a: §359), and Wittgenstein wants to highlight the absurdity of thinking that such animal reactions are grounded in knowledge or ratiocination: 'The squirrel does not infer by induction that it is going to need stores next winter as well. And no more do we need a law of induction to justify our actions or our predictions' (1977a: §287).

Wittgenstein sought to stress the primacy of animality over reason in another area: namely, the nature of pain-behaviour, and particularly our grounds for believing that people other than ourselves are in pain. It is worth remembering that Wittgenstein regards the verbal expression of pain as a *replacement for* non-linguistic behaviour, rather than a *description of* it (cf. Wittgenstein 1958: §244). Goethe's theme is here paramount. The deed (in this

instance, the natural expression of pain) is primary; the verbal articulation is 'grafted on to' the primitive reaction. Wittgenstein's
account of pain-behaviour thus turns the Cartesian view on its
head. Descartes held that feelings are hidden from others until
language is learned and then used to describe what is occurring
inside. Wittgenstein, on the other hand, wants to stress that to be
hidden is not the natural state of our feelings; instead, as a child
matures, it learns to suppress its natural reactions, and to hide its
emotions and feelings.

Likewise, primitive reactions are fundamental to our perception
of the pain of *others*. In his reflections on this, Wittgenstein is once
again combating what he considers to be over-rationalistic accounts
of why we judge other people to be in pain, such as the argument
from analogy: when I am in pain, I groan or writhe, so when I see
someone exhibiting similar behaviour, I conclude, by analogy with
my own case, that their behaviour is an outward expression of an
inner pain. In *Zettel* Wittgenstein argues against this view (cf.
Wittgenstein 1981: §537), stressing instead the role of primitive,
instinctive behaviour:

> It is a help here to remember that it is a primitive reaction to tend,
> to treat, the part that hurts when someone else is in pain; and not
> merely when oneself is. (Wittgenstein 1981: §540)

> Being sure that someone is in pain, doubting whether he is, and
> so on, are so many natural, instinctive, kinds of behaviour
> towards other human beings, and our language is merely an
> auxiliary to, and further extension of ... primitive behaviour. (For
> our *language-game* is behaviour.) (Instinct) (Wittgenstein 1981:
> §545)

Thus, I tend someone who is in pain, *not* because I have an intellectual conviction that he is suffering: my actions are, instead, a
natural *response* to that person's behaviour, to his cries, writhing
and moans. And it is these tending acts which are fundamental
here. The language of tending arises out of the behaviour and does
not *inform* it: in other words, the primitive reactions are 'the proto-
type of a way of thinking and not the result of thought'
(Wittgenstein 1981: §541).

This is such a fundamental aspect of Wittgenstein's later work,
pervading so much of his thought, that it would be bizarre if the

idea of primitive reactions did not enter into his considerations of the nature of religious belief. And indeed, the contention that religious doctrines, religious systems, are grounded in primitive reactions is explicitly present in the *Remarks on Frazer*. In order to make sense of what Wittgenstein says there, we need to understand the kind of analogy which can be drawn between the language of pain and the language of religion. We have seen how the language of pain is said to develop out of instinctual, non-linguistic behaviour. Similarly the language of religion (the articulation of religious *beliefs*) is an extension of certain primitive reactions, say a natural expression of wonder or of fear. Note, however, that the religious belief is not *equivalent* to that expression of wonder (the expressivist view). Rather, just as instinctive pain-behaviour opens up a logical space whereby a greater articulation can occur, so the primitive religious reaction opens up a conceptual space, making possible the articulation of thoughts about the meaning and ultimate end of life, making possible new experiences, new ways of relating to the world.

Hence, one of the most memorable aspects of the *Remarks on Frazer* is Wittgenstein's characterization of rites as 'Instinct-actions', actions which are neither informed by nor grounded in reason or thought. Wittgenstein elaborates on this theme when speaking of procedures surrounding the lighting of the 'need-fire', a fire ritual resorted to in times of crisis. Frazer details the complex rules governing who may make the need-fire: 'Sometimes it was said that the two persons who pulled the rope which twirled the roller should always be brothers or at least bear the same baptismal name' (Frazer 1922: 640). Wittgenstein comments:

> One can very well imagine that – and perhaps the reason given might have been that the patron saints would otherwise pull against one another, and that only one could direct the matter. *But this too would only be a later extension of instinct.* (Wittgenstein 1979c: 80, emphasis added)

This is an extraordinary remark, contending that quite intricate religious systems have developed out of primal instincts, out of primitive reactions. Wittgenstein is not of course being reductionistic: it is certainly not being claimed that a fully-developed religion essentially *is* a pre-reflective response to the world. No, Wittgenstein is not here guilty of the genetic fallacy. What he is saying is that it is inconceivable that an elaborately worked-out doctrinal system could come into existence without the initial, affective, primitive reactions he emphasizes. To this extent, Wittgenstein's considerations amount to a variation on R. R. Marett's famous dictum that 'savage religion is not so much thought out as danced out' (Marett 1914: xxxi). In both cases, what is being challenged is the view, predominant in the intellectualist tradition, that religious rituals are grounded in antecedent quasi-scientific beliefs. In Marett and Wittgenstein this picture is reversed: what is fundamental, what is primary, is the action: *in the beginning was the deed.*

We will need to return to this theme of the primacy of instinct in later chapters. Here, however, our focus must be on the explanatory status of these pre-rational ritual impulses which are seen to underlie religion. And what is typical in the Wittgensteinian picture is that it is *these* primitive reactions which are held to be beyond explanation: 'I do not know how any further justification could be given of these reactions, or how any alternative account could explain them away' (Phillips 1988: 281). So if we are urged 'to look at what happens as a "proto-phenomenon"', then this proto-phenomenon is the reaction itself, and it is *this* which is closed to further explanation. That reaction is itself 'precisely the explanation wished for' (Wittgenstein 1979c: 72). Phillips assents wholeheartedly to this view, criticizing Edwyn Bevan's explanations of religious symbols and expressions because these obscure from us 'the naturalness of religious responses' (Phillips 1981: 193). But this raises the question of what exactly is *wrong* with an attempt to explain the reactions lying at the root of religious belief: is it (logically) impossible to attempt to explain them, just futile to try to, or, as Phillips' tone often suggests, that it simply displays a lack of sensibility to attempt to do so?

5.3 EXPLAINING THE RITUAL IMPULSE

The Wittgensteinian position, as we have seen, places its full stop at our primal, ceremonial impulses, those primitive reactions which are branded 'proto-phenomena'. Such ur-phenomenal reactions cannot, it is claimed, be explained; they are somehow irreducible. A Wittgensteinian account of religion will, then, reach its bedrock (and no further) at those impulses which are manifested in religious practices. These reactions take on the character of 'the given' ('what has to be accepted'), and are not something further to be explained. What must be achieved in an account of a religious practice is an evocation of the ceremonial impulse which gives rise to it. Hence, Paul Johnston, linking appeasement rituals with our own ceremonial inclinations, writes:

> We may come to understand an appeasement ritual by connecting it up with occasions when we too feel actions of appeasement would be appropriate. Why people should perform such acts at all, however, is left unexplained, and someone to whom the notion of appeasement means nothing is simply left with the fact that human beings act in this way. (Johnston 1989: 31)

'We can only *describe* and say human life is like that.' But why *should* we be content with description alone here? As Cioffi says, 'Might not the ritual impulse be explained as well as the ritual?' (Cioffi 1990a: 4). I want here to pursue that question.

Modern ethology is a discipline from which just such an explanation of the ritual impulse has been offered. In the work of Konrad Lorenz and of Walter Burkert, we find an explanatory account of ritual which is particularly apposite here. By that it is meant that, although they have radically opposing conceptions of the nature of human action (contrast Lorenz's stress on 'the determination of [human] behaviour by natural laws' (Lorenz 1967: 191) with the position presented in *The Idea of a Social Science*), these writers share with Wittgenstein a belief in the primacy of actions over beliefs in the sphere of religion. Thus, Burkert's aim is to explain 'the development and function of ritual ... without recurring to "ideas" or "beliefs"' (Burkert 1979: 50). Instead of concentrating on ratiocinative elements, then, these writers look to the primitive reactions underlying more sophisticated religious constructions.

Thus far, the rejection of intellectualist tenets and the appeal to primitive reactions provide common ground on which both Wittgensteinians and biological ethologists stand. However, a closer look at the latter position reveals stark differences, for Lorenz's desire is to explain ritual as a phylogenetic phenomenon. His researches continue studies initiated by Julian Huxley, who

> discovered the remarkable fact that certain movement patterns lose, in the course of phylogeny, their original specific function

and become purely 'symbolic' ceremonies. He called this process ritualization and used this term without inverted commas; in other words, he equated the cultural processes leading to the development of human rites with the phylogenetic processes giving rise to such remarkable 'ceremonies' in animals. (Lorenz 1967: 47)

Following this suggestion, Lorenz provides many examples of 'rituals' culled from the animal kingdom, of which the most celebrated is his extended treatment of the 'triumph ceremony' of greylag geese (cf. 1967: 150–86). Here, by means of aggressive behaviour against a non-existent trespasser, and by triumphant cries after its 'repulsion', a pair of greylags reinforce their bond of companionship. In order, however, to observe the ethological approach at its most incisive, we would do well to turn to the examples provided by Burkert in *Structure and History in Greek Mythology and Ritual*.

Burkert is keen to stress the promise of the biological perspective for an understanding of human ritual, and he provides examples from Greek ritual which, though previously mystifying, can be illuminated by ethology. The first example to be considered here is the herm, described by Burkert as 'a rather dignified, usually bearded, head on a four-cornered pillar and, in due place, an unmistakeable, realistically molded, erect phallus' (Burkert 1979: 39). These pillars were set up outside houses, at crossroads, at the frontiers of settlements, and so on. Burkert considers previous interpretations of the herm, that it is a fertility symbol or an apotropaic sign, and both are found wanting. It is, he claims, from ethology that an answer to the problem of the herm can be given:

> There are species of monkeys, living in groups, of whom the males act as guards: they sit up at the outposts, facing outside and presenting their erect genital organ ... The basic function of sexual activity is suspended for the sake of communication; every individual approaching from the outside will notice that this group does not consist of helpless wives and children, but enjoys the full protection of masculinity.
>
> With man, at least in the more civilized areas of the historical epoch, there is only the artifact left, instead of real action. (Burkert 1979: 40)

Thus, the presence of a herm was a warning: a message of potency. Ethology, it is claimed, is similarly successful in its treatment of another problematic ritual: that of libation, the ceremonious pouring out of liquids. This has generally been taken as a rite of 'offering'. Yet 'libation is quite a peculiar way of "giving": you pour out wine on the soil, and there it stays: How are the gods in heaven to get any of it?' (Burkert 1979: 41). The biological perspective offers a different picture:

> Marking a territory by pouring out liquids is a 'ritual' behaviour quite common in mammals, especially predators ... Beneath the level of highly developed civilization even in twentieth-century folk customs there is 'ritual behaviour' at frontiers or boundary stones quite similar to what the dog does ... In fact divers species of mammals have evolved special glands for scent marking; cultural evolution has supplied man with utensils for similar functions. (Burkert 1979: 43)

Burkert's reflections on this (and indeed on the herm) are exemplary of his general view of the nature of ritual, which is seen as 'action redirected for demonstration' (Burkert 1979: 37). These actions are developed from biological impulses, and subsequently formalized, with exaggeration and repetition producing a theatrical effect. There is, patently, an explicit functionalism in the views of Burkert and Lorenz: ritual has a purpose, and it is generally that of creating and sustaining a bond between communities of people (and, indeed, of animals). The functionalist thesis can be observed in Lorenz's talk of 'group cohesion' and the controlling of aggression (Lorenz 1967: 65–6) and in Burkert's statement that the message transmitted by ritual 'seems to be concerned mainly with the solidarity of the group and the exclusion of others' (Burkert 1979: 48).

It is, however, not the functionalism of the phylogenetic approach which is of interest here, but rather the connected issue of the status of those animal reactions which the Wittgensteinian considers ur-phenomenal. Let us review the ethological case. What underlies rituals are certain instincts which spring '"spontaneously" from the inner human being' (Lorenz 1967: 41). These primitive actions are not, however, simply 'to be accepted'. For the ethologist, these 'innate rites' (1967: 61) can be explained phylogenetically, for they serve a purpose in the evolution of the species (by controlling aggression, creating bonds, and so on). So when Johnston says that an appeasement ceremony is something that human beings do and *that is all there is to say*, the ethologist will take issue with him. Indeed, Lorenz considers just such a ceremony – the ritual of smoking the pipe of peace – and is not prepared simply to say 'this is what human life is like'. Rather, he imaginatively speculates as to the origin of the ceremony, postulating two war-weary neighbouring chiefs who come together in order to negotiate peace. In such a situation of obvious tension, the chiefs search for a 'displacement activity' and find this in the act of packing and lighting a pipe: 'Who does not know it, the heavenly, tension-relieving catharsis of smoking?' (1967: 62). In subsequent meetings, two pipes are replaced by a single one, and 'in the course of generations the original gesture of embarrassment developed into a fixed ritual which became law for every Indian and prohibited aggression after pipe-smoking' (1967: 62). It would be hard to confer veridicality on such speculation, but what *is* offered by Lorenz here, by his talk of displacement activities, is an alternative to the Wittgensteinian prohibition on explanation. Whereas Johnston claims that someone perplexed by the notion of appeasement is just left with the fact that this is how humans happen to act, Lorenz believes that he can pursue understanding further, by indicating to the confused how such rites serve to inhibit aggression and thereby have a phylogenetic purpose. For the ethologist, then, the 'primitive reactions' spoken of by Wittgensteinians are not ur-phenomenal, since they *can* be understood in terms of something else: namely, in terms of the underlying theory of evolution.

We can infer that Phillips for one would be wholly opposed to explanations of this kind, and his reason for this might well be the same as that which he brought against Bevan: 'the explanation takes us away from the naturalness of the expression' (Phillips 1981: 194). But *do* Burkert's explanations take us away from natu-ralness of expression? On the contrary! The ethological approach is concerned, possibly more than any other, to stress how religious actions are the natural and spontaneous outpourings of human being. Nevertheless, a theory which describes religion wholly in terms of its cohesive function is anathema to the Wittgensteinian, for it bypasses the concepts of the religious themselves, and is reductionistic in the sense of deriving religious phenomena from nonreligious phenomena.

Although Phillips' rejection of such theories of religion is unambiguous, when we observe what Wittgenstein himself said about such matters we find a less clear-cut picture. On the one hand, his critical remarks on Darwin would seem to be applicable also to Lorenz's evolutionary perspective on religion. Here we find intolerance of phylogenetic explanations. Hence, Wittgenstein contended that 'Darwin, in his "expression of the Emotions", made a mistake similar to Frazer's, e.g. in thinking that "because our ancestors, when angry, wanted to bite" is a sufficient explanation of why we show our teeth when angry' (Moore 1959b: 316). This statement raises questions which are not subsequently answered by Wittgenstein: why *is* Darwin's explanation of the development of facial expressions mistaken, and why is this 'mistake' similar to that allegedly made by Frazer in his account of the Beltane festival? Regarding this second question, one possible answer is that Frazer, too, is keen to employ an evolutionary perspective, exhibited in the aim of the comparative method to trace the intellectual evolution of mankind, and it is *this* which Wittgenstein objects to.

But there is another answer to this, one which also addresses the first question, and which suggests that it is not so much a matter of Wittgenstein *prohibiting* explanation, but rather of him simply not being *interested* in it. Criticizing Darwin, Wittgenstein writes:

> Striking an object may merely be a natural reaction in rage. A tendency which has come into vogue with the modern sciences is to explain certain things by evolution. Darwin seemed to think that an emotion got its importance from one thing only, utility. A baby bares its teeth when angry because its ancestors did so to bite. Your hair stands on end when you are frightened because hair standing on end served some purpose for animals. The charm of this outlook is that it reduces importance to utility. (Wittgenstein 1982b: 34)

There is an implicit criticism here of the Darwinist 'cult of the useful' (Spengler 1926: 156), but it is not this which is of concern. The important thing is that Wittgenstein is considering the issue of *striking objects in rage*, a subject he broaches in the *Remarks*, where he considers explanations of beating the ground. Here the ambivalence we have spoken of is explicit, for to begin with he speaks in a highly negative manner, claiming that 'an historical explanation, say, that I or my ancestors previously believed that beating the ground does help is shadow-boxing, for it is a superfluous assumption that explains *nothing'* (Wittgenstein 1979c: 72). Having said this, however, Wittgenstein offers a more measured view, stressing only the *difference* between the historical explanation and his programme of 'making clear' (bringing the phenomenon 'into connection with an instinct which I myself possess'). Thus he states merely that 'a further investigation about the history of my instinct moves on another track' (1979c: 72). And if *this* is what Wittgenstein thinks, then there is nothing illicit or futile about a scientific investigation into ritual, or about a phylogenetic explanation of the ritual impulse. I suggest, then, that Wittgenstein's impatience with the evolutionary perspective is simply due to a lack of shared interests and goals. Hence, in Waismann's notes we read:

> If I were told anything that was a *theory*, I would say, No, no! That does not interest me. Even if this theory were true, it would not interest me – it would not be the exact thing I was looking for. (Waismann 1979: 116)

Even if it were true. Thus the possibility is left open that there *could* be true theories, true explanations. Here the ambiguity in Wittgenstein's reflections on explanation emerges, for while his comments on Darwin do seem to manifest intolerance, at other times he seems merely to stress that he is not interested in these questions, that they are outside the scope of his concerns. In this sense, his non-explanatory perspective seems less like that of Phillips and more akin to C. S. Lewis' who, in *An Experiment in Criticism*, writes:

> I am describing and not accounting for myths. To inquire how they arise – whether they are primitive science or the fossil remains of rituals, or the fabrications of medicine men, or outcroppings from the individual or the collective unconscious – is quite outside my purpose ... I deal only with that part of the iceberg which shows above the surface ... No doubt there is plenty down below. The desire to investigate the parts below has genuinely scientific justification. (Lewis 1961: 44–5)

Wittgenstein's prohibition on explanation seems thus a rather bizarre one, informed only by personal preference. And if this is the case, then it raises a significant question about the project of the *Remarks on Frazer*.

6
The Frontiers of the
Remarks

6.1 DISCONTINUITY THESES

The findings of the previous two chapters – that the concept of perspicuous representation is not wholly adequate as a anthropological tool, and that Wittgenstein has only idiosyncratic reasons for rejecting explanation – raise a significant question about the project of the *Remarks on Frazer's Golden Bough*. Attention to these discrepancies may lead us to think that, as an alternative to the intellectualist programme of a Frazer, Wittgenstein's suggestions for anthropology are rather poor. Indeed, a number of writers have gone so far as to suggest that Wittgenstein's purpose in writing on ritual is radically discontinuous with Frazer's; that while Frazer is trying to understand why primitive peoples engage in magical activity, Wittgenstein is not interested in this matter at all, and that his aims lie elsewhere. If this contention were true, it would mean that it would be futile to attempt to extricate an interpretation of religion from the *Remarks on Frazer*. As my intention in this book is to do precisely that, it will, therefore, be crucial to devote some attention to the discontinuity thesis in order to see whether my plans are torpedoed. I want here to consider two very different discontinuity theses, those of Rush Rhees and Frank Cioffi.

Rhees' denial that Wittgenstein's notes make a contribution to the study of religion could not be more emphatic:

> Why should Wittgenstein discuss Frazer's account of the rituals and magic of primitive peoples? *Not because it throws light on religion.* Wittgenstein mentions religion in his introductory remarks, but as part of his general discussion ... *And clearly he is not discussing history or anthropology.* (Rhees 1971: 18, emphases added)

Rather, Wittgenstein is said to be reflecting on Frazer's material in order to consider specifically metaphysical problems. Focusing on

Wittgenstein's desire to consider 'metaphysics as a kind of magic', Rhees contends that when we read Frazer we are struck, perhaps horrified, by the rites he describes. Metaphysical statements, such as 'substance is indestructible' or 'I can be certain only of my own existence', can have the same effect on us. And as with magic, metaphysical problems cannot be solved by any kind of historical or scientific theory; they are not that kind of problem. Rather, they are examples of the 'mythology in our language' (Rhees 1971: 18). This mythology is 'not a *blunder*' (Rhees 1971: 22); and it is nothing to laugh at. (Compare with Wittgenstein's comment on the rule at Nemi: 'This is what took place here; laugh, if you can' (Wittgenstein 1979b: 3).)

As well as indicating the curious depth of metaphysical problems, Wittgenstein's reflection on magical phenonema has also the purpose of elucidating other aspects of philosophy and language. Hence, Rhees directs our attention to the following passage:

> What we have in the ancient rites is the practice of a highly cultivated gesture-language.[1]
>
> And when I read Frazer I keep wanting to say: All these processes, these changes of meaning, – we have them still in our word-language. If what they call the 'Corn-wolf' is what is hidden in the last sheaf; but also the last sheaf itself and also the man who binds it, we recognize in this a movement of language with which we are perfectly familiar. (Wittgenstein 1979b: 10–11)

Here Wittgenstein is reflecting on certain strains of ritual thought documented by Frazer in *Spirits of the Corn and of the Wild*. It is the belief among certain rustic peoples that the animating spirit of the crops may be embodied in animal form, say as a cock, a hare or a dog. And when the wind blows through the corn fields, setting the field in motion like a sea, the peasants may say 'The Wolf is in the corn', or 'The big Dog is there'. This conception of the animal embodiment of the corn-spirit is to the fore during the harvest, when the corn is reaped. As the harvesters fell the crop, the spirit is chased out of the corn, and retreats into that left standing, until its final home is the last bunch. Everyone fears to reap this, for they say that the Wolf is sitting in it. But the Wolf is not just in that last sheaf; the last sheaf is itself called 'the Wolf', as is the man who finally reaps it (cf. Frazer 1922: 448–50; Frazer 1936g: 270–305).

Wittgenstein's response to this material does not function as a criticism of Frazer's interpretation of these beliefs, nor is he advancing a competing interpretation of the referent of the term 'Corn-wolf'. No, he seems concerned solely with the similarities between those peasant beliefs and aspects of our language. The same changes of meaning we observe in the harvest rite are present in language in the form of such grammatical features as *metonymy* (substitution of a word referring to an attribute for the thing that is meant: for example, the crown is not just what the monarch wears, but the monarch *himself*). Such reflections are, for Rhees, illustrative of the project of the *Remarks on Frazer*: Wittgenstein is concerned, not with the inherent nature of religious actions and beliefs, but with their resemblance to conspicuous features of language and philosophy.

In assessing Rhees' case, it has to be said that his claim that Wittgenstein's notes are not an attempt to throw light on religion or anthropological matters is either an exaggeration, or else simply mistaken. It is certainly true that Wittgenstein often appeals to rituals in order to illuminate aspects of our language.[2] It is also true that the *Remarks* deal in large part with problems of philosophy, and that Wittgenstein's reading of Frazer helped to mould his mature thought (we noted this earlier, with specific reference to perspicuous representation). To say, however, that the *Remarks* have little to do with magic or religion seems excessive. Even if, as Rhees suggests, the ritual examples culled from Frazer are used purely to illuminate the illusions of metaphysics, then there must be some thesis presented regarding magic which serves as the focus of the comparison. In other words, if metaphysics is like magic, then magic must be like metaphysics. A post-Rhees examination of the *Remarks* still, then, supports the *prima facie* impression that one of Wittgenstein's principal concerns in writing on *The Golden Bough* is to correct what he sees as a distorted theory of ritual, and to make pregnant suggestions as to how the subject should accurately be viewed.

Cioffi's radical challenge is more persuasive than Rhees', and arises from a perception that the *Remarks on Frazer*, if understood as a contribution to the anthropology of religion, are incoherent and defective. For Cioffi, Wittgenstein does not present a coherent view of magic, nor does he offer an adequate method for understanding the rationales behind magical action. The process of 'making clear', as we saw in Chapter 4, cannot hope to produce a veridical account of a primitive practice: we cannot infer from the rationales for our own quasi-ritualistic acts (kissing photographs) the motives behind ritual practices in other cultures (burning in effigy). So Wittgenstein's anthropological project of reconstituting the rationales of ritualists founders on an inadequate hermeneutical method.

Yet the characteristic feature of Cioffi's interpretation of the *Remarks* is to deny that such a reconstitution *is* Wittgenstein's primary purpose. Rather, 'since perspicuity bears so tenuous a relation to historicity' (Cioffi 1990b: 69) (that is, that the process of making an opaque practice clear to us may not succeed in uncovering the actual rationale of that act), Cioffi claims that the *Remarks* 'should not be read for the light they shed on ritual practices' (Cioffi 1990b: 69). So, having detected inconsistencies and inadequacies in Wittgenstein's surface argument, Cioffi looks more closely at it and finds a rather different purpose. Cioffi describes this change of purpose as a 'dismissal of the hermeneutic project for that of self-understanding' (Cioffi 1990a: 11), a change of project 'which involves dismissing clearly empirical questions and raising in their stead questions which can be treated as epistemically discontinuous with those raised by Frazer' (Cioffi 1990a:11). Wittgenstein's concern is summed up neatly by Cioffi thus:

> The predominant value of Wittgenstein's remarks is not their contribution to the explanatory tasks of anthropology or prehistory but ... the light they shed on our relation to exotic practices. (Cioffi 1990b: 69)[3]

The pattern which Cioffi discerns in the *Remarks* runs like this: we experience wonderment and perplexity when we read the tales of extraordinary customs chronicled in *The Golden Bough*; such perplexity leads us to reflect on those eccentric personal-ceremonial acts each of us performs; this reflection does not, however, illuminate the rationales of the exotic rites; rather, we reflect on our own ritualistic actions *for their own sake*. We can see how this diagnosis fits a familiar example from the *Remarks*: Wittgenstein begins by thinking about something Frazer has documented – the homoeopathic magic of effigy-burning – and this leads him into consideration of why it is that we kiss pictures of those we love. He does not subsequently return to the issue of primitive magic; having proceeded to our own actions, his meditation is complete.

Connected with this self-serving reflection is the way in which

Cioffi sees Wittgenstein's enterprise with regard to ritual phenomena to be of a piece with his aesthetic enquiries. In what sense, then, is an investigation into the Nemi rite or homoeopathic magic an aesthetic question which should be resolved by methods other than the empirical ones employed by Frazer? The answer is here provided by Wittgenstein's insistence that 'an aesthetic explanation is not a causal explanation' (Wittgenstein 1966: 18). So when Wittgenstein speaks of 'the sort of explanation one is looking for when one is puzzled by an aesthetic impression' (1966: 21), what is he trying to find if it is not a causal explanation?

Cioffi feels the answer to this lies where Wittgenstein compares expressions of aesthetic puzzlement with a remark such as 'What is it I wanted to say?', and he notes a connection between such a question and a remark from the *Investigations*:

'So you really wanted to say ... ' – We use this phrase in order to lead someone from one form of expression to another. (Wittgenstein 1958: §334)

Cioffi's exegesis is illuminating:

This suggests to me that the kind of remark which Wittgenstein thinks aesthetic puzzlement calls for is one which, though it may seem to be describing or explaining a certain past state of mind, is really prolonging an experience in a particular direction; like ... the estranged couple who say they never loved one another: statements which, though apparently descriptive of the past, really serve to orient their utterers to a projected future. (Cioffi 1969: 198)

Applying this to the *Remarks on Frazer*, perhaps Wittgenstein is not implying that burning in effigy can be understood by uncovering the reasons why we kiss pictures of loved ones. Rather, he is responding to the perplexity felt through a reading of exotic rites and 'prolonging that experience in a particular direction'; namely toward our own personal-ritualistic acts. Thus, when Wittgenstein characterizes as an *explanation* the process of bringing a ritual action 'into connection with an instinct which I myself possess' (Wittgenstein 1979c: 72), he should not be taken to be accounting for the existence of the exotic rite. Instead, 'the explanation which resolves this particular difficulty' (Wittgenstein 1979c: 72) is an aesthetic explanation, the features of which have been noted above. So with respect to ritual phenonema, Wittgenstein is directing our attention, not to how such practices originate, nor to the beliefs underlying them, but to how we stand to such phenomena, how our 'crush of thoughts' (Wittgenstein 1979b: 3) is to be unpacked.

Cioffi's analysis thus gives a different slant on the character of the disagreement between Wittgenstein and Frazer. The conflict is not primarily to do with the *nature* of ritual practices, but rather with the path an investigation should take when one is confronted with such phenomena. Whereas Frazer sees the need for empirical enquiry and historical reconstruction, Wittgenstein stresses the need for 'consolation' or 'solace'. Cioffi maintains that this amounts, not to two different answers to the same question ('Why ritual?'), but, instead, to two epistemically distinct questions *about* ritual. The first of these questions may be characterized in terms of 'They-discourse' and has the form 'Why do exotic peoples engage in such-and-such a ritual?' The second question may be termed an example of 'We-discourse': 'Why do such accounts of ritual *impress us?*'[4] On this view, it is maintained that Frazer's procedure, while not illegitimate, is, perhaps, *misplaced*:

> Wittgenstein may just be calling attention to an error which there is a natural tendency to make. The error in question might be described as looking for consummation in the wrong place; an instance of which is asking for the etiology of a phenomenon where what we really want is an analysis of the impression produced on us by the phenomenon. For example, we often think we are interested in the past when it is really the experience of pastness which absorbs us. (Cioffi 1969: 197)

Wittgenstein, then, on Cioffi's view, feels that the problems arising out of the subject of ritual do not call for empirical enquiry, that certain phenomena – say, human sacrifice, or exotic ritual magic – do not present themselves to us merely as things to be explained. It is felt that 'what we want with respect to certain phenomena are not their causes, but their bearings' (Cioffi 1984: 171).

Consider how this theme emerges explicitly in the *Remarks*. Opposing the idea of an explanation of a ritual, Wittgenstein says: 'for someone broken up by love an explanatory hypothesis won't help much. – It will not bring peace' (Wittgenstein 1979b: 3). Yet this comment is somewhat bewildering. Why should reflection on how *we* stand to something like human sacrifice, why we are fascinated by ritual slaughter, bring *peace* of all things? Is it not rather the case that it will trouble us less if we confine it to the errors of our forefathers? Will this not ameliorate our dismay? Certainly. So the kind of peace that Wittgenstein wishes to bring is not the variety which will result in us sleeping easily at night. Rather, it is the peace which comes from bringing an end to our epistemic cravings. ('The real discovery is the one that makes me capable of stopping doing philosophy when I want to' (Wittgenstein 1958: §133).) This desire for epistemic peace might be seen as a bizarre obfuscation, for when one takes up Wittgenstein's methods (rather than, say, those of Frazer) it may be felt that 'we have abandoned thinking for brooding' (Cioffi 1984: 172).

On Cioffi's view, then, the *Remarks on Frazer's Golden Bough* are an attempt at self-clarification, and, as such, Wittgenstein's enterprise is discontinuous with that of social anthropologists. He is not attempting to reconstruct the rationales of the participants in exotic ceremonies, and his appeals to our own personal-ceremonial actions do not serve to illuminate such rationales. Wittgenstein is engaged in an aesthetic project, and his elucidations of rituals are aesthetic explanations. Such explanations consist in using an example of ritual phenomena as a springboard for reflection on the strangeness of our own lives ('prolonging an experience in a particular direction').

6.2 THE *REMARKS ON FRAZER* AND THE STUDY OF RELIGION

Given the problems we have encountered with Wittgenstein's methodology, it may seem that the choice facing us is this: Wittgenstein is either propounding the kind of abortive hermeneutics encapsulated in the notion of 'making clear', or he is, as Cioffi suggests, concerned with self-clarification. Cioffi is undeniably correct to stress the failure of Wittgenstein's hermeneutic project. Yet this failure and our inability to determine the rationales of primitive ritualists by pure acts of imagination does not by itself entail that Wittgenstein's project has no anthropological significance nor any relevance for the study of religion. Besides those comments which address our own reactions to the material accumulated by Frazer, there are also incisive remarks which address the nature of ritual (though without speculations as to the motives informing particular rituals). And it is these remarks which provide the backbone of Wittgenstein's contribution to the study of religion.

We must state first of all, however, that there is no use pretending, as some of Wittgenstein's followers do, that the *Remarks on Frazer* constitute an exercise in social anthropology, for when Wittgenstein is engaged in an investigation he does not proceed as a comparativist would. Instead of appealing to actual rites, actual tribes, or actual languages, when Wittgenstein wishes to clarify a feature of our lives he invariably *invents* a practice or a language with which to contrast it. We may wish to attribute this to the fact that Wittgenstein was 'ethnographically naive' (Pitkin 1972: 102), yet in the context of the *Remarks on Frazer* a more sympathetic construction is possible.

This interpretation can be based on the following remark:

> Just how misleading Frazer's accounts are, we see, I think, from the fact that one could well imagine primitive practices oneself and it would only be by chance if they were not actually to be found somewhere. That is, the principle according to which these practices are ordered is much more general than Frazer shows it to be and we find it in ourselves: we could think out for ourselves the different possibilities. (Wittgenstein 1979b: 5)

The idea contained here is similar to a central feature of Paul Ernst's thinking, when he writes of 'the many possible myths which can be schematised and found in reality' (Ernst 1910: 291). Goethe (1970: 310) says something similar about the *Urpflanze*. In the tradition of Ernst and Goethe, then, Wittgenstein is concerned, not primarily with what rituals (or myths or folk-tales) exist, but with what *possible* rituals *there could be*. 'Our investigation ... is directed not towards phenomena, but, as one might say, towards the *"possibilities"* of phenomena' (Wittgenstein 1958: §90). Now this is not simply an idle exercise, since, as Rodney Needham (1985: 163) has pointed out, for a number of fields of social life (for example, descent systems) we can 'think out for ourselves the different possibilities' and find them in reality. This reveals something about the nature of those systems, and, indeed, about human thought.

In this largely *a priori* vein of assessing the possible forms ritual might take, Wittgenstein wants to map out the contrasts of values we find in magical and religious phenomena. This desire is exhibited when he considers the ways in which a divine king may be treated by his people:

> We can readily imagine that, say, in a given tribe no-one is allowed to see the king, or again that every man in the tribe is obliged to see him. And then it will certainly not be left more or less to chance, but the king will be *shown* to the people. Perhaps no-one will be allowed to touch him, or perhaps they will be *compelled* to do so. (Wittgenstein 1979b: 5)

With his thoughts still on the possibilities of ritual, Wittgenstein continues:

> Think how after Schubert's death his brother cut certain of Schubert's scores into small pieces and gave to his favourite pupils these pieces of a few bars each. As a sign of piety this action is *just* as comprehensible to us as the other one of keeping the scores undisturbed and accessible to no-one. And if Schubert's brother had burned the scores we could still understand this as a sign of piety. (Wittgenstein 1979b: 5)

It would, of course, not be a sign of piety had the scores been left to be kicked about on the floor or used as scrap paper. Wittgenstein's conclusion: 'The ceremonial (hot or cold) as opposed to the haphazard (lukewarm) is a characteristic of piety' (Wittgenstein 1979b: 5).

This, then, constitutes the paradox of the *Remarks on Frazer*: there is something peculiar about Wittgenstein's technique which makes us want to say that he is not engaged in anthropology, yet at the same time he does make illuminating comments about ritual which make us loath to accept the discontinuity thesis in its entirety. What, then, is the status of the *Remarks* and in what relation does Wittgenstein's project stand to the study of ritual?

In order to answer this question we can note how similar in form are the *Remarks* to a short story by Jorge Luis Borges. In 'Doctor Brodie's Report', Borges relates the content of a manuscript he has 'discovered' (invented). This manuscript, written by one David Brodie, a missionary who preached the Christian faith in Africa, tells of the social and ritual practices of the 'Mlch', a savage tribe whose customs are revolting to us:

They imbibe the milk of cats and chiropterans ... While eating, they normally conceal themselves or else close their eyes. All other physical habits they perform in open view ... So as to partake of their wisdom, they devour the raw corpses of their witch-doctors and of the royal family. (Borges 1985: 92)

The Mlch are proscribed from lifting their eyes to the stars, and they worship a god called 'Dung' who is depicted as a stunted and mutilated figure. The god thus exhibits the same features as the kings of the Mlch. A man is elected to the kingship at birth by virtue of the presence on his body of certain distinguishing marks. Once chosen, the king is blinded, gelded and his hands and feet are amputated. He is then confined to a cavern and kept from view, shown to the people only in times of war.

Borges' tale is fictional, yet this fake ethnography is instructive nonetheless. Although the Mlch do not exist and Borges is thus not describing the practices of a real people, Brodie's report illustrates the possibilities of ritual by presenting us with invented customs. Borges writes that 'it is a known fact that the word "invention" originally stood for "discovery"' (Borges 1985: 101), implying that although he has merely invented the Mlch, his characterization of their practices are in a certain sense a discovery, an elucidation of the ritual propensities of mankind.

Wittgenstein's enquiry, I suggest, is of the same genre as Borges' tale, and thus he does make what we might call 'discoveries' about ritual. First, he illustrates the possible forms ritual action may take, and this is done, not by appeal to actual rites, but by 'thinking out for ourselves the different possibilities'. In doing so, he shows not just our own 'inwardness' with rituality, but also indicates something about ritual itself: namely, the principles (the 'unknown law') according to which it is structured (the hot and the cold, for example). And this is indeed crucial for the study of religion, for, as Peter Byrne writes:

we need some conceptual knowledge that is at least *a priori* relative to any particular phase of the religious life in history. This conceptual knowledge is a general understanding of religion as an aspect of human life and of the general character of religious systems. It is a knowledge of the human religious condition. (Byrne 1989: 236)

It is, then, as a form of conceptual evidence, as a series of observations on general patterns of religious thought and action, that Wittgenstein's thoughts have significance for the study of religion. Secondly, and as we have already seen, Wittgenstein is keen to stress the primacy of deed over deliberation in ritual. This crucial feature of his account is not the result of any thorough investigation of exotic phenomena. Rather, it is the product of a particular philosophical view of the way human beings act, one which stresses 'primitive reactions' and the instinct component of human behaviour. These two factors – form and instinct – are certainly relevant to any study of religion. Wittgenstein's concern in the *Remarks* is with the possibilities of action naturally performed by that strange ritual creature: man. And this is indeed what we must now focus upon: Wittgenstein's analysis of the natural history of a ceremonial animal.

Part III
The Natural History of a Ceremonial Animal

7

'Metaphysics as a Kind of Magic'

7.1 THE POETIC CONCEPTION: WITTGENSTEIN, CHESTERTON, ERNST

One purpose of the argument of Chapter 3 was to suggest that the *Remarks on Frazer* cannot be construed as the sketch of an expressive interpretation of magic and religion. This conclusion was reached, not by reflection on Wittgenstein's thoughts on ritual, but, rather, by attention to his later philosophy of language. It would be incomplete to assume, however, that this constitutes the sole reason for denying the near-habitual expressivist appellation. On the contrary, a deeper reading of Wittgenstein's notes on *The Golden Bough* provide us with ample evidence of an account of ritual far different from the standard expressivist view; the view, that is, that rituals aim at no concrete ends and are rather acts of personal and/or social catharsis. In this chapter, I will begin to examine what I take to be the core notions of the *Remarks*, starting with Wittgenstein's striking comparison of magic with metaphysics. And one fruitful way to commence this analysis is by comparing his views on magic with those of G. K. Chesterton.

When reading Chesterton's remarks on magic and folklore, one is frequently struck by his rebuke for the worth of the scientific method in examining the affairs of human beings. He claims that 'the same frigid and detached spirit which leads to success in the study of astronomy or botany leads to disaster in the study of mythology' (Chesterton 1905: 142). A scientific account of folk belief will not just be futile, but also distorting:

This total misunderstanding of the real nature of ceremonial gives rise to the most awkward and dehumanized versions of the conduct of men in rude lands or ages. The man of science, not realizing that ceremonial is essentially a thing which is done without a reason, has to find a reason for every sort of ceremonial, and, as might be supposed, the reason is generally a very absurd one – absurd because it originates not in the simple mind of the barbarian, but in the sophisticated mind of the professor. (Chesterton 1905: 144)

The view of 'the man of science', that the beliefs involved in magic and religion are somehow hypothetical, creates the mistaken impression that we are here dealing with something rationally thought out. But a magical belief is the product neither of ratiocination nor of cool reflection:

We may say, if we like, that it is believed before there is time to examine it. It would be truer to say that it is accepted before it is believed. (Chesterton 1930: 118)

Chesterton's rebuke for the scientific method's approach to magic is comparable, not only with Wittgenstein's criticism of *The Golden Bough* (these affinities being obvious), but also with Paul Ernst's rejection of the rationalistic interpretation of folk tales. While Frazer is the object of both Wittgenstein's and Chesterton's scorn, part of Ernst's *Nachwort* to his 1910 edition of Grimm's *Kinder-und Hausmärchen* addresses the interpretation of the miracles of the Gospel offered by the nineteenth-century theologian Heinrich Paulus. Central to Paulus' enterprise is a rejection of the supernatural, so anything of this character needs to be eliminated from an account of the life of Christ. Hence, the walking on the water was an illusion, the raising of Lazarus from the dead is explained in terms of premature burial, and so on. For Ernst, accounts such as Paulus' are misplaced. An understanding of the miracles of the Gospel and of the events in folk tales, legends and sagas, has nothing to do with asking questions such as 'How could this have happened?' Nevertheless, Ernst maintains, this is the spirit of the enquiries of the day, and reflecting on the 65th tale of the *Gesta Romanorum* (which centres on certain mysterious messages on a crossroads signpost), Ernst contrasts the attitudes of 'yesterday' with those of 'today':

Here Fantasy is set a task: Why is the King out riding? What do the four inscriptions mean? Who wrote them? ... Fantasy does not come into play in the understanding of such a story today, because the first thought is: can this story actually be true? Who is telling it? What purpose can the narrator have? In short, today, criticism is instantly awoken and the credibility of the olden days is quite missing. (Ernst 1910: 301)

An understanding of folk tales is, claims Ernst, not to be obtained by such rationalistic questioning, but by inwardly grasping their significance. The battle is between scientific rationalism on the one hand, and *poetry* on the other:

They [folk tales] are poetry and should be understood as such: we should feel them, take them into ourselves and let them have their effect on us. (Ernst 1910: 271)

This is plainly the thrust of Chesterton's remark that 'all this mythological business belongs to the poetical part of man' (1930: 116).

Chesterton's own strategy for understanding magical practices is founded on the belief that one can know a great deal of anthropology simply because one is oneself human. Once this is recognized, he says, then the temptation to look for a scientific solution to the problem of, say, totemism disappears:

The secrets about which anthropologists concern themselves can best be learnt, not from books or voyages, but from the ordinary commerce of man with man. The secret of why some savage tribe worships monkeys or the moon is not to be found even by travelling among those savages and taking down their answers in a note-book, although the cleverest man may pursue this course. The answer to the riddle is in England; it is in London; nay, it is in his own heart. (Chesterton 1905: 143)

This amounts to the idea that the nature of any form of ceremonial can be accounted for by attention to our own ritual inclinations and to the nature of human beings as such. The way to understand primitive rituals is by analogy with the rituals performed in our own society: placing flowers on a grave, kneeling to pray, decorating our homes at Christmas, and so on. We have previously had cause to note that this kind of hermeneutic is inadequate, yet the important point to extract from Chesterton's musings here is that rituals are 'exceedingly natural and obvious' things to do. This does not make the rituals of ourselves or of primitives any less mysterious or awesome, however:

We do not understand, it is true, the emotion which makes us think it obvious and natural; but that is because, like all the important emotions of human existence, it is essentially irrational. (Chesterton 1905: 145)[1]

The contention that ritual everywhere has a common foundation (human nature) allows Chesterton to account for the similarity of world myths, not by recourse to any dissemination theory, but simply by appeal to 'something in our nature and conditions' (Chesterton 1930: 118). Here we may find another point of contact with Ernst, who, when considering the striking similarity of the tales and sagas of different nations, speaks of a 'spontaneous origination in specific peoples, through a development of the motif according to the general laws of logic and the association of perspectives' (Ernst 1910: 272; cf. Wittgenstein 1979b: 13).

Chesterton wants to move away from the notion that myths are simply allegories or metaphors, for this explanation does not capture the force of those tales told. 'Father Christmas is not an allegory of snow and holly; he is not merely the stuff called snow afterwards artificially given a human form, like a snow man. He is something that gives a new meaning to the white world and the evergreens' (Chesterton 1930: 120). This choice of example is, however, weak, and fails to achieve the result that Chesterton aims for. No one seriously thinks of Santa Claus as 'an allegory of snow and holly', for he is plainly to be identified with Saint Nicholas. A better example would be that of the Green Man, a perennial character in British folklore. If one finds oneself in a forest at the beginning or height of spring, one will be aware of the very *greenness* of everything, and the thought may present itself that there is some being, some spirit, responsible for the growth of the trees, the moss, the ferns. Perhaps, however, one would reject the idea that this spirit of vegetation – the Green Man – is to be regarded as a real individual, and instead view such a belief as allegorical, symbolic of nature's regeneration, and so on. But one may shy from this account also, feeling that it fails to make perspicuous how our perception of the rising of the sap has been altered. The problem here is that there is no ready-made category into which we can place the idea.

Moreover, Chesterton thinks that it is dangerous to assume that these things *could* be classified, for this would foster the belief that they can be *comprehended*. And it is this which lies at the heart of his criticism of *The Golden Bough*, for the feelings which are aroused in us by certain notions in magic and folk tales (say, the idea of an external soul) are essentially incomprehensible: 'we do not know what what these things mean, simply because we do not know what we ourselves mean when we are moved by them' (Chesterton 1930: 121). This thought leads Chesterton to a reflection which must surely rank as his most pregnant contribution to the study of magic:

> Suppose somebody in a story says 'Pluck this flower and a princess will die in a castle beyond the sea,' we do not know why something stirs in the subconsciousness, or why what is impossible seems also inevitable. Suppose we read 'And in the hour when the king extinguished the candle his ships were wrecked far away on the coast of the Hebrides.' We do not know why the imagination has accepted that image before the reason can reject it; or why such correspondences seem really to correspond to something in the soul. (Chesterton 1930: 121)

Howard Mounce makes the point well (and this reinforces what was said earlier about misplaced rationalism) that the success of these sentences depends not upon their being 'true', but rather upon a certain fascination that they cast over us. To attempt to account for their meaning by saying 'Plucking a flower killed a princess because it was a signal to a band of assassins who immediately rode off to see to her death' (Mounce 1973: 358) would only serve to destroy the magic of the sentence, and make it commonplace. Chesterton believes that the importance of ideas such as those expressed in his two fairytale sentences lies not in their relation to factual events. The depth they possess has to do with 'why something stirs in the subconsciousness' when we hear them. As he says, our reason will reject these ideas, but not before the imagination has accepted them, and it this non-rational (or more specifically, *pre*-rational) part of us which is bound up with ritual and belief. The depth of magical beliefs is then due to the depth of the human soul:

> Very deep things in our nature, some dim sense of the dependence of great things upon small, some dark suggestion that the things nearest to us stretch far beyond our power, some sacramental feeling of the magic in material substances, and many

more emotions past finding out, are in an idea like that of the external soul. (Chesterton 1930: 121)

The view that great things depend upon small does seem to be one of the major features of magical thought, in practice as well as in the tales that Chesterton speaks of. Consider the example given by Frazer of the talismanic sword possessed by the Cambodian 'King of Fire':

> If the Fire King draws the magic sword a few inches from its sheath, the sun is hidden and men and beasts fall into a profound sleep; were he to draw it quite out of the scabbard, the world would come to an end. (Frazer 1936b: 5)

Now there certainly is a sense in which what is important or deep in magic is contained in this example. A rationalist may see it simply as an error (for of course, the withdrawl of a sword cannot bring about the end of the world). Chesterton, however, like Ernst, would feel that the meaning of the story about the Fire King's sword is not to be addressed in this way. Rather than concerning ourselves with whether or not the sword could have this property, we should reflect on the fascination that envelops us when we entertain the possibility that it *might*. Such a belief *is* absurd, but it is precisely this expression of what is impossible which is so fascinating. So note how Chesterton's procedure is largely psychological: he attempts only to show how the ideas contained in magic and folklore affect, fascinate and appeal to the human soul. The magic sword is something which, however unreasonable, grasps the imagination. For Chesterton, as indeed for Wittgenstein, *this* is what should be of interest to us, for that which appeals to us will also be that which created the associated belief and practice. In Wittgenstein's words: 'What strikes us in this course of events as terrible, impressive, horrible, tragic, &c., ... *that* is what gave birth to them' (Wittgenstein 1979b: 3).

7.2 WITTGENSTEIN, MAGIC AND METAPHYSICS

The same poetic understanding of religious and magical belief which informs the writings of both Chesterton and Ernst is also encountered in Wittgenstein. He too abhors the rationalistic interpretation of ritual, and propounds instead the view that magic is more of an imaginative and poetic affair than writers like Frazer presume. We find elements of this view in a passage from *Culture and Value*, where Wittgenstein speaks of a miracle as being 'a *gesture* which God makes'. An instance of this is said to be that of God making the trees around a saint bow in reverence after he has spoken.

> The only way for me to believe in a miracle in this sense would be to be *impressed* by an occurrence in this particular way. So that I should say e.g.: 'It was *impossible* to see these trees and not feel that they were responding to the words.' ... And I can imagine that the mere report of the *words* and life of a saint can make someone believe the reports that the trees bowed. (Wittgenstein 1980a: 45)

What this passage seems to suggest is that a religious belief is not accepted through reasoning, but rather because it is felt to be *appropriate*: it is felt that such an event (trees bowing in reverence) is *fitting*. But to repeat: this is not a rational belief. Its poetry is accepted before questions of rationality are brought to bear on it. To recall Chesterton's words, 'it is accepted before there is time to believe it' (Chesterton 1930: 118).

Confirmation that Wittgenstein *is* saying something like this about magic can be found in *On Certainty*. Wittgenstein is discussing the set of propositions which Moore in his 'Defence of Common Sense' claims to *know* to be true. Moore 'knows' that 'the earth had existed ... for many years before my body was born' (Moore 1959a: 33). As part of his critique of this contention, Wittgenstein writes:

> May someone have telling grounds for believing that the earth has only existed for a short time, say since his own birth? – Suppose he had always been told that – would he have any good reason to doubt it? Men have believed that they could make rain; why should not a king be brought up in the belief that the world began with him? And if Moore and this king were to meet and discuss, could Moore really prove his belief to be the right one? I do not say that Moore could not convert the king to his view, but it would be a conversion of a special kind; the king would be brought to look at the world in a different way.

We may pause here to note just two things. First, Wittgenstein's remark that 'men have believed that they could make rain' does contrast sharply with those passages in the *Remarks* which seem to suggest that primitives consulting a rain-maker do not really think that he can make rain. Wittgenstein's candid 'anti-instrumentalism' can perhaps be revised in light of this. Secondly, his comment about the conversion of the king being of 'a special kind' makes the point that the change from a religious to a secular world-view (or *vice versa*) is not a case of recognizing the previous view as being mistaken. Having made these points, Wittgenstein continues:

> Remember that one is sometimes convinced of the *correctness* of a view by its *simplicity* or *symmetry*, i.e. these are what induce one to go over to this point of view. One then simply says something like: '*That's* how it must be.' (Wittgenstein 1977a: §92)

This idea that certain views are accepted because of their seemliness is a frequent theme in Wittgenstein's writings. For instance, he contends that although Darwinism is accepted as 'obviously' true, it is based on only very thin evidence. Indeed, he says, it is accepted because of its charm, rather than because of evidence in its favour: 'In the end you forget entirely every question of verification, you are just sure that it must have been like that' (Wittgenstein 1966: 26–7). He expresses similar thoughts with regard to psychoanalysis. Contrary to Freud's feeling that 'strong prejudices work against the idea of psycho-analysis' (Wittgenstein, in Malcolm 1984: 100–1), Wittgenstein maintains that its explanations are 'adopted because they have a peculiar charm' (Wittgenstein 1966: 25):

> The attractiveness of the suggestion, for instance, that all anxiety is a repetition of the anxiety of the birth trauma, is just the attractiveness of a mythology ... There is an inducement to say, 'Yes, of course, it must be like that'. A powerful mythology. (Wittgenstein 1966: 51–2)[2]

Here we see the attractiveness of certain (putative) scientific explanations likened to the charm of mythology. From here it is but a short step to the contention that magical and religious beliefs too are accepted because of their charm.

Consider how this emerges in another passage from *Culture and Value*:

'Yes, that's how it is,' you say, 'because that's how it *must* be!'
(Schopenhauer: man's real life span is 100 years.)
   'Of course, that's how it must be!' It is just as though you have
understood a creator's *purpose.* You have grasped the *system.*
   You do not ask 'But how long do men actually live?' which
strikes you now as a superficial matter; whereas you have understood something more profound. (Wittgenstein 1980a: 26)

Wittgenstein's remark here emphasizes the depth of a particular
picture over and against the humdrum (though accurate) reality of
the lifespan of a human being. So how does this relate to belief? The
answer must be something like this. Wittgenstein is noting the
poetic charm of Schopenhauer's statement, and how it is capable of
being intuitively accepted. The force of this can be well brought out
by reflection on an example, discussed by Frazer, and taken from
the folk-beliefs of certain communities living in the coastal regions
of Britain. It is said in these parts (up until very recently at least) that
people are born when the tide comes in and die when it goes out.
Frazer is quick to point out that this belief is the result of a mistaken
application of the Law of Similarity, so that instead of seeing the ebb
and flow of the tide as a mere symbol, 'they discern a real agent'
(Frazer 1922: 34). However, given an interpretation of the poetic-
seemliness form, an explanation in terms of error may be seen to be
gratuitous. Rather, one need only to note how certain ideas exercise
a fascination on our minds and compel us to accept them. 'It is very
interesting that pictures do *force* themselves on us' (Wittgenstein
1956: 7). An idea such as that of the tide's control over life and death
may be particularly attractive due to its possession of the kind of
symmetry spoken of by Wittgenstein. Grasping the idea of death at
the ebbing tide may lead one to feel that a deeper understanding of
the nature of life has been achieved. Consider again Wittgenstein's
comment on Schopenhauer, recast in the light of this example:

   'Yes, that's how it is,' you say, 'because that's how it *must* be!'
   (People are born when the tide comes in and die when the tide
   goes out.)
      'Of course, that's how it must be!' It is as though you have
   understood a creator's *purpose.* You have grasped the *system.*
      You do not ask 'But do people really die thus?' which strikes
   you now as a superficial matter; whereas you have understood
   something more profound.

To think in such ways about the relation of the tide to life and death is to view the world from a particular perspective, to see it as, in some sense, crafted. (Imagine a world in which the tide did have such control over death. It would perhaps have the character of a novel or fairy-tale. There, death would never be accidental, but rather *ordained*. 'A creator's purpose.') Nevertheless, to view the world as crafted is neither reasoned nor reasonable. Rather, it is an example of those forms of thought which somehow manage to force themselves on us: it is perhaps natural to think in ways which have a kind of poetry about them.

Significantly, the feeling that 'This is how things must be' is, for Wittgenstein, characteristic not only of religion, but of metaphysics also. Regarding this latter, he says:

A simile that has been absorbed into the forms of our language produces a false appearance, and this disquiets us. 'But *this* isn't how it is!' – we say. 'Yet *this* is how it has to *be*!' (Wittgenstein 1958: §112)

That Wittgenstein did see fundamental affinities between magic, religion and metaphysics is attested to by the introductory comments in the *Remarks on Frazer*. Here the connection is made explicit:

I think now that the right thing would be to begin my book with remarks about metaphysics as a kind of magic.

But in doing this I must neither speak in defence of magic nor ridicule it.

What it is that is deep about magic would be kept.—

In this context, in fact, keeping magic out has itself the character of magic.

For when I began in my earlier book to talk about the '*world*' (and not about this tree or table), was I trying to do anything except conjure up something of a higher order by my words? (Wittgenstein 1979b: vi)

The drawing of a comparison between magic and metaphysics is not peculiar to Wittgenstein. Often the analogy is intended to throw contempt on one and, by implication, on the other (cf. Carnap 1935: 28). And as Wittgenstein himself is so harsh in his condemnations of metaphysics, one might think that his desire to illuminate it by comparison with magic would presuppose a belief in the worthlessness or confusion of this latter. Hence, Wittgensteinians are often loath to entertain this comparison, so entrenched are their opinions of the depth of magic as opposed to the futility of metaphysics. For instance, Baker and Hacker say that the utility of Wittgenstein's desired comparison is called into doubt by great differences between the two fields. For example, ritual has 'a deep expressive role in the life of the community' (Baker and Hacker 1984b: 274), and although rituals may die, this is not due to their being 'illusory or nonsensical' (1984b: 274). The case is the opposite, they maintain, with regard to a metaphysical belief, which plays no central role in a community and which is rejected when its true nature is recognized. In short, magic is symbolic, metaphysics not. Reflecting on the magic/metaphysics comparison, then, Baker and Hacker say that 'Wittgenstein did not try to develop this thought, perhaps advisedly' (1984b: 273). But this is mistaken. Wittgenstein *does* develop this idea in the *Remarks on Frazer*, and his thoughts on this matter are not at all barren, as we may have been led to suspect.

A first indication that Wittgenstein did not abandon the comparison can be seen when he writes: 'A whole mythology is deposited in our language' (Wittgenstein 1979b: 10). Although I will later suggest a different interpretation of this remark, it has to be said that Wittgenstein's comment is generally taken to refer to those aspects of our language which 'bewitch' our intelligence and lead to metaphysics (cf. Wittgenstein 1958: §109). Hence, Baker and Hacker see the remark as being of a piece with Wittgenstein's attack on the 'confusions' involved in metaphysics: 'It is the task of philosophy to work against the myth-building tendency of our understanding' (Baker and Hacker 1984b: 271; cf. Kenny 1982: 13). Such views can be labelled 'Nietzschean' interpretations of the 'mythology in language' remark, for the comment is perhaps inspired by a passage in 'The Wanderer and his Shadow,' where Nietzsche writes:

> Through words and concepts we are still continually misled into imagining things as being simpler than they are, separate from one another, indivisible, each existing in and for itself. A philo-sophical mythology lies concealed in *language* which breaks out again every moment, however careful one may be otherwise. (Nietzsche 1986: 306, §11)[3]

Here, the view that philosophical problems are produced by the misleading forms of language is explicitly stated. It is important to note that the idea of being misled by language is present also in Ernst's *Nachwort*, and that, in the so-called 'Big Typescript', the final section of the chapter on the nature of philosophy is entitled *'Die Mythologie in den Formen unserer Sprache (Paul Ernst)'* (Wittgenstein 1993: 196).[4] Indeed, Wittgenstein always maintained that the idea of being 'misled by the form of expression of our language' (Wittgenstein 1974b: 159) was inspired by Ernst, and meant to acknowledge his influence in the preface to the *Tractatus*, where it is written that 'the reason why [philosophical] problems are posed is that the logic of language is misunderstood' (Wittgenstein 1961b: 3).

Such thoughts are certainly present in the *Nachwort*, but there Ernst is not discussing metaphysics, but rather certain notions in primitive and folk belief, such as 'the idea that apparently lifeless objects possess a soul', the totemic notion that clans are descended from animals and plants, and so on. Considering these beliefs, Ernst entertains the view as to whether such ideas arise 'from the interpretation of a misunderstood tendency of the language' (Ernst 1910: 273). As such, he contends that 'it is not observation' which inclines a clan to believe that it was descended from, say, the white wolf: 'rather it is the logical progression out of words and concepts' which decides the belief (Ernst 1910: 274). Ernst maintains that while such beliefs are confused, they are also 'the most meaningful sign of human worth' (1910: 274). He writes:

> The animal lives completely within the world of his senses but man creates even at such early stages his own world, which can completely contradict his external experience. He does not bow down and say: such is experience; rather, he commands: this is how experience will be; and precisely because in doing so he enters into a confused state, into the insoluble, the nonsensical, he develops even higher. (Ernst 1910 : 275)

In other words, religious concepts express the way things 'must be'. Such a thought seems remarkably of a piece with our earlier reflections on the notion of death at ebb tide, and reveals great contiguity between the thought of Ernst and that of Wittgenstein.

Indeed, if we turn to the *Remarks on Frazer*, we find consideration of the very idea that religious and magical concepts arise out of a mistaken understanding of the logic of language and are, as a consequence, similar in kind to the propositions of metaphysics. Wittgenstein's reflections here amplify the contention of the 'Lecture on Ethics': 'I want to impress on you that a certain characteristic misuse of our language runs through *all* ethical and religious expressions' (Wittgenstein 1965: 9). Thus, following his remark that a mythology is deposited in language, Wittgenstein writes:

> To cast out death or to slay death; but he is also represented as a skeleton, as in some sense dead himself. 'As dead as death.' 'Nothing is so dead as death; nothing is so beautiful as beauty itself.' Here the image which we use in thinking of reality is that beauty, death, &c. are the pure (concentrated) substances, and that they are found in the beautiful object as added ingredients of the mixture. – And do I not recognize here my own observations on 'object' and 'complex'? (Wittgenstein 1979b: 10)[5]

There is much to unpack here. Wittgenstein is commenting on Frazer's account of the custom of 'Carrying out Death'. This European Lenten observance involves the making of an effigy of Death – sometimes out of straw and fastened to a pole; in other places, a doll covered by a shroud and carried in a tiny coffin – which is paraded around the village of the celebrants accompanied by a song such as the following:

> *Now carry we Death out of the village,*
> *The new Summer into the village,*
> *Welcome dear Summer,*
> *Green little corn.*
> (Frazer 1922: 360)

At the close of the celebration, Death is ritually slaughtered, either burned or flung into water, and the celebrating children return to the village singing that Death has left the village and that they have *'brought Life back'* (Frazer 1922: 360).

Consideration of this case leads Wittgenstein to reflect on the similarity of this custom to certain philosophical doctrines. He is here referring explicitly to the Platonic notion that properties are ingredients of things. In the *Blue Book*, Wittgenstein speaks of this doctrine as being one of the confused philosophical tendencies which leads one into the 'complete darkness' of metaphysics. He says:

> The idea of a general concept being a common property of its particular instances connects up with other primitive, too simple, ideas of the structure of language. It is comparable to the idea that *properties* are *ingredients* of the things which have the properties; e.g. that beauty is an ingredient of all beautiful things as alcohol is of beer and wine, and that we therefore could have pure beauty, unadulterated by anything that is beautiful. (Wittgenstein 1969: 17)

What Wittgenstein sees in the custom of 'Carrying out Death', then, is the application of a primitive (perhaps an over-simplified) language in which notions and words such as 'death' and 'life' are seen as pure qualities, or reified forms, existing in abstraction from objects exhibiting signs of life or death. The peasants in the European custom are misled by the substantive 'death'. In Waismann's words: 'When we deal with a substantive, we involuntarily think of the case in which the word is correlated with an object, in the same way that the name of a person is connected with the person ... We look for a "being" which will fit the word in question, we people the world with aetherial beings to be the shadow-like companions of substantives' (Waismann 1965: 81). A tendency to see abstract nouns as independent existents informs the drift to metaphysics. Wittgenstein appears to be saying that it also forms the basis of (at least some) religious and magical beliefs.

Wittgenstein is here sketching a conception of religious thought which had been given more detailed expression by the school of 'Mythological Folklorists'. For example, by closely binding together the sciences of language and of religion, Max Müller stressed that what needed to be clearly understood was the 'dependence of early religion on language' (Müller 1893: 90). Moreover, what was stressed was the *misunderstandings* involved in this dependence: mythology was seen 'as an inevitable disease of language' (Müller 1893: 101). Thus, Müller considers the 'peculiar difficulty which the human mind experiences in speaking of collective or abstract ideas' (Müller 1968: 73), such as 'virtue', 'summer' or 'winter'. 'Virtue' (or indeed 'death') is nothing individual: 'it is a quality raised by language into a substance' (Müller 1968: 69). It is precisely this idea of the reification of qualities which Wittgenstein employs in his analysis of 'Carrying out Death'.

Further similarities can be noted by reflection on the technique of another member of the School, Abram Smythe Palmer, as exhibited in his book *Folk-Etymology, a Dictionary of Verbal Corruptions or Words Perverted in Form and Meaning, by False Derivation or Mistaken Analogy*. An example of Palmer's technique:

> ENGLAND. So far back as the time of Procopius England was popularly regarded by the people on the opposite shore of the continent as the land of souls or departed spirits. It is still believed in Brittany that a weird boat laden with souls is ferried across the English channel every night ... It has been conjectured that this superstition arose from a misunderstanding of *England*, formerly *Engeland*, as *engle-land*, 'the Angel land', *engel* being an angel in German, A.Saxon, &c. (Palmer 1882: 111)

Consider in this context the corrupted understanding of the word *Lammas*. Originally meaning 'loaf-mass' and thus referring to a first-fruits festival, this meaning became forgotten, and collapsed into the rather obvious *Lamb-Mass*, hence the practice of bringing live lambs into church on that day (cf. Brand 1848: i 348). An example such as this may serve to illustrate Ernst's contention that religious concepts arise when 'the linguistic logic of the past is no longer understood and is alluded to by invention' (Ernst 1910: 308). A more pertinent example, however, is provided by Wittgenstein himself:

> Suppose a race calls itself 'the children of Israel'. Originally, I suppose, that did not mean the descendants of a man called Israel. No, 'descendants' or 'children' meant the same as the 'tribe', viewed as a temporal phenomenon. As if the development of π was called 'the children of π'.
>
> Now suppose that 'by a misunderstanding' the expression was interpreted as the children or descendants of one Israel, so that there was talk of a man Israel who was their ancestor: the question is, In what sort of cases is it right to talk of a misunderstanding, and in what cases just of a figure of speech? Prima facie, we should expect all sorts and degrees. And that, in certain religions, what was originally a figure of speech would exuberate into full misunderstanding. (Perhaps with the help of philosophers.) (Wittgenstein MS 116, 283–5; quoted in Rhees 1982: 97)

Whatever conclusions we draw from this, there may be thus some benefit in noticing the affinities between Ernst's 'misunderstood tendency of the language', Müller's 'disease of language' and Wittgenstein's 'mythology in the forms of our language'. Wittgensteinians sceptical of the worth of a magic/metaphysics comparison will be even less pleased by the thought that magic arises from a 'disease of language'. If religious and magical beliefs are the result of linguistic confusion, then this surely entails that we should rid ourselves of them. Although rejecting this account of religion, Phillips does feel that the metaphysics comparison illuminates the character of *superstition* (cf. Phillips 1976: 110). In maintaining this, Phillips makes a move which is typical of Wittgensteinians (cf. Ray 1990: 476), marking off 'true' religion (or 'true' magic) from 'false' or 'superstitious' practices.

This is an unfortunate and unworkable comparison. One *may* wish to say that a man who genuinely concerns himself with, say, avoiding walking under ladders or not stepping on cracks in the pavement, is confused (though perhaps not *philosophically* confused!). But the account given by Phillips of ways of acting as seemingly trivial as these is inadequate. The feeling that something important depends on the performance of something apparently insignificant is, as Chesterton urged, a feeling from the very depth of the human soul. Consider the common 'superstition' of refraining from lighting a cigarette from a candle. Why do we need to say that this is a confused action? Is there not a strange depth to the notion that such an act would result in the death of a sailor? Actions such as this do not seem to be any different in kind from the examples given by Chesterton of deep magical beliefs or folk-tale motifs, and indeed are illustrative of the kind of residual magical *thoughts*, devoid of institutionalized *practice*, which are rife in our society. Such strange ways of thinking and acting form as much a part of a 'natural history of human beings' as do more large-scale religious systems. Phillips' understanding of religion may have no place for these actions simply because it is too high-minded, whereas these minor, a-rational acts perhaps maintain some genuine affinity with magical thought (cf. Clack 1995: 113–14).

Perhaps another reason why Phillips' religion/superstition distinction should be rejected is that it is hard to find a non-pejorative application of the term 'superstition'. That Roman Catholicism, primitive religions, and even Fabian socialism have at one time or other been thus labelled should serve to illustrate that the term is more often than not used as 'little more than a verbal bludgeon to trounce one's ideological opponents' (Jahoda 1970: 2). In the absence of any positive category of 'the superstitious', we should be wise to avoid as much as possible the use of the term.

Sadly, Wittgenstein himself uses the term in contradistinction to 'religion', describing superstition as 'a sort of false science' (Wittgenstein 1980a: 72). A similar distinction is employed in the *Remarks*:

> We should distinguish between magical operations and those operations which rest on a false, over-simplified notion of things and processes. For instance, if someone says that the illness is moving from one part of the body into another, or if he takes measures to draw off the illness as though it were a liquid or a temperature. He is then using a false picture, a picture that doesn't fit. (Wittgenstein 1979b: 5)

Our main problem of interpretation is concerned with to what this is meant to refer. In other words, which elements of ritual are to be labelled 'false'? Those which, like 'Carrying out Death', exhibit metaphysical features? Wittgenstein does not speak in a disparaging way about the Lenten rite, although he does so about a comparable practice:

> The scapegoat, on which one lays one's sins, and who runs away into the desert with them – a false picture, similar to those that cause errors in philosophy. (Wittgenstein 1993: 197)

Rhees spells out why this is for Wittgenstein a false and misleading picture:

> 1 'Children carry the sins of their fathers.'
> 2 'A goat, when consecrated, carries the sins of the people.'
> In the first sentence 'carry' is used in the sense of the whole sentence. In the second sentence 'carry' seems to mean what it does in 'The goat carries on his back the basket in which we put our firewood'; and yet it *cannot* mean that. (Rhees 1982: 82)

Rhees says that the first sentence does not jar, that the picture of a man carrying his own sins like a burden is not misleading (Bunyan). Thus we should not think of Christ's act of atonement, his shouldering of sin, as a jarring symbolism. What Wittgenstein is referring to in his criticism, says Rhees, is the *literal* scapegoat: an *animal* which takes the burden of the community's sins. 'What would it mean to say that a goat has to bear its *own* sins, let alone that it has to bear the sins of *people*?' (Rhees 1982: 82).

So the point which Rhees seems to be making has to do with the possibility of *consciousness of sin*. While it is meaningless to think that human sins can be placed on a goat, the symbolism of the human scapegoat taking on the sins of a community does not so jar. Rhees may be thinking here of something like the events of Conrad's novel *The Rover*, set in the aftermath of the French Revolution. The central female character, Arlette, is spoken of as having 'the sin of all the murders of the Revolution on her shoulders' (Conrad 1992: 225), and again, as 'like the scapegoat charged with all the murders and blasphemies of the Revolution' (1992: 232). Her burden is, however, taken from her by Peyrol, the old sea rover, who sacrifices himself to the guns of the English so that Arlette can marry and the sick community be rejuvenated. The plot of *The Rover* adequately illustrates the distinction Rhees stresses: one can make sense of the actions of a person who knowingly shoulders the guilt of a society. This cannot be done in the case of an animal scapegoat: consciousness of sin, and of responsibility, has no application here.

Yet this is only superficially plausible. What is important here is not the issue of consciousness, but that of *carrying*, and it is the same feature which characterizes 'Carrying out Death': how can something which is abstract (sins, death) be physically carried? The real issue is not whether what carries the sins is human or animal, but the kind of misuse of language involved in talking in such a manner. For Rhees speaks about human scapegoats as though their act of taking on the burden of guilt was as spontaneous as that of Peyrol, who acts 'on a sudden impulse of scorn, of magnanimity' (Conrad 1992: 260), contending that this is what confers sense on such an action. Yet as Frazer shows, expulsions of scapegoats (whether human or animal) were periodically and *habitually* performed in many cultures, and the poor wretches who were expelled (or slaughtered) generally had little say in the matter (cf. Frazer 1936i: *passim*). Thus, the self-giving act which Rhees supposes the human scapegoat to perform is little more than a fantasy on his part. Thus, if we press the point and abandon Rhees' human/animal distinction, should we say that Wittgenstein is really contending that the ceremonies involving the expulsion of scape-goats (which, it must be remembered, are widespread and a fundamental part of *many* religions) are 'misleading pictures' worthy of scorn?

Perhaps a typical Wittgensteinian like Phillips would claim that this is the case. He certainly wishes to say that the idea of the scape-goat is a meaningless 'confusion which springs from a misunderstanding of the logic of our language' (Phillips 1988: 308). But if the isolable aspect of the ritual which evokes such scorn is the idea of 'carrying' something abstract, then this entails that there are *many* other rituals (including 'Carrying out Death', and those forms of sympathetic magic resting on the principle of personification) which must also be treated with disdain and labelled as 'superstition'. And this, for the reasons given earlier, would surely be bizarre. Now certainly we have seen that Wittgenstein presents the possibility of understanding (at least some) magical rituals in terms of a 'misuse' or 'misunderstanding' of language. Our concern must now be to show how he can maintain this while at the same time wishing to keep in his account a sense of the depth and profundity of magic.

7.3 'PROFOUND, PROFOUND': THE PHILOSOPHY IN RUMPELSTILTSKIN

Phillips' distaste for a magic/metaphysics comparison can be put down to his belief in the confusion and worthlessness of metaphysics. However, in this respect he is only *partially* expressing a Wittgensteinian concern. For while it is certainly true that Wittgenstein wishes to stress 'the senselessness of metaphysical turns of phrase' (Wittgenstein 1974b: 129), he also maintains that there is a great depth to metaphysics. For example, he often spoke of metaphysics in terms of a 'running up against the limits of language'. This tendency of human beings, which produces supposedly 'senseless' utterances, is not, however, to be ridiculed. In one of the conversations recorded by Waismann, Wittgenstein says: 'I do not scoff at this tendency in man; I hold it in reverence' (Waismann 1979: 118). Similarly, Rhees notes Wittgenstein's remark that 'You can't say "etsch, etsch!" to philosophical problems, they are too strong' (Rhees 1971: 24). This entails, then, that the comparison of metaphysics with magic is not necessarily one which intends to show how the latter is worthy of contempt.

One way in which we can illustrate the profundity of both metaphysics and magic is by juxtaposing some philosophical difficulties surrounding names and the act of naming, with a comparable area of sympathetic magic, that to do with magic in names, about which Wittgenstein comments:

> Why should it not be possible that a man's own name be sacred to him? Surely it is both the most important instrument given to him and also something like a piece of jewelry hung round his neck at birth. (Wittgenstein 1979b: 5)

Here Wittgenstein is commenting on a most conspicuous aspect of magical thought, one that is explored in great depth by Frazer and other writers. It is a feature of primitive thought that names are not regarded simply as personal signifiers, aids to discourse and recognition, but rather are bound up in an integral manner with the person. The primitive believes that his name is as much in need of protection as his body, and, for fear of damage being inflicted on him by an enemy, will not allow his name to become common knowledge.[6]

Wittgenstein wants to show that such beliefs are not alien and bizarre, but are, in fact, wholly familiar to us. Beyond the ejaculation concerning the sanctity of names, however, no examples of the 'naturalness' of this belief in our lives are forthcoming. Such examples are not, though, hard to find. Consider how serious it is when a Member of Parliament is 'named' by the Speaker of the House; or how we feel that when our name is mocked, or else made the subject of a pun, then it is we ourselves who are being ridiculed; or even how terrifying we find the idea of having our name removed and replaced with a number.

Our immediate purpose here is not, however, to focus upon the naturalness of name magic. Rather, we wish to illuminate the character of a magic/metaphysics comparison, and here we need to emphasize how the belief in a magical connection between name and thing named is mirrored in philosophy. Our task is here made simple, for Wittgenstein frequently characterizes the philosophical treatment of naming in terms of magic. This emerges most explicitly in the *Brown Book*, where Wittgenstein reflects on the temptation there is 'to imagine that giving a name consists in correlating in a peculiar and rather mysterious way a sound (or other sign) with something' (Wittgenstein 1969: 172). Concerning this 'delusion', Wittgenstein proceeds to say: 'One could almost imagine that naming was done by a peculiar sacramental act, and that this produced some magic relation between the name and the thing' (Wittgenstein 1969: 172). By means of an invented language-game, he attempts to show how this conception of a magical relation is confused: in the language-game, 'the relation of the name of a person to the person here consists in the person having been trained to run up to someone who calls out the name' (Wittgenstein 1969: 172). This stress on *training* and *praxis* is intended to disperse the aura of mystery (the 'occult process' (Wittgenstein 1958: §38)) surrounding the naming relation. Wittgenstein's picture thus stands full square against the 'primitive philosophy' which 'condenses the whole usage of the name into the idea of a relation, which thereby becomes a mysterious relation' (Wittgenstein 1969: 173).

If it is Wittgenstein's contention that philosophers tend to see a mysterious relation between a name and the thing named, and that in so doing they propound a 'primitive philosophy', then the passage from this view to an interpretation of name magic is relatively smooth. For the sorcerer believes that by acting on the name of his intended victim (say, by writing the name on an effigy to be burned) he can injure the person. Hence we can say that the 'confusion' involved in this is that of confounding the name with its bearer (cf. Wittgenstein 1958: §40). If this *is* his contention, then Wittgenstein is giving voice to a common thought in anthropology, one which can be detected, for example, in the writings of Horton (1970: 156) and Skorupski (1976: 144–8). It is, however, C. R. Hallpike's neo-Piagetian analysis of primitive thought which provides the most detailed treatment of savage reification of words and names. Both children and primitives, Hallpike contends, suffer from an 'implicit confusion of subjective and objective' (Hallpike 1979: 385), which is termed by Piaget 'conceptual realism'. One particular species of this is 'nominal realism', and is the condition whereby the primitive fails to recognize 'that names and words are quite distinct from their referents and are conventional in origin' (Hallpike 1979: 385). Thus, the primitive (or child) fails to distinguish 'between the sign and the thing signified' (Hallpike 1979: 386). 'Words (including names, a concept which the child finds easier to understand than "word") are regarded as a part of the things they denote' (Hallpike 1979: 386). Hallpike says that if we survey the writings of the Pre-Socratic philosophers we find ample evidence of this form of conceptual realism – Wittgenstein would perhaps contend that such a doctrine did not stop there, but progressed well into the theories of the philosophers of our time. If this is the direction in which Wittgenstein's reflections on name- and word-magic marches, then we seem left with a similar conclusion as in the case of 'Carrying out Death': that magical beliefs arise out of a misunderstanding of the logic of language, in this instance due to a failure to recognize the conventional nature of personal signifiers. And this is true: the *Remarks on Frazer* do suggest such an account. Nevertheless, Wittgenstein knows all too well that it will not do to use such reflections in order to excoriate magical thought, or to locate it simply in the infancy of human thought. These forms of thinking are too tenacious and, Wittgenstein would say, too *deep*. It is hard to say precisely in what this depth lies, but we can at least indicate the direction of Wittgenstein's thoughts on this matter. First, there are numerous places in his writings where he considers the relation of composers' names to their music (cf. Wittgenstein 1980a: 24–5; Wittgenstein 1982a: §§72–3), and where he ponders on the link between people and their signatures. This he explicitly links with 'magic that is done with pictures, hair etc.' (Wittgenstein 1980c: §336).

Most telling, however, is his response to the tale of Rumpelstiltskin. In this tale, collected by the Brothers Grimm, the power of the dwarf lies in the secrecy of his name, such that when it is guessed by the miller's daughter, Rumpelstiltskin has to give up his nefarious claim to her first-born. As Edward Clodd makes clear in his extended study of the Suffolk variant of the tale, *Tom Tit Tot*, this prominent motif of the tale has its roots in savage philosophy, in the belief, noted earlier, that one's name is an integral part of oneself, and that an enemy's knowledge of it can cause harm to the bearer. The central idea in the tale of Rumpelstiltskin is, then, the same as those 'metaphysical' aspects of magic under consideration here. Wittgenstein's reaction to the tale, as recorded by Fania Pascal, indicates the depth he feels magic to possess, even if it is based on the kind of linguistic misunderstanding that he and Ernst speak of. Thus, after reading out Rumpelstiltskin's words 'And oh! I am glad that nobody knew / That the name I am called is Rumpelstiltskin', he responded: 'Profound, profound' (Pascal 1984: 20). Pascal says that she could not share Wittgenstein's vision of the profundity in the tale, and it is, indeed, hard to say where it lies. If pressed, however, we should have to say that the depth in the word-magic to which the tale of Rumpelstiltskin gives expression lies in the strong feeling we have that our words can influence events, that one's name is not simply an 'aid to reference', but is bound up with one's personality, even one's soul (cf. Clodd 1898: 231–8). Beattie's reminders of our shameful feelings after wishing death on someone belong to these reflections, as does Freud's idea of 'the omnipotence of thought'. The profundity of such thoughts, even if pathological, has to do with our inarticulate sense of the dark depth of the soul – of our *own* souls even – and should remind us of Chesterton's reflections on the curious depth of certain folk-tale motifs. More significantly, perhaps, we have begun to touch upon themes of Wittgenstein's treatment of ritual – and of its depth – which emerge strongly in his notes on human sacrifice. The time to examine these remarks is almost upon us, but we should first note one surprising upshot of this chapter's investigations.

7.4 WITTGENSTEIN AND FRAZER: BEYOND EXPRESSIVISM AND INSTRUMENTALISM

The preceding examination of the metaphysics/magic comparison entertained in the *Remarks* uncovered two features of Wittgenstein's reflections on magical thought which tend to go unspoken. First, and with regard both to the custom of 'Carrying out Death' and to the scapegoat ritual, we noted how Wittgenstein emphasizes that, in magical thought, there is a tendency to reify words and concepts, such as 'Death' and 'Sin', which thence are perceived as capable of being 'carried'. Secondly, and similarly, the phenomenon of name- and word-magic, when illuminated by a comparison with metaphysics, exhibits a tendency to 'confuse' a name with its bearer.

We earlier noted how Wittgenstein was saying nothing new in all this, and how these thoughts are similar to those of, for example, Max Müller. Moreover, and perhaps surprisingly, his thoughts are little different from those of Frazer himself. Consider how Frazer introduces the idea of the scapegoat:

I have sought to trace this curious usage to its origin, to decompose the idea of the Divine Scapegoat into the elements out of which it appears to be compounded. If I am right, the idea resolves itself into a simple confusion between the material and the immaterial, between the real possibility of transferring a physical load to other shoulders and the supposed possibility of transferring our bodily and mental ailments to another who will bear them for us. (Frazer 1936i: v)

Similarly, what he writes about name-magic should bring to mind the magic/metaphysics comparison:

Unable to discriminate clearly between words and things, the savage commonly fancies that the link between a name and the person or thing denominated by it is not a mere arbitrary and ideal association, but a real and substantial bond which unites the two in such a way that magic may be wrought on a man just as easily through his name as through his hair, his nails, or any other material part of his person. (Frazer 1922: 244)

It is not meant to be suggested that Wittgenstein is guilty of the same mistake as that committed by Frazer. For the latter, primitives mistook ideal connections for real ones because they were at a low stage of mental development and were fundamentally dim-witted. Against this, Evans-Pritchard made the sensible observation that such a 'mistaking' of connections did not occur in the everyday activities performed by primitive people but rather occurred 'only when evoked in specific ritual situations' (Evans-Pritchard 1965: 29). Wittgenstein, of course, makes the same point when commenting that the savage 'cuts his arrow with skill and not in effigy' (Wittgenstein 1979b: 4). What is important, however, is to note that when Wittgenstein talks of the logic of magical thought as exhibited in something like the scapegoat rite, he expresses this in similar terms to those employed by Frazer.

And this is not an isolated instance. Numerous passages in the *Remarks* give the lie to the received opinion that Wittgenstein is unhesitatingly opposed to Frazer, challenging his views incessantly. Take the following remark:

In magical healing one *indicates* to an illness that it should leave the patient.
    After the description of any such magical cure we'd like to add: If the illness doesn't understand *that*, then I don't know *how* one ought to say it. (Wittgenstein 1979b: 6–7)

What is being stated by Wittgenstein here does not run counter to an instrumentalist conception of magic; in fact, it *suggests* an instrumental rationale for the action. Nature is being impelled, by a process of mimesis, to follow man's bidding. And this, of course, is exactly what Frazer would conclude about magical healing. Blinded by the received view that Wittgenstein is utterly dismissive of instrumentalism, one may claim that his remark about magical cures is eccentric and unrepresentative. Nothing could be further from the truth. Just two more examples:

> Eating and drinking have their dangers, not only for savages but also for us; nothing more natural than wanting to protect oneself against these. (Wittgenstein 1979b: 6)

> People at one time thought it useful to kill a man, sacrifice him to the god of fertility, in order to produce good crops. (Wittgenstein 1982b: 33)

Such thoughts contrast sharply with the view that ritual is 'expressive', and indicate that Wittgenstein believes, with Frazer, that (at least some) rites are intended to ward off unwanted events or to bring about desired ends.

This is not to say that there are not great differences between the respective approaches of Frazer and Wittgenstein, yet these should not be understood in terms of a disagreement over whether magic is instrumental or not. We can begin to indicate the possible nature of their disagreement by considering a remark from the later set of notes, which shows Wittgenstein still concerned with the relation between magic and metaphysics. This remark arises as a reflection on Frazer's discussion of the primitive conception of the soul. Frazer informs us that: 'The Malays conceive the human soul as a little man, mostly invisible and of the bigness of a thumb, who corresponds exactly in shape, proportion, and even in complexion to the man in whose body he resides' (Frazer 1922: 179). Wittgenstein comments:

> How much more truth there is in this view, which ascribes the same multiplicity to the soul as to the body, than in a modern watered-down theory.
>   Frazer doesn't notice that we have before us the teaching of Plato and Schopenhauer.

We find every childlike (infantile) theory again in today's philosophy, only not with the winning ways of the childlike. (Wittgenstein 1979c: 74)

There is an error here. Frazer *does* recognize the teachings of Plato and other metaphysicians, if not in this case then in those of other magical views. Time and again he tries to illuminate magical thought by juxtaposing it with that of such philosophers as Pythagoras, Empedocles, and even Herbert Spencer (cf. Frazer 1936h: 300–5). Consider another case where the magical view can be likened to a philosopher's theory. In his chapter on the 'Homoeopathic Magic of a Flesh Diet', Frazer documents how certain peoples believe that by eating the flesh of a certain animal they will acquire its physical qualities. Hence, 'in Northern India people fancy that if you eat the eyeballs of an owl you will be able like an owl to see in the dark' (Frazer 1922: 496), and 'in British Central Africa aspirants after courage consume the flesh and especially the hearts of lions, while lecherous persons eat the testicles of goats' (Frazer 1936h: 142). Such crude views can certainly be juxtaposed with Feuerbach's (perhaps equally crude) materialist proposition that man is what he eats (cf. Kamenka 1970: 110–13).

There is, however, something more pertinent which can be gleaned by reflection on the principles of magical diets, for it presents in a stark manner a feature of Wittgenstein's thought on ritual belief which is not shared by Frazer. This has to do with an area which was explored earlier in connection with Chesterton: that of the spontaneous, pre-reflective acceptance of magical ideas. How natural the idea seems that one wishing to be brave should eat the flesh of the most courageous of animals, the lion! Again, how easy it is to accept the notion that in order to harm one's enemy one should destroy an image of him. Wittgenstein is not objecting to the view that primitives intend to harm their enemies through their magic (and if he is then he is surely mistaken); he is rather claiming that such actions have not arisen through an elaborate procedure of hypothesis-forming and subsequent testing. What Wittgenstein is opposed to is the kind of theory voiced by Eliade, who writes:

When a sorceress burns a wax doll containing a lock of her victim's hair she does not have in mind the entire theory underlying that bit of magic – but this fact does not affect our understanding of sympathetic magic. What does matter to our understanding is to know that such an action could only have happened after people had satisfied themselves by experiment, or established theoretically, that nails, hair, or anything a person has worn preserve an intimate relation with their owner even when separated from him. (Eliade 1987: 9)

Wittgenstein certainly opposes this view, for what did we establish theoretically before we kissed the photograph of our loved one? Nothing, for there is no testing of this kind involved here. We kiss the pictures or the names of those we love, throw darts at photographs of the politicians we despise, and so on, because these are perfectly natural things for us to do, and not because we have reached a belief in their efficacy by means of a sustained and elaborate process of ratiocination.

The two themes we have here noted – the legitimacy of instrumentalism and the unratiocinated nature of rituals – come together perfectly in Wittgenstein's response to Frazer's description of the mode of life of the Mikado, obliged to sit motionless on his throne for some hours every morning, so that 'he could preserve peace and tranquility in his empire' (Frazer 1922: 169). Wittgenstein writes:

When a man laughs too much in our company (or at least in mine), I half-involuntarily compress my lips, as if I believed I could thereby keep his closed. (Wittgenstein 1979c: 73)

The purpose of this reminder is not to show that Frazer is wrong in attributing to the ancient Japanese the belief that the Mikado's movements had control over the stability of the empire. On the contrary, Wittgenstein is attempting to show just how *natural* it is for a person to act on the principles of imitative magic. Wittgenstein is wanting to maintain, as Frazer had, that 'the principle of mimicry is implanted ... deep in human nature' (Frazer 1936i: 374) and is used frequently when attempting to achieve some concrete end, such as making someone be quiet. But Wittgenstein's stress on the involuntary character of the ritual – on its status as a primitive reaction – still necessitates a rejection of intellectualism: ritual actions are not 'thought out', not based on beliefs.

It is in this, then, that the difference between Frazer and Wittgenstein lies. Frazer, thinking that all human thought and activity corresponds to some degree to scientific endeavour naturally thinks that magical action must be arrived at by the same process by which science advances, namely hypothesis and experiment. Thus, for Frazer magic arises through ratiocination. Wittgenstein, on the other hand, insists that magical practices are of a spontaneous, unratiocinated character, and feels that accounts which set up an elaborate network of theories underlying these practices are simply gratuitous. Nevertheless, the spontaneous/ratiocinative contrast, which goes beyond the debate on instrumentalism, is a rather subtle – if crucial – distinction, and one which undermines the very rigid dichotomies so enthusiastically employed by both hostile and friendly commentators on the *Remarks*. Indeed, when we turn to the later set of notes on *The Golden Bough*, as we now shall, we observe, more clearly than ever, that the frequently drawn opposition between Wittgenstein and Frazer is more apparent than real.

8

Frazerian Reflections: Wittgenstein on Beltane and Human Sacrifice

Hitherto, we have been concerned largely with themes thrown up in the first set of *Remarks on Frazer's Golden Bough*, questions to do with the principles of magic, with anthropological method, with expressive and intellectualist interpretations of religious rites, and so on. In those notes written in the early 1930s, Wittgenstein surveyed many aspects of *The Golden Bough* and was savagely critical of Frazer. When, however, we turn to the later notes, written around 1948, we find a very different picture. Here, Wittgenstein is discussing only one aspect of *The Golden Bough* – namely, Frazer's characterization of the Beltane fire-festival – and, furthermore, no vicious attacks on Frazer are launched. Indeed, the argument of the later set of notes is in places not dissimilar to the oft-voiced comments made in *The Golden Bough* about religion's roots in human nature. Although these remarks have a small scope, they are of great interest and significance. Accordingly, the entirety of this chapter will be given over to a examination of Wittgenstein's thoughts on the fire-festivals of Europe. First, however, we should familiarize ourselves with the nature of the Beltane festival and with what Frazer has to say about it.

8.1 THE FESTIVAL OF BELTANE

The pagan Celtic year was divided into two main periods, winter and summer, and the dawn of each was marked by great festivities. The new year was celebrated at the beginning of November, and it was on Hallowe'en, or *Samhain* (originally the first of November, rather than the thirty-first of October) that one of these two festivals occurred. The other took place six months later on the first of

135

May; that is, on May Day, or *Là Beltain*. These dates do not coincide with the equinoxes and solstices of the solar year, nor with the sowing and reaping of the agricultural year. Rather, they mark changes in temperature: May Day ushering in the warmth and returning greenery of summer, and Hallowe'en signalling the harsh onslaught of the cold winter months. It is these dates which mark the respective periods when the cattle of the herdsman can graze in the open and when they need to be returned to the stall. Thus, the bisection of the Celtic year into two halves at the beginning of May and the beginning of November can be dated to a time when the Celts were a pastoral people, dependent for their subsistence on their herds.

The character of Hallowe'en and the importance it had for the Celts is not alien to us, for much of it is preserved in our modernday entertainments at the end of October. It did, however, possess a seriousness which does not figure in the festivities of today. For the Celts, *Samhain* marked the end of the old year and the beginning of the new. As such, this night was dangerous, for it was felt that the very fabric of time was then breached. Spirits were abroad, and just as the cows were brought back to the security of the stall, so dead ancestors returned to the warmth of their old homes, to sit by the fireside and partake of food and company. Again, the souls of those who were to die in the coming year could be seen, and hence, rites of divination were commonly enacted on Hallowe'en, with the intention of ascertaining who would live to see another new year and who would not. Witches and fairies too were let loose at *Samhain*, and many a precaution needed to be taken to protect oneself against their baleful influence. A central aspect of the festival was the lighting of bonfires on hills, a feature which this winter festival shares with its summer counterpart, Beltane.

Like Hallowe'en, May Day has preserved some of its special character, although it is not so widely celebrated as it was in times past. May Day was then celebrated as the beginning of summer; garlands were made, and houses and doorways were adorned with the newly sprouting vegetation (indeed, so much so that John Aubrey lamented the damage done to so many hawthorn trees in Woodstock (cf. Aubrey 1972: 137)). A tree was felled and set up as a maypole, around which the folk danced and sang. It was a day of great licence, the excesses of which could provoke many a puritan to bewail the fact that of many young women revelling in the woods, few 'returned home againe undefiled' (Brand 1848: i 213).

Such was the nature of May Day in England. Yet it is the Scottish Beltane festivities which concern both Frazer and Wittgenstein, and particularly the lighting of great fires on this day. In his description of the Beltane fire-festival, Frazer quotes from a number of detailed accounts of the celebration as it was performed in the late eighteenth century. The following passage (John Ramsey's account) illustrates well the character of the festival:

> Towards the close of the entertainment, the person who officiated as master of the feast produced a large cake baked with eggs and scalloped round the edge, called *am bonnach beal-tine* – *i.e.*, the Beltane cake. It was divided into a number of pieces, and distributed in great form to the company. There was one particular piece which whoever got was called *cailleach beal-tine* – *i.e.*, the Beltane *carline*, a term of great reproach. Upon his being known, part of the company laid hold of him and made a show of putting him into the fire; but the majority interposing, he was rescued. And in some places they laid him flat on the ground, making as if they would quarter him. Afterwards, he was pelted with egg-shells, and retained the odious appellation during the whole year. And while the feast was fresh in people's memory, they affected to speak of the *cailleach beal-tine* as dead. (Frazer 1936j: 148)

Frazer sees in such a celebration the remnants of an older and more serious rite, and in piecing together the original nature of the Beltane festival, he relies on Tylor's notion of 'survivals'. In *Primitive Culture*, Tylor had noted that there are many customs and traditions, such as the idea that May marriages are unlucky, which persist among people even when their meaning has been forgotten. He went on:

> Now there are thousands of cases of this kind which have become, so to speak, landmarks in the course of culture. When in the process of time there has come general change in the condition of a people, it is usual, notwithstanding, to find much that manifestly had not its origin in the new state of things, but has simply lasted on into it. On the strength of these survivals, it becomes possible to declare that the civilization of the people they are observed among must have been derived from an earlier state, in which the proper home and meaning of these things are

to be found; and thus collections of such facts are to be worked as mines of historic knowledge. (Tylor 1891: i 71)

Frazer views the Beltane festival as it was performed in the eighteenth century as just such a 'mine of historic knowledge', a mitigated survival of an earlier rite. Hence, he addresses the problem of discovering the form and meaning of the ritual from which the entertainment of the eighteenth century was descended. Frazer considers and rejects Wilhelm Mannhardt's 'solar theory' of the fire-festivals, whereby the fires lit on May Day and Hallowe'en, and at Midsummer and Midwinter, were, in their original form, 'sun charms ... intended, on the principle of imitative magic, to ensure a needful supply of sunshine for men, animals, and plants by kindling fires which mimic on earth the great source of light and heat in the sky' (Frazer 1936j: 329). In its place, Frazer accepts Edward Westermarck's 'purificatory theory', the contention of which is that the fire-festivals are 'designed to burn up and destroy all harmful influences' (Frazer 1936j: 329). Such an interpretation seems particularly apposite in the case of the Beltane fires when we remember that the eve of May Day is Walpurgis Night, 'a night of considerable importance and much anxiety to the Highland farmer, ... on which all the tribes of witches, warlocks, wizards, and fairies, in the kingdom, are to be reviewed by Satan and his chief generals in person, and new candidates admitted into infernal orders' (Stewart 1823: 258–9). Thus, Frazer suggests, the chief evil which is to be destroyed by the purification rites of Beltane is that of *witches*:

> Again and again we are told that the fires are intended to burn or repel the witches; and the intention is sometimes graphically expressed by burning an effigy of a witch in the fire. Hence, when we remember the great hold which the dread of witchcraft has had on the popular European mind in all ages, we may suspect that the primary intention of all these fire-festivals was simply to destroy or at all events get rid of the witches, who were regarded as the causes of nearly all the misfortunes and calamities that befall men, their cattle, and their crops. (Frazer 1936j: 342)

Thus, the first stage of Frazer's reconstruction of the Beltane festival shows how the game-like diversion of May Day was previously a deadly serious ritual intended to protect the lives and crops of the

Highlanders. The second stage indicates that the pretence of throwing one of the assembly into the fire, or the presence of a burning effigy therein, are remnants of a more chilling occurrence: that previously human beings thought to be witches, or else representing evil forces, were *really* burned in the flames. As Frazer says, there are 'unequivocal traces' of human sacrifice in the Beltane tomfoolery (Frazer 1936k: 31).

Thus, Frazer's contention is clear: what remained of the Beltane festival in the eighteenth century, when it was reported by the likes of Ramsey and Thomas Pennant, was the survival of an earlier and sinister practice of sacrificing those human beings regarded by the celebrants of the rite as witches.

8.2 A DENIAL OF HISTORICAL UNDERSTANDING?

The crux of Frazer's position regarding the Beltane festival is, then, this: that the Highland custom constitutes the remains of an earlier rite in which people regarded as witches were burned in the festival's fires. Now what must surely strike us about this contention is its very *reasonableness*. Indeed, the thought is not peculiar to Frazer, for many writers have simply taken it for granted that human sacrifice once took place around the Beltane fires (cf. Hutton 1996: 225; Ross 1990: 134; Scott 1902: iv 154). It does, however, appear that Wittgenstein is objecting to this idea, for in the notes of his lectures recorded by Moore, Wittgenstein states that 'it was a mistake to suppose that why, e.g., the account of the Beltane Festival "impresses us so much" is because it has "developed from a festival in which a real man was burnt". He accused Frazer of thinking that this was the reason' (Moore 1959b: 315). This apparent criticism emerges also in the *Remarks*, where Wittgenstein writes:

> What is sinister, deep, does not lie in the fact that that is how the history of this practice went, for perhaps it did not go that way; nor in the fact that perhaps or probably it was that, but in what it is that gives me reason to assume it. (Wittgenstein 1979b: 16)

> May we not have been led into a mistake because we were over-impressed by historical considerations? (Wittgenstein 1979b: 15)

The implication of such remarks would seem to be that Frazer's attempt to reconstruct the original form of the Beltane rite is mistaken. Hence Rudich and Stassen's judgement that 'Wittgenstein's attack on Frazer's work is really an attack on the very idea of historical understanding' (Rudich and Stassen 1971: 88). On this view, Wittgenstein is criticizing the doctrine of survivals, and rejecting the commonly held assumption that one can explain a practice by uncovering its origins in an earlier stage of society. Dispensing with Frazer's project of historical reconstruction, Wittgenstein offers instead, Rudich and Stassen claim, a doctrine of 'plausibility'. When confronted by something disturbing (like Ramsey's description of the Beltane festival), we need to rid ourselves of our uncomfortable curiosity and achieve inner satisfaction. As, however, there may be many plausible explanations and antecedents of the phenomenon, none of which may be conclusive or convincing, Wittgenstein is said to maintain that 'each person applies the one which maximizes his inner satisfaction' (Rudich and Stassen 1971: 88). He therefore attributes the interpretation of Beltane as the remnants of a bloody sacrifice to Frazer's 'predilection for prehistoric horror stories':

> He thinks the custom for drawing lots (pieces of cake one of which contains a button) in order to choose the one who will run three times through a bonfire can be explained with equal plausibility as a manner of celebrating a button-maker's birthday. (Rudich and Stassen 1971: 88-9)

It is hard to find a more perverse and erroneous reading of Wittgenstein's argument. The remark to which Rudich and Stassen are referring is (presumably) the following:

> Here something looks like the ruins of a casting of lots. And through this aspect it suddenly gains depth. Should we learn that the cake with the knobs in a particular case had originally been baked, say, in honour of a button-maker on his birthday and the practice had then persisted in the district, it would in fact lose all 'depth', unless this should lie in the present form of the practice itself. (Wittgenstein 1979b: 15)

Such a remark does not lead us to the 'plausibility' conclusion. On the contrary, Wittgenstein is stating that if this *were* the history of the practice, then it would be less likely to make such a disturbing impression on us. Indeed, Wittgenstein never speaks of 'plausibility', nor of applying the most personally 'satisfying' interpretation, but rather contends that we are *obliged* to view the Highland rite in terms of human sacrifice, that this is 'the direction in which we *ought* to see it' (Wittgenstein 1979b: 14, emphasis added). It should thus be clear from what Wittgenstein says that anyone who seriously thought that the Beltane festival was to do with the celebration of a button-maker's birthday would have made a mistake, or have been shallow and unperceptive. As Wittgenstein straightforwardly says, 'it is clear that what gives this practice depth is its *connection* with the burning of a man' (Wittgenstein 1979b: 14).

So Wittgenstein is not dismissing the worth of historical enquiry, though it certainly is true that this does not take centre-stage in his own analysis of the Beltane festival. But his worries about 'historical considerations' seem less informed by a belief in their worthlessness than by a feeling that meticulous attention to history may lead us away from what is important or 'impressive' in (in this instance) the Beltane fires. And we will shortly see what Wittgenstein has to say on that matter. But it is also true that he thinks a stress on historical enquiry may lead one into certain errors. Wittgenstein wants to effect a distinction between the *meaning* of the Beltane custom on the one hand, and its *original form* on the other. Frazer had not done this, for having raised the question 'What is the meaning of burning effigies in the fire at these festivals?' (Frazer 1936k: 21), his answer focuses on the burning of witches. This carries with it the implication that if this was the original meaning of the rite, then it must be the meaning of the eighteenth-century custom also. But of course, the attempt to equate the *origins* or *causes* of a phenomenon with its *meaning* is what is known as the genetic fallacy, a crude example of which would be to say that because human beings were originally apes, we still are, essentially, apes. Wittgenstein may, then, simply be drawing attention to the danger of committing this logical blunder if one becomes 'over-impressed by historical considerations'.

Nevertheless, Wittgenstein does not have a wholeheartedly sceptical attitude toward historical enquiry. Consider the following remark, where he suggests how such enquiry may alter our conception of a practice:

If it were the custom at some festival for men to ride on one another (as in horse-and-rider games), we would see nothing more in this than a way of carrying someone which reminds us of men riding horses. But if we knew that among many peoples it had been the custom, say, to use slaves as mounts and to cele-brate certain festivals mounted in this way, we should then see in the harmless practice of our time something deeper and less harmless. (Wittgenstein 1979b: 14)

Similarly, our merriment at the election of the Mock Mayor of Ock Street or our pleasure in eating gingerbread men may be tainted (or even *deepened*) if we were to be informed that such things were perhaps vestiges or survivals of the practice of human sacrifice. Wittgenstein denies none of this: far from historical enquiry being impossible in these matters, it may be highly informative and provide enlightenment regarding certain customs which, like the Beltane festival in recent times, seem 'too meaningless to have been invented in this form' (Wittgenstein 1979b: 17). Such historical investigations may reveal familiar and homely customs to have a very sinister past, and thus, perhaps, a sinister character for us today. Yet what is crucial for Wittgenstein is that no historical research is required in order to show that the Beltane festival is sinister:

> Even if its ancient origin and its descent from an earlier practice is established by history, it is still possible that there is nothing sinister at all about the practice today, that no trace of the ancient horror is left on it. Perhaps it is only performed by children now, who have contests in baking cakes and decorating them with knobs. So that the depth lies solely in the thought of that ances-try. Yet this ancestry may be very uncertain and one feels like saying: 'Why make what is so uncertain into something to worry about?' (like a backwards-looking Kluge Else). But worries of that kind are not involved here. (Wittgenstein 1979b: 15)[1]

Wittgenstein is saying something like this: one may imagine that a game, say football, was, in the distant past, a bloody and brutal affair in which the side defeated in the contest was slaughtered in order to propitiate the spirits of the corn. This is certainly not unimaginable, yet, in the absence of any historical evidence, 'why make something so uncertain into something to worry about?' Yet there is plenty to worry about when we reflect on the Beltane custom as it was performed in the eighteenth century. In contradistinction to the football example, the Beltane custom *is* sinister, and does not need historical investigation to prove it so. This theme emerges again when Wittgenstein notes that when we read Ramsey's account of the festival we seem to be unavoidably led to the conclusion that these celebrations are a survival of sacrificial practices:

> Here it seems as though it were the hypothesis that gives the matter depth. And we may remember the explanation of the strange relationship between Siegfried and Brunhilde in our *Niebelungenlied*. Namely that Siegfried seems to have seen Brunhilde before. (Wittgenstein 1979b: 14)[2]

When two lovers say they knew each other in a former life, this is not (generally) meant to be anything other than a pure expression of love. Similarly with the Beltane custom: the May Day rite strikes us as having been descended from sacrifice, but, says Wittgenstein, this need not be the case. The connection is a formal, and not a historical one (cf. Wittgenstein 1979b: 9). Thus the association with sacrifice is part of the physiognomy of the rite, and is not external to it: what strikes us when we hear of the custom is that its *theme* is the burning of a man. Whether or not the Beltane festival is descended from an actual practice of sacrifice is thus insignificant when compared with the impression made on us by an account of it.

So Wittgenstein is not attacking the idea of survival in culture, nor is he sceptical about the worth of historical investigation as such. What is at stake is the meaning of a particular phenomenon or group of phenomena: the fire-festivals of Europe. What we see in Wittgenstein's notes is the idea that, if we wish to understand why the Beltane festival is a sinister affair, an historical-genetic explanation of these festivals is superfluous:

> The question is: is what we may call the sinister character of the Beltane fire festival as it was practised a hundred years ago – is this a character of the practice in itself, or only if the hypothesis regarding its origin is confirmed? I think it is clear that what gives us a sinister impression is the inner nature of the practice as performed in recent times, and the facts of human sacrifice as we know them only indicate the direction in which we ought to see it. (Wittgenstein 1979b: 14)

As Cioffi has illustrated, Wittgenstein is drawing a distinction between two kinds of sinister ritual phenomena: (i) those whose sinister nature can only be seen by paying attention to their origins or to their primordial meaning, and thus whose 'depth lies solely in the thought of its ancestry'; and (ii) those rituals which exhibit 'a physiognomy of terror' (Cioffi 1981: 218), and whose sinister character is obvious, independent of historical enquiry. It is Wittgenstein's point, then, that the Beltane festival clearly belongs to class (ii); that its meaning is revealed, not by its history, but directly, through its 'inner nature', the features of which we must now examine.

8.3 SOMETHING DEEP AND SINISTER

Wittgenstein contends, then, that the sinister nature of the Beltane festival is immediately apparent, and that one does not need to discover that it descended from an archaic rite of human sacrifice in order to recognize this.[3] It is to this end that he asks rhetorically: 'When I see someone being killed – is it simply what I see that makes an impression on me or does this come with the hypothesis that someone is being killed here?' (Wittgenstein 1979b: 17). The question thus arises: what is it about the physiognomy of the festival – about its 'inner nature' – that creates such a sinister impression? The answer to this lies in Wittgenstein's remark that, regardless of whether or not the Beltane festival is a survival of a bloody rite, 'the facts of human sacrifice ... indicate the direction in which we ought to see it' (Wittgenstein 1979b: 14). In other words, the Highland custom strikes us as being *like* human sacrifice, and it is this which imbues it with its sinister atmosphere.

Wittgenstein, however, realizes that this is not the end of the investigation, for a subsequent question still needs to be asked:

What makes human sacrifice something deep and sinister anyway? Is it only the suffering of the victim that impresses us in this way? All manner of diseases bring just as much suffering and do *not* make this impression. (Wittgenstein 1979b: 16)

We can sharpen up Wittgenstein's point by reflecting, not on the differences between sacrifice and illness (a comparison which does not quite achieve what Wittgenstein wants it to), but between two forms of *killing*. One instance of killing may simply be a murder, carried out for such reasons as financial gain, revenge, passion, or the like. Accounts of such an act may concern us, but contrast that feeling with the dismay likely to be engendered were we to hear of a man being flayed or burned alive as part of a religious ceremony. Again, consider two forms of cannibalism. One occurs when, in times of severe hardship, a community resorts to eating some of its members. Were we to hear of such an event, it would no doubt strike us as tragic, but we would be unlikely to regard what the survivors of the famine did as 'sinister'. This form of cannibalism contrasts all too starkly with the ritual variety, partaken of to mark special days or victory in battle, in which the most appalling of sufferings is heaped upon the poor victim, often obliged to construct the oven to be used in the roasting of his own body, or made to watch as his severed limbs were eaten before him by the company (cf. Hogg 1958: 29–30). Yet, Wittgenstein contends, it is not simply the infliction of abominable pain which marks off the ritual killing. Rather, in a time of plenty, and performed not with distaste but with relish, it is the 'queer pointlessness' of the act which creates the sinister impression and 'could make us uneasy' (Wittgenstein 1979b: 18).

We may pause here to note that the category of 'queer pointlessness' could be extended to encompass the totality of the ritual field. Wittgenstein, as Cioffi notes, has an 'anti-utilitarian view of rituality' (Cioffi 1981: 230), and if this is the case, then ritual contrasts with those activities of life the purpose of which is immediately apparent (hunting prey, ploughing a field, and so on). Against these examples, ritual actions exhibit a greatly differing form, one which is not adequately accounted for by saying (as is often done) that they can be marked off by their 'formality'. Many ritual acts possess no formality at all (decorating a house with greenery, gaily throwing herbs across a fire (cf. Frazer 1936j: 182)), while their *purpose* is not immediately apparent.

And concerning the Beltane rite, Wittgenstein certainly contends that it is this peculiar lack of purpose which produces in us an uneasy feeling:

> The Beltane festival as it has come down to us is the performance of a play, something like children playing at robbers. But then again it is not like this. For even though it is prearranged so that the side which saves the victim wins, there is still the infusion of

a mood or state of mind in what is happening which a theatrical production does not have. And even if it were a perfectly cool performance we should be uneasy and ask ourselves: What is this performance trying to do, what is its point? And apart from any interpretation its queer pointlessness could make us uneasy. (Which shows the kind of reason that an uneasiness of this sort can have.) (Wittgenstein 1979b: 17–18)

This, then, is one aspect of human sacrifice, and of the Beltane festival, which creates the sinister impression. Yet there is another feature of sacrifice, preserved in the Highland celebrations, which serves to produce the sinister atmosphere which Wittgenstein speaks of. This feature is what Cioffi has aptly called 'the eruption of the demonic into the quotidian' (Cioffi 1981: 223). This can be elucidated by reference to two facets of the Beltane rite: the use of a cake to determine the victim; and the atmosphere of merrymaking which provides the environment for the mock sacrifice.

It is a common feature of the accounts of the Beltane festival drawn upon by Frazer that the 'devoted' person who is to be 'sacrificed' is selected by a drawing of lots. To this end a cake is used, a certain piece of which is marked in order to denote the victim. Wittgenstein finds this particularly chilling:

> The fact that for the lots they use a cake has something especially terrible (almost like betrayal through a kiss), and that this does seem especially terrible to us is of central importance in our investigation of practices like these. (Wittgenstein 1979b: 16)

Because cakes play a particular role in our lives, marking birthdays, weddings, and other joyful occasions, their removal from this role and subsequent utilization in the selection of a victim of sacrifice seems peculiarly troubling. Something which we have been brought up to view in a particular way and which has certain familiar and convivial characteristics and associations is here employed in the most bloody of actions. Small wonder we feel uneasy.

Similar points can be made about the overall ambience of the custom, for what contrasts sharply with the mock killing is the *jollity* of the celebrations, seen in the fact that the participants seem to be thoroughly enjoying themselves. It is this uneasy balance between violence and merriment which impresses us here, and it comes to the fore in certain accounts of actual human sacrifice. Hence, a description of the crowd of Mesopotamians set to be dispatched to an early grave as 'a very gaily dressed crowd' (Woolley 1954: 70) produces anxiety: why should these folk whose lives are about to be sacrificed be adorned in such a frivolous manner? In like fashion, Frazer's account of 'Killing the God in Mexico' presents to us a description of a carnival atmosphere in which the most dreadful acts occur. Here, the human representative of the Goddess of Salt, Huixtocihuatl, leads the dances of the festival. On the eve of her death, she dances ceaselessly until the moment when she is seized by the priests who cut open her breast and tear out her heart. When the killing was done, 'the salt-makers who had witnessed the sacrifice went home to drink and make merry' (Frazer 1936i: 284).

A further example. Frazer quotes A. E. Housman's description of 'the pious orgy at Naples', in which the festivities taking place in the streets culminated in the slaughter of a number of people. Housman even notes that 'in honour of my presence they murdered a few more than usual' (Frazer 1936j: 221). Once again, it is the notion of a particular feast or popular day being celebrated with 'fireworks, bonfires, *and assassinations*' (Frazer 1936j: 220, emphasis added) which is worrying. The notions of celebration and murder seem to be at odds, and this generates a disturbing impression. (Wyndham Lewis' depiction of the battles of the First World War as 'carnivals of mass murder' (Lewis 1967: 85) has much the same effect.) Our familiar notion of a carnival is subverted by its age-old forms as described by Frazer, and we no longer feel at home with it. We begin to detect the sinister in what once seemed to us the most genial of entertainments. Wittgenstein writes:

> The concept of a 'festivity'. We connect it with merrymaking; in another age it may have been connected with fear and dread. (Wittgenstein 1980a: 78)

And furthermore, the idea of a festivity in which death habitually results, and often through pure chance (the drawing of lots), may graphically (or subconsciously) remind us of the contingencies of our own existence, or even of the nature of human life itself. This representation of our life as an uneasy celebration terminated by pain and bloodshed would certainly be enough to create the sinister impression which an account of a festival such as Beltane engenders.

These, then – the 'queer pointlessness' of the custom and the disconcerting compound of celebration and carnage – are the reasons for the sinister impression occasioned by the account of the Beltane festival. They form part of the physiognomy of the rite, of its 'inner nature'. But there is another aspect of the sinister inner nature of the Highland custom that we have barely touched on yet. It concerns the nature of the celebrants themselves:

> When I speak of the inner nature of the practice I mean all those circumstances in which it is carried out that are not included in the account of the festival, because they consist not so much in particular actions which characterize it, but rather in what we might call the spirit of the festival: which would be described by, for example, describing the sort of people that take part, their way of behaviour at other times, i.e. their character, and the other kinds of games that they play. And we should then see that what is sinister lies in the character of these people themselves. (Wittgenstein 1979b: 14)

This remark requires greater elaboration, for it illuminates not only Wittgenstein's thought on the impression caused by an account of the festival, but throws light also on his idea that the nature of religious actions are not to be understood by reference to anything external to human beings. Rather, the nature of religion mirrors the nature of man.

8.4 A SAVAGE AND CEREMONIAL ANIMAL

Attention to the nature of the Beltane festival and to rites centred on human sacrifice should alert us to the inadequacy of the standard expressivist interpretation of ritual. Recall how this model in its received 'Wittgensteinian' mode goes: Frazer is wrong to look for instrumental motives behind ritual actions, for magic is not informed by quasi-scientific reasoning. In order to understand a ritual all we need to know are the perennial hopes and fears of human beings, and how the attitudes of the ritualists are expressed in their ceremonies. A magical action, such as burning in effigy, is not an attempt to achieve an empirical end: like kissing a photograph of one's beloved, 'it aims at some satisfaction and achieves it'. While such an account has a certain *prima facie* plausibility with respect to individual acts of homoeopathic magic and divination, it runs into serious difficulties when applied to something as terrible as the Beltane festival. For instance, Richard Bell's standard Wittgensteinian analysis of the Highland celebration badly hits the buffers when he maintains, juxtaposing an account of Beltane with examples of kissing photographs and the like, that: 'Understanding the fire-festivals is like that – they aim at nothing other than the satisfaction of those who participate in them' (Bell 1978: 123).

Such an account reflects a sadly reflex embracing of Wittgenstein's thought that, with regard to ritual, 'we act in this way and then feel satisfied'. And as an account of (even mock) human sacrifice, it is hopelessly inadequate. When considering the full horror of the Beltane festival and the idea of the burning of a man which it manifests, is it really a helpful or perspicuous analogy that we kiss pictures of those we love? May not this lead us into misunderstandings of Beltane; say, a *taming* of the phenomenon? Kissing the photograph of a loved one may indeed bring satisfaction if we are apart from them. But is it adequate to say that the act of throwing someone into a fire simply brings satisfaction? This is surely questionable, and it is a point that even the purportedly 'insensitive' Frazer managed to grasp, for when writing of the ritual of Attis, the author of *The Golden Bough* clearly saw that this was an awful ceremony, the facts of which are untameable.

The greatest festival of the year at Hierapolis fell at the beginning of spring, when multitudes thronged to the sanctuary from Syria and the regions round about. While the flutes played, the drums beat, and the eunuch priests slashed themselves with knives, the religious excitement gradually spread like a wave among the crowd of onlookers, and many a one did that which he little thought to do when he came as a holiday spectator to the festival. For man after man, his veins throbbing with the music, his eyes fascinated by the sight of the streaming blood, flung his garments from him, leaped forth with a shout, and seizing one of the swords which stood ready for the purpose, castrated himself on the spot. Then he ran through the city, holding the bloody pieces in his hand, till he threw them into one of the houses which he passed in his mad career. The household thus honoured had to furnish him with a suit of female attire and female ornaments, which he wore for the rest of his life. When the tumult of emotion had subsided, and the man had come to himself again, the irrevocable sacrifice must often have been followed by passionate sorrow and lifelong regret. (Frazer 1922: 349–50).

'We act in this way and then feel satisfied'? Such a horrific narrative should illustrate the inadequacy of any account which claims that the 'point' of all religious rites is to do with satisfaction.

But Wittgenstein's account is not of this kind. In the second set of *Remarks*, Wittgenstein is concerned to stress the full horror of the Beltane rite, and his reflections lay no stress on the idea that anything as banal as 'satisfaction' might lie at its heart. Indeed, in stark opposition to Bell's interpretation, Wittgenstein maintains that our understanding of a rite in which a man or an effigy is burned in a fire cannot simply stop once we have claimed 'thus people celebrate':

> The fact that on certain days children burn a straw man could make us uneasy, even if no explanation [hypothesis] were given. Strange that they should celebrate by burning a *man*! What I want to say is: the solution is no more disquieting than the riddle. (Wittgenstein 1979b: 18)

It seems likely that what Wittgenstein meant to write here was: 'The solution is no *less* disquieting than the riddle'. And the point, then, is this: if we fall back on a celebratory account of the Beltane (and kindred) fires, this does not arrest our unease. For if human beings *celebrate* in this manner, or if this is the way they might satisfy their impulses, then this is a highly disturbing fact indeed. (Recall Housman's statement that his presence in Naples was 'honoured' by more murders than usual.)

This, then, is where Wittgenstein's attributing the sinister nature of the Beltane rite to the demeanour of its celebrants comes into play. If the festival is sinister, savage even, then this cannot be put down to anything other than the character of those people taking part. He writes:

> If I see such a practice, or hear of it, it is like seeing a man speaking sternly to another because of something quite trivial, and noticing in the tone of his voice and in his face that on occasion this man can be frightening. The impression I get from this may be a very deep and extremely serious one. (Wittgenstein 1979b: 16)

When we hear of horrific acts, of orgies of violence, we may sense an immense distance separating ourselves from other human beings, the perpetrators of those events. Our world may then begin to appear less homely, more threatening. We are surrounded, not by friends, but by monsters, potential assassins.

To get entirely clear about the distinctiveness of Wittgenstein's position on this matter, we may note how different his stance is from Frazer's when the latter accounts for the sacrificial practices of the ancient Mexicans by claiming that they 'sprang in great measure from a mistaken theory of the solar system' (Frazer 1936a: 315). Wittgenstein is saying that it is implausible to put the full horror of mass sacrifice down to an inadequate grasp of science, or to other 'purely speculative errors' (Frazer 1936a: 315). To account for the phenomenon of human sacrifice one needs to understand the kind of creatures human beings are. Thus, the enquiry must turn upon 'the thought of man and his past ... the strangeness of what I see in myself and in others, what I have seen and have heard' (Wittgenstein 1979b: 18).

In part, Wittgenstein's remark is meant as another indicator of why Beltane strikes us as being a 'deep and sinister' business. The thought of man's past, presented to us by the age-old air of the festival; the thought of long-dead ancestors performing similar rites; the character of their lives and their relation to ours: all of this is enough to make our heads whirl. Here, 'one might speak ... of a feeling "Long, long ago", for there is an expression of voice and mien which goes with narratives of past times' (Wittgenstein 1982a: §840). The fascination of antiquity is encapsulated in customs such as the Beltane festival, and through it we half sense an affinity with those who have gone before us. The sinister aspect of this reflection lies in the perception that man's past is the scene of countless bloody rituals. When we read, for example, of the building of the Avebury monuments that 'burials, perhaps even sacrifices, accompanied the setting up of some of the stones' (Sharp 1989: 97), we are, even in the absence of hard evidence, unsurprised; what we *know* about human beings and their history, the ways in which they have celebrated important events, thrusts upon us 'the overwhelming probability of this idea' (Wittgenstein 1979b: 17).

With an argument such as this there is a great temptation to consign the brutalities of human sacrifice to the past or to savage peoples. So Westermarck, for instance, contends that with the growth of enlightenment, folk 'lose faith in this childish method of substitution, and consequently find it not only useless, but objectionable' (Westermarck 1906: 468). Thus, when Wittgenstein says that 'what is sinister lies in the character of these people themselves', a case could still be made for saying that the menacing demeanour of these people's activities, and thus of themselves, is an idiosyncrasy of this particular community in their stage of social evolution – but that we ourselves are not so harmful. Other of Wittgenstein's comments, however, belie this comforting assumption:

> There is one conviction that underlies the hypotheses about the origin of, say, the Beltane festival; namely that festivals of this kind are not so to speak haphazard inventions of one man but need an infinitely broader basis if they are to persist. If I tried to invent a festival it would very soon die out or else be so modified that it corresponded to a general inclination in people. (Wittgenstein 1979b: 16–17)

The fact that a custom like Beltane has been so tenacious and persisted through centuries makes it practically inconceivable that it could be an isolated eccentricity, the idiosyncrasy of a particular group in a particular period. Moreover, its continuing presence as an apparently meaningless survival reveals all too starkly that the strangeness and violence of the festivity come very easily to the participants. To apply one of Marett's principles, which states that survivals are 'symptomatic of those tendencies of our common human nature which have the best chance of surviving in the long run' (Marett 1920: 2), we can say that the Beltane festival reveals an aspect of our nature which we would rather remained hidden. Fergus Kerr makes the point well when, criticizing Frazer's hypothesizing as an attempt 'to evade the truth about ourselves', he states that Wittgenstein's purpose in writing as he does about the Beltane custom is to show 'what human beings are like: *das Seltsame* is in us all' (Kerr 1986: 161). Viewed in this manner, Wittgenstein's theme is perhaps a variation on the chilling words of Sir Thomas Browne: 'The heart of man is the place the Devils dwell in; I feel sometimes a Hell within myself' (Browne 1927: 73).

This, then, is held to be Wittgenstein's great achievement: he points to our savage inheritance, to the fact that, while we may appear civilized beings, underneath our rational exteriors are strange and passionate creatures with violent propensities. Hence his desire to place the Beltane festival next to an example of one of our number reacting sternly to another. Viewed in this manner, Wittgenstein's project in the second set of *Remarks* mirrors the theme of Conrad's *Heart of Darkness*, in which two Europeans – Marlow and the mysterious Mr Kurtz – experience 'the awakening of forgotten and brutal instincts' within themselves (Conrad 1983: 107). The point here is that savagery is not something alien to us – something from another age or a distant continent – but is dormant, and within us. John Buchan broaches this notion also. In his novel *The Power House*, the anarchist Andrew Lumley declares to Edward Leithen: 'You think that a wall as solid as the earth separates civilisation from Barbarism. I tell you the division is a thread, a sheet of glass' (Buchan 1916: 64).

The conclusion which is often drawn from this is that Wittgenstein differs from Frazer in not being frightened to look within himself and to find affinities with the perpetrators of barbaric sacrifices. Frazer, we are frequently told, lacked this courage. Witness Christopher Cherry's analysis:

> Frazer conceals from himself his (and our) 'kinship to those savages' by methodological deceit, by pretending, against all the indications, that their preoccupations are remote from ours and can be made intelligible to us, if at all, only through dispassionate historical speculation. (Cherry 1984: 273)

The understanding of *The Golden Bough* displayed by such a comment is remarkably superficial. Undoubtedly, Frazer often *does* exhibit the kind of detached attitude to understanding rituals that Cherry speaks of. Yet this is only half the story, constituting what we might term the 'plain text' of *The Golden Bough*. Co-existent with this there is Frazer's subtext, itself stressing the fragility of civilization. It is this implicit theme which inspired the likes of Buchan and Conrad, and if we want to maintain that *their* concerns are identical with Wittgenstein's, then we must concede that the differences between *him* and Frazer must, on this matter, be marginal. Frazer writes:

> It is not our business here to consider what bearing the permanent existence of such a solid layer of savagery beneath the surface of society, and unaffected by the superficial changes of religion and culture, has upon the future of humanity ... We seem to move on a thin crust which may at any moment be rent

by the subterranean forces slumbering below. (Frazer 1936a: 236)

We would be hard pressed to find a better characterization of Wittgenstein's argument than this vision of dormant subterranean forces bursting through the veneer of civilization.

Seen in this way, the view that the respective views of Frazer and Wittgenstein are fundamentally at odds is rather inaccurate. At any rate, Frazer's subtext is far removed from the idea of mistaken theories which so annoyed Wittgenstein in the first set of notes. This subtext, in its representation and evocation of horrors, has been likened to the vision of St Anthony and the nightmarish fantasies of Bosch (cf. Vickery 1973: 119). Furthermore, one of Frazer's undoubted achievements in *The Golden Bough* is (perhaps accidentally) to present a picture of faith and ritual as 'indigenous to humanity, virtually biological' (Trilling 1966: 17), and if this is the case, his view cannot be that dissimilar from Wittgenstein's portrayal of ritual as the spontaneous (and perhaps biologically based) reactions of a ceremonial animal. We can, given this, approach an interpretation which does not drive a wedge between Frazer and Wittgenstein. Seen in this manner, the remarks on Beltane constitute a series of what we may term 'Frazerian reflections'; observations on the indigenous and savage ritual expression of mankind. Remember that in these later notes Wittgenstein does not criticize Frazer's 'lack of spirituality': perhaps by 1948 he had read beyond the plain text and encountered the Bosch-like vision of dionysiac impulses which had earlier inspired Conrad.

Whether or not we are willing to accept this view of 'two Frazers' and of Wittgenstein's acceptance of the subtext of *The Golden Bough*, Wittgenstein's reflections on the Beltane festival leave us once again with the distinctive picture of the ritual life of mankind which we have discerned elsewhere in the *Remarks on Frazer*. Ritual actions are seen to be instinctual in character; primitive reactions, which, because prior to ratiocination, give us immediate access to the nature of human beings. In this manner, then, we can legitimately say that religion is first and foremost an expression of human nature. So when we turn our minds to an aspect of ritual as horrifying as human sacrifice, we are led inexorably into thoughts of those smouldering and sinister traits of character which lie within each one of us. And to this end, ritual holds up a mirror to a distressing aspect of our common natures. With Schopenhauer (1897: 22), our judgement may well be: *l'animal méchant par excellence!* .

9

'The Collapse into the Inorganic'

With this chapter, my analysis of Wittgenstein's *Remarks on Frazer's Golden Bough* is concluded. I have surveyed the themes of these two sets of notes, and have, whenever necessary, appealed to other of his writings and to those of other theorists, in order to clarify or expand upon certain suggestions. My evaluation has differed from those of the majority of commentators, and particularly from those who claim to follow Wittgenstein. For these followers have often contended that Wittgenstein's criticisms of Frazer are unanswerable and that in the place of the theory he demolished, Wittgenstein presented an expressive account of magic and religion, whereby the reasons for such rites are located in a catharsis of emotion or in the expressing of attitudes towards the world. Rejecting the comparative method, Wittgenstein is said to have presented an invaluable and original anthropological method of analysis: perspicuous representation. This book has challenged these contentions. Many of Wittgenstein's criticisms of Frazer have been shown to be inconclusive and unsatisfactory. The expressivist thesis was seen to be no more plausible than instrumentalist alternatives, and more importantly, it was shown that Wittgenstein himself cannot have been propounding such a view. Likewise, the concept of a perspicuous representation was examined and found to have not inconsiderable difficulties.

The *Remarks on Frazer* do not comprise a comprehensive account of magic and religion. What we are offered instead is a series of striking suggestions and reflections on the nature of ritual and religion. Binding all these suggestions together, though, is the contention that ritual actions are the perfectly natural expressions of a 'ceremonial animal'. Basic religious and magical actions constitute the pre-reflective, spontaneous outpourings of human nature. When we destroy photographs of those we have loved and who have spurned us; when we engage in personal-idiosyncratic acts of divination; when we place flowers on a grave; when we refuse to walk under a ladder; when a person is sacrificed; such ritual actions are a central part of the natural history of man, a ceremonial animal, and they are as essential to our natural history as spinning a web is to the natural history of a spider. And it is this notion of spontaneous expression which, as we saw in previous chapters, unites Wittgenstein's treatment of homoeopathic magic, of human sacrifice, and of the relation between magic and metaphysics. This final chapter will begin with a further consideration of this unifying motif, but as we will see, to view religion purely in terms of spontaneous human expression would be to overlook a vital element: namely, the role of cultural considerations. Accordingly, I want to approach the *Remarks* from a different angle and place Wittgenstein's comments on magic and religion in the wider environment of his view of human culture. In so doing, it will be possible both to clarify certain matters which seem oblique and obscure in the notes on *The Golden Bough*, and to indicate a view of religion held by Wittgenstein which is perhaps more ambitious than the conclusions of the previous chapters (though accurate in their portrayal of the *Remarks*) would suggest.

9.1 'IF FLEAS DEVELOPED A RITE IT WOULD BE BASED ON THE DOG'

At the close of Chapter 6 it was claimed that Wittgenstein's enquiry is centred on the possibilities of ritual phenomena. In sketching these possibilities, he is concerned not just with contrasts (above/below) but with those 'very general facts of nature' which inform the structure and content of a ritual. In this matter, Wittgenstein's treatment of ritual is not unlike his treatment of all other human practices and activities, stressing that the conceptual structures involved in these practices (and the practices themselves) are not *necessary* ('absolutely the correct ones' (Wittgenstein 1958: 230)) but rather *natural*, and are fitting, given the features of the world in which we live. Wittgenstein commonly imagines familiar features of our world to be different, noting how many of our concepts and practices would be rendered redundant as a result. For example, if we lived in a world in which objects were constantly changing their length and mass, our procedures of measuring and weighing would be of no use (cf. Wittgenstein 1958: §142); and if things were always changing colour, we would find our colour-grammar impractical. Moreover, our practices and conceptual structures are dependent not just upon features of the world in which we find ourselves. It is *our own* natures also which just as much dictate the form of these concepts. This extends not just to expressions of emotion, changes in which would produce, for example, differing notions of tragedy and comedy in dramatical writing, but even to mathematics, which is generally regarded as independent of any contingency. Thus, Wittgenstein calls mathematics 'an anthropological phenomenon' (Wittgenstein 1956: 180), and stresses the natural capacities of human beings which permit calculation to occur. If these capacities were absent there could be no mathematics. Hence, were we, like other animals, unable to distinguish a triangle from a rectangle, then we could not engage in geometry.

In like manner, the possibilities of ritual expression are demarcated by features of the world and of human life. We can reflect on this idea by noting the contrast drawn by the ethnologist Adolf Bastian between *Elementargedanken* ('elementary ideas') and *Völkergedanken* ('ideas of the peoples') (cf. Bastian 1895: *passim*). The latter ideas are those which concern a particular nation or group of people, and we shall return to these later in this chapter. Yet we should first note how Wittgenstein mirrors Bastian's appeal to the notion of 'elementary ideas', which arise from pan-human, transcultural experience: those very facts of human life in the world which provide the environment for ritual actions and beliefs. Thus:

> That a man's shadow, which looks like a man, or that his mirror image, or that rain, thunderstorms, the phases of the moon, the change of seasons, the likenesses and differences of animals to one another and to human beings, the phenomena of death, of birth and of sexual life, in short everything a man perceives year in, year out around him, connected together in any variety of ways – that all this should play a part in his thinking (his philosophy) and his practices, is obvious, or in other words this is what we really know and find interesting. (Wittgenstein 1979b: 6)

Here Wittgenstein is noting that whole range of familiar phenomena around which man's expressions of 'natural piety' are focused. Winch refers to such features of the world as 'limiting notions', and we need only to think of examples of ritual in order to recognize how these notions form the backbone of such acts. Consider how many of the customs of folk life are fixed in the calendar, marking changes of season so crucial to the lives of an agrarian community. Consider also how the phenomenon of sexual life enters into ritual, in the form of bacchanalian coupling during May Day festivities, or the presence in pre-Reformation churches of 'exhibitionist' carvings. It was Drury's account of his 'shocking' encounter in Egypt with a similarly explicit representation (a bas-relief of the god Horus in the act of ejaculation) which provoked the following response from Wittgenstein:

> Why in the world shouldn't they have regarded with awe and reverence that act by which the human race is perpetuated? Not every religion has to have St. Augustine's attitude to sex. Why, even in our own culture marriages are celebrated in a church; everyone present knows what is going to happen that night, but that doesn't prevent it being a religious ceremony. (Drury 1984: 148)

This is a perspicuous comment on the character of natural piety. Every individual has entered the world as a result of the activity celebrated in the Horus figure. It is, then, perfectly natural for a religious symbol to have sexual life as its focus.

The thought that it is such inescapable features of human life which form the character of religious observance was, it seems, constantly in Wittgenstein's mind during the composition of his notes on Frazer. Thus:

> It was not a trivial reason, for really there can have been no *reason*, that prompted certain races of mankind to venerate the oak tree, but only the fact that they and the oak were united in a community of life, and therefore it was not by choice that they arose together, but rather like the flea and the dog. (If fleas developed a rite, it would be based on the dog.) (Wittgenstein 1979c: 72–3)[1]

Frazer himself would have recognized the force of this observation, for he too stresses how 'profoundly influenced by physical environment' the religion of a people is (Frazer 1936e: v), and manages to convey with some awe the impressive extent of the diffusion of the oak tree: 'long before the dawn of history Europe was covered with vast primaeval woods, which must have exercised a profound influence on the thought as well as on the life of our rude ancestors who dwelt dispersed under the gloomy shadow or in the open glades and clearings of the forest' (Frazer 1936b: 350). The difference between Wittgenstein and Frazer on this matter once again amounts to a conflict over the degree of *reasoning* involved in religious concept-formation. Thus, Frazer looks for reasons why the oak was so venerated (locating this in its association with the sky, the rain, the thunder, and, consequently, with Zeus), whereas Wittgenstein stresses the non-ratiocinative nature of this worship ('no *reason*'). I have, time and again in this book, emphasized that this is where the true difference between Wittgenstein and Frazer lies: not in the latter's belief that rites aim to achieve some end, but in the fact that he contends that such actions come about through a process of reasoning akin to hypothesis-forming and experimentation. It is the gratuitousness of the reasons Frazer gives for primitive observances – so ubiquitous in *The Golden Bough* – which stands in such stark contrast to the conception of natural piety. So, for example, Frazer, concerned to discover why it is that the need-fire is held to be unable to kindle if any other fire remains alight in the neighbourhood, embarks on a most tortuous explanation. Primitives and peasants alike, he contends, conceive of fire 'as a unity which is broken up into fractions and consequently weakened in exact proportion to the number of places where it burns; hence in order to obtain it at full strength you must light it only at a single point' (Frazer 1936j: 298). The explanation thus implies that the ritualists act from a (quite sophisticated) opinion they hold about fire, and this, of course, Wittgenstein denies (cf. Wittgenstein 1979b: 12).

Wittgenstein's alternative picture stresses the spontaneity of ritual acts. It is of course true that fire is astounding and it is one of those very general facts of nature which 'make an impression on the awakening mind of man' and thus tends to give rise to ritual action (Wittgenstein 1979b: 6). Indeed, Wittgenstein appeals to the nature of fire in the following remark, which surely ranks as one of the most incisive (and chilling) comments on the nature of the fire-festival sacrifices:

> That fire destroys things *completely*, unlike battering or tearing them to pieces, must have astonished men. (Wittgenstein 1979c: 81)

Of course, animals appear to be astounded by fire as well. (At the very least, their reaction to fire is striking.) But man is 'a ceremonial animal', what Marett (1933: 3) called *homo religiosus*, and thus those things which astound and impress him are likely to be the focus of his spontaneous actions. This is not to say that man *must* find fire mysterious or build it into his rituals,[2] for the forms of ritual are not *compelled* by those perennial features of the world highlighted by Wittgenstein. The limiting notions, which due to their familiarity may not be a cause of wonder at all, do, however, form the background to our lives, and it should not therefore be surprising that human ritual expression is centred upon birth, sex, death, the weather, the natural world, and so on.

Wittgenstein's form of the *Elementargedanken* argument rests ultimately on the notion that our fundamental ways of acting are, in a sense, primal and not grounded in reason. Such a contention is not peculiar to his treatment of *ritual*, for, as we saw earlier, it is distinctive of Wittgenstein's thought that he traces our concepts and practices back to unratiocinated primitive reactions, natural human capacities and characteristics. Thus, in his discussion of rule-following in the *Investigations*, he notes that, given the usual kind of training, children learning arithmetic will generally continue a particular series in the correct way. If confronted with a pupil who continually failed to act in accord with the rule (or made his actions accord with a different rule), 'such a case would present similarities with one in which a person naturally reacted to the gesture of pointing with the hand by looking in the direction of the line from finger-tip to wrist, not from wrist to finger-tip' (Wittgenstein 1958: §185). And as Wittgenstein is at pains to point out, 'it is part of human nature [as opposed to the nature of, say, cats] to understand pointing with the finger in the way we do' (Wittgenstein 1974b: 94). Thus, the agreement of human beings in rule-following (and hence in language-use) is due to nothing other than shared natural capacities, and indeed the very existence of our linguistic practices *presupposes* such regularity in human behaviour. The agreement, then, is not arrived at by a process of reasoning, but is *prior* to all reasoning; it 'is not agreement in opinions but in form of life' (Wittgenstein 1958: §241).

It is important here to consider a little more the issue of the role of human nature in rule-following and forms of life, and it needs to be established whether Wittgenstein views this nature in either predominantly biological or else cultural terms. John Hunter has claimed that it is a view of the biological nature of human beings which constitutes the idea of a form of life. Describing a form of life as 'a biological or organic phenomenon' (Hunter 1971: 278), he maintains that we should define it as 'something typical of a human being', like growth or nutrition. While there is support for this interpretation from the pages of the *Investigations* (cf. Wittgenstein 1958: §25), it may be wise to suggest that although the idea of reactions typical of all human beings does enter into it, the concept is not exhausted by this. For when Wittgenstein speaks of a form of life, he is principally concerned with spelling out, not the biological, but rather the *cultural* features of human beings. Thus, considering a tribe with whom we 'cannot find our feet', Wittgenstein puts their alien forms of life down, not to a difference in biological nature (they are human), but to 'an education quite different from ours' (Wittgenstein 1981: §387). This leads Baker and Hacker to suggest that the differing forms of life of different human groups are the 'product of nurture not nature' (Baker and Hacker 1988: 242), that the concept of a form of life is a cultural and not a biological one,[3] and that even when Wittgenstein does talk of the 'natural history' of human beings, it is 'the history of a convention-forming, concept-exercising, language-using animal – a cultural animal' that he is interested in (1988: 241). The balance between the biological and the cultural (between natural capacities and train-ing) in respect of forms of life mirrors to an extent the balance between *Elementar-* and *Völkergedanken*, between universality and specificity: the facts of human life certainly influence what can be said in religion (if human beings did not die, there would be no need in religion for talk of a life beyond the grave), but the *forms* which religion takes in different cultures will largely be conven-tional. We should now turn to these conventional factors, and analyse the cultural dimension of Wittgenstein's view of religion.

9.2 EXPRESSION-MEDIA

To reiterate, Wittgenstein stresses that there are inescapable features of human life and of the environment in which human lives are enacted which, though not strictly dictating the forms of religious expression, nevertheless provide the context of meaning for them. When a perennial feature of human life (say, death) becomes the focus of the ritual imagination, that magico-metaphysical imagination spawns rites such as 'Carrying out Death', born out of a 'misunderstanding of the logic of language'. Furthermore, the fact that *Elementargedanken* are universal takes us some way towards understanding a problem that has constantly dogged theorists of religion: namely, the similarity which exists amongst the rituals of many different peoples. Given the impelling framework of the world and of human life, such similarities can be attributed, at least to an extent, to these features. No appeal need thus be made to diffusionist theory, for the emphasis is placed on 'a spontaneous origination in specific peoples' (Ernst 1910: 272). Yet, and as Wittgenstein himself is keen to note, there are great differences, as well as similarities, amongst the rites of different peoples. Here, Bastian's notion of *Völkergedanken* serves to direct our attention to the various ways in which different peoples impress their own character upon these basic human experiences. I want to explore further the way in which the character of a people enters into its religious practices and to contend that part of Wittgenstein's purpose in writing on *The Golden Bough* is to show that a people's character is *manifested* through its religious practices and beliefs.

Wittgenstein's appeal to both species of *Gedanken* is mirrored in Michael Oakeshott's conception of religion. In those remarkable pages of *On Human Conduct* which treat of faith, Oakeshott contends that religious belief has the purpose of providing 'a recon-ciliation to the unavoidable dissonances of a human condition' (Oakeshott 1991: 81). Religion arises out of a feature of the human condition which is anything but contingent, and which is described by Oakeshott as 'the hollowness, the futility of that condition' (Oakeshott 1991: 83). The thought that human life is surrounded by evanescence and mutability is a principal image in the religious imagination ('Knit me that am crumbling dust'), and this is far from being an accidental feature. Yet along with the contention that reli-gion is framed by limiting notions, Oakeshott also stresses that a religion is a species of what I shall call 'expression-media': 'Every religion, each with its own image of deity and of self, has its own idiom of faith which reflects the civilization of the believer' (Oakeshott 1991: 86). Oakeshott's account of religion, then, has the same two-fold structure as Wittgenstein's: religion springs from the inescapable condition of human being in the world, and it reveals the nature of the *Volk* who participate in it.

That second aspect emerges in the *Remarks* when Wittgenstein considers the problem which Frazer set himself: namely, the nature of the rule at Nemi. Whereas Frazer's procedure is to uncover the motives which led to the institution of the practice, Wittgenstein's contention is that the Nemi rite should be seen, not as the result of erroneous hypothesizing, but as involving the manifestation of certain ideas and values:

> Put that account of the King of the Wood at Nemi together with the phrase 'the majesty of death', and you see that they are one. The life of the priest-king shows what is meant by that phrase.
> If someone is gripped by the majesty of death, then through such a life he can give expression to it. (Wittgenstein 1979b: 3)

It may appear that the tone of Wittgenstein's remarks here is individualistic, for he speaks of some *one* giving expression to the idea of 'the majesty of death'. This, however, should not be so construed, for Wittgenstein prefers to speak of 'the religious practices of a *people*' (1979b: 2) and not of one person. Indeed, as we saw in a previous chapter, he rejects any notion that religious rites could be 'haphazard inventions of one man', for they 'need an infinitely broader basis if they are to persist' (Wittgenstein 1979b: 17). Wittgenstein's suggestion can be pieced together thus: the collective religious practices of a people (a nation or a culture) make manifest the values and ideals which lie at that culture's heart.

Though perhaps only implicitly present in the notes on Frazer, this idea is, however, prominent in the thought of those two writers – Paul Ernst and Oswald Spengler – whose influence, more than that of any other, is dominant in the *Remarks*, and Wittgenstein would no doubt have been familiar with this principal contention of *Lebensphilosophie* (cf. Schatzki 1991: 326–7). Ernst sees the folktales (and hence, the folk-*beliefs*) of a culture as the repository of its moral values ('*sie enthalten unsere Ethik*' (Ernst 1910: 271)), yet it is in Spengler that we encounter a greater statement of this view. Indeed, it is from *The Decline of the West* that the phrase 'expression-media' is taken. It arises in the context of Spengler's discussion of 'the idea of the Macrocosm, actuality as the sum total of all symbols in relation to one soul' (Spengler 1926: 165), involving:

> the possibility of making intelligible what one has created in the style of one's own being, through expression-media such as language or art or religion, by means of word-sounds or formu-

lae or signs that are themselves also symbols. (Spengler 1926: 165)

Spengler's contention is that the 'soul' of a culture is 'manifested in the men, customs, deities, root-words, ideas, buildings and acts of it' (Spengler 1926: 165). Of course, this conception is not peculiar to Spengler, for we find it in the writings of other major thinkers in the German tradition, notably Herder and Hegel. Herder locates the determinants of a *Volk* community, not in racial characteristics or other physical factors, but in a shared language, traditions, folklore and customs. Thus the folkways of a people mirror its form of humanity. Similarly, Hegel's contention in *The Philosophy of History* is that the spirit of a nation is manifested in every expression of that nation's life: 'Its religion, its polity, its ethics, its legislation, and even its science, art, and mechanical skill, all bear its stamp' (Hegel 1956: 64).

The idea which is present in all these writers is, then, that the soul (or spirit) of a culture (or nation, or *Volk* community) can be detected by attention to its religious practices, its legislative systems, artistic styles, and even to its mathematics (cf. Spengler 1926: 58–59; 101–2):

But the prime symbol does not actualize itself; it is operative through the form-sense of every man, every community, age and epoch and dictates the style of every life-expression. It is inherent in the form of the state, the religious myths and cults, the ethical ideals, the forms of painting and music and poetry, the fundamental notions of each science – but it is not presented by these. Consequently, it is not presentable by words, for language and words are themselves *derived* symbols. Every individual symbol tells of it, but only to the inner feelings, not to the understanding. (Spengler 1926: 175)

Here we may detect a substantial likeness between Spengler's contention that the values of a culture cannot be stated in propositional form (any attempt to do so results in 'a helpless stammering' (Spengler 1926: 190)), and a central element of Wittgenstein's early philosophy, namely the thought that value is inexpressible. Indeed, it is possible to offer an interpretation of Wittgenstein's thoughts on the Nemi rite consonant with the Tractarian distinction between showing and saying.

In the *Tractatus*, Wittgenstein held that both logical form and 'the mystical' were 'transcendental' (Wittgenstein 1961b: 6.13; 6.421) and hence inexpressible. Though both are unsayable (unlike the propositions of natural science), each *shows itself*, logical form through the character of and relation between propositions (cf. Wittgenstein 1961b: 4.121–4.1211), and 'the mystical' through deeds and art. Paul Engelmann provides us with the best example we have of the mystical 'showing' itself. In 1917, Engelmann sent Wittgenstein a copy of Ludwig Uhland's poem 'Count Eberhard's Hawthorn', a simple verse relating the tale of a crusader who, while in Palestine, cuts a sprig from a hawthorn tree, carries it with him through the wars, and on his return home plants it. It grows into a fine tree, and in his old age the knight sits under the hawthorn and recalls his years as a crusader. Wittgenstein was enthusiastic, praising the poem and seeing a mediation of the mystical through it:

> The poem by Uhland is really magnificent. And this is how it is: if only you do not try to utter what is unutterable then *nothing* gets lost. But the unutterable will be – unutterably – *contained* in what has been uttered! (Engelmann 1967: 7)

Just as Uhland's poem mediates depth and value, so the Nemi rite makes manifest the deeply held values of the community of believers.

This is certainly one way of making sense of what Wittgenstein has to say about the rule at Nemi: Wittgenstein *is* concerned to stress what is deep about the practice, and he *does* see the values of the community as manifested in the rite that occurred in the sacred grove. There is, however, a problem in applying the showing/saying distinction to what Wittgenstein says about the priest-king. And the problem lies in the claim that the values of the community cannot be stated and can only be shown or manifested in a practice. For, of course, Wittgenstein himself has no difficulty in articulating the value which lies at the heart of the Nemi rite: he describes it as 'the majesty of death'. Skorupski's criticism of Beattie mirrors this point. Discussing the symbolist theme that ritual is a way of saying metaphorically what cannot be said literally, Skorupski says that the value which the symbolist manages to uncover in any rite 'usually turns out to be something which the ritualist has more than enough linguistic resources to cope with himself' (Skorupski 1976: 41).

But as we have seen, Wittgenstein himself does not make this error in the *Remarks* and is not led into saying that the values exhibited by the Nemi rite are inexpressible. Rather, and in the spirit of Hegel, he may be maintaining that the manifestation of a culture's values is supervenient upon (for example) ritual actions, and that whereas ritualists may be totally unaware that they are doing something with this level of meaning, *observers* can detect those values which are therein revealed (recall Wittgenstein's treatment of the Beltane festival). An analogy with the artistic creations of a given period can perhaps illuminate this. Baroque portraiture was not a self-conscious exhibition of the values of its time. Yet its particular style enables a thinker like Spengler to trace features of that culture's soul which could give rise to such a work (cf. Spengler 1926: 270–3). Thus, the values of a culture are open only to one who is *outside* that culture (or otherwise independent of it) (cf. Spengler 1928: 275)), or to one observing his own culture when it is in a state of decline: 'The owl of Minerva begins its flight only with the onset of dusk' (Hegel 1991: 23).

It may be objected that I have simply restated a version of the expressivist account of the *Remarks*, such an account as was earlier discredited. This would be an over-hasty criticism provoked solely by the use of the word 'expression'. The expressivist thesis is concerned with the possibility of emotional catharsis or generation during a rite. The media account, by contrast, lays no stress on individual or group needs and emotions, but on the manifestation of values. One may feel that there is only the scantest of evidence that such an account is held by Wittgenstein. Nevertheless, the expression-media thesis does capture the essence of what Wittgenstein has to say, as we will shortly see, about trends in philosophy and architecture. It also presents us with a stark view of religion as a purely human creation, and if religions are primarily expressions of human nature, then it is also surely true that these expressions are shaped by convention and tradition and reveal as much about the collective representations of a culture as they do about untrammelled human nature.

9.3 'A WHOLE MYTHOLOGY IS DEPOSITED IN OUR LANGUAGE'

Whatever the rights and wrongs of attributing to Wittgenstein a form of the expression-media thesis, a consideration of the affinities between his critique of Frazer and Spengler's idea serves to illuminate one important feature of the *Remarks*. Part of the force of Spengler's point is that no individual is free to choose the religion he follows, any more than he is free to choose his mother-tongue, for such things are part of the cultural tradition into which he is born (cf. Wittgenstein 1958: 230). An individual's language and religion flow into him with his mother's milk. To this extent, the acceptance of a religion is not so much to do with the weighing up of possible routes to salvation offered by competing theoretical systems, as it is a mark of one's being part of a tradition, part of a common cultural life. That Wittgenstein presents a version of this Romantic view can be attested to by offering, as promised in an earlier chapter, an alternative interpretation of one of the crucial comments of the *Remarks on Frazer*: '*In unserer Sprache ist eine ganze Mythologie niedergelegt'* (Wittgenstein 1967: 242).

In Chapter 7, we located the meaning of that phrase in a Nietzschean-style comment on the illusory character of metaphysical propositions. Language, Nietzsche claimed, had concealed within it 'a philosophical mythology' which constantly caused confusion, and it is such a mythology which Wittgenstein maintained led to metaphysics. In the context of the *Remarks on Frazer* we noted how this argument emerges in Wittgenstein's treatment of the Lenten custom of 'Carrying out Death'. And certainly, the implications of what we can call the 'Nietzschean view' of this enigmatic aphorism are present in the *Remarks*, as well as in Wittgenstein's analyses of traditional philosophical problems. Nevertheless, it should be stressed that there is another, and radically different, construction that can be put on the thought that our language contains a mythology. For the accuracy of the Nietzschean interpretation needs to be questioned. As we saw earlier, Nietzsche's comment has a conspiratorial air, while Wittgenstein only uses the word '*niedergelegt'* which has the implication that something is being 'stored', or 'laid down' (as wine is 'laid down').

What we can glean from this is that Wittgenstein is not (or at least not *primarily*) using the phrase to refer to a misunderstanding of the logic of language. No, the remark is bedfellow, not with the contention that philosophical problems arise from misunderstandings, but with his view, quoted by Rhees, that 'our language is an embodiment of ancient myths' (Rhees 1982: 69). Thus, what Wittgenstein appears to be saying is that we have deposited in our language (as fossils are deposited in rock strata) the remnants of a mythology, the beliefs of previous times. When we speak of 'fate taking a hand', or of fearing 'the wrath of the gods', we bring out of storage the mythology of our ancestors. All of this is entirely consonant with Wittgenstein's overall view of language, which he likened to a city:

> Our language can be seen as an ancient city: a maze of little streets and squares, of old and new houses, and of houses with additions from various periods; and this surrounded by a multitude of new boroughs with straight regular streets and uniform houses. (Wittgenstein 1958: §18)

Both in this passage, and in the comment from the *Remarks*, Wittgenstein is proclaiming the depth of language. We see in it remnants of ancient beliefs, proverbs and lore; of historical occurrences; of gods and mythical events. For example, Frig, the ancient English Goddess of the Earth, though now long forgotten and about whom little is known, shows herself in words commonly used: Friday is the 'Day of Frig', and the names of old towns – Froyle, Frobury and Fryup – attest to the ancient worship of her. Indeed, a survey of the place-names of Anglo-Saxon origin reveals much about our ancestors' beliefs: 'The gods of the English still in place-names retain a firm hold on the countryside' (Branston 1974: 38). This is one reason why Robert Louis Stevenson was so entranced by maps, and why Wittgenstein is so keen to stress the need to 'plough over the whole of language' (Wittgenstein 1979b: 7). It is in such a manner that we should understand Wittgenstein's hatred of a purely invented language, which could bear no witness to the history and philosophy of a people:

> Esperanto. The feeling of disgust we get if we utter an *invented* word with invented derivative syllables. The word is cold, lacking in associations, and yet it plays at being 'language'. A system of purely written signs would not disgust us so much. (Wittgenstein 1980a: 52)

Think of how such common phrases as being 'sold down the river' or 'burying the hatchet' have their origins in historical events and in customs (in these instances, the slave trade and American Indian rites of peace). Wittgenstein recognized that an invented language, a language which was 'inorganic',[4] could have no elements with such historical depth as this. The 'stenographer' of the *Tractatus* was rightly criticized for dehistoricizing language (cf. Kerr 1986: 66–8). The recognition that 'our language is an embodiment of ancient myths' rectifies that error.

The view that a mythology is laid down in language is not an uncommon one, and Wittgenstein's version of this view is certainly not as elaborate as that of Usener, who held that it was necessary for all general terms in language to pass through a mythic stage. As Cassirer summarizes, 'the fact that in the Indo-Germanic languages abstract concepts are usually denoted by feminine nouns ... proves, according to Usener, that the idea this feminine form expresses was originally not conceived as an abstractum, but apprehended and felt as a female *deity*' (Cassirer 1953: 42). Wittgenstein does not give voice to such a view in the *Remarks*, although this is certainly one way in which his observation could have proceeded. As it stands, however, his remark serves, first, to direct our attention to the fact that the shared tradition of a people is embodied in their language, and secondly, as advice that knowledge of a people's mythology can be obtained by surveying their language. In both respects Wittgenstein here resembles Herder. In his 'Essay on the Origin of Language', Herder is at pains to stress that the language of a people 'is its collective treasure, the source of its social wisdom and communal self-respect' (Herder 1969: 165), and that through that language an individual is linked with past generations. Like Usener, Herder sees the very forms of a people's language as arising from their mythological inheritance:

> Everything is humanized, personified to man and woman; everywhere gods and goddesses act as malicious or benevolent creatures. The roaring storm and the gentle zephyr, the clear spring of water and the mighty ocean – their whole mythology is disclosed in these sources, in the *verba* and *nomina* of the ancient languages. (Herder 1969: 143)

The similarity of this to Wittgenstein's remark is striking. The idea to be culled from this convergence, as well as from all that has gone before, is that for Wittgenstein the distinctive mythology, religious practices and other folkways of a people are part of a tradition which links those people with their ancestors and which is the decisive interconnecting link between members of that community.

Furthermore, as this mythology is taught to each member with the learning of their mother-tongue and is preserved within it, it can be surveyed by considering the ancient elements of that organic phenomenon, a language. It is important to note that this Herderian reading of the comment that 'a whole mythology is deposited in language' is not just *different* from the Nietzschean interpretation offered in Chapter 7, but *opposed*. As Cassirer has shown, the Romantic view that language is 'a faded mythology' is wholly rejected by Müller who, stressing 'the *factual* primacy of verbal concepts over mythic ones' (Cassirer 1953: 85), saw mythology as the *corruption* of those factual concepts. Yet Wittgenstein does appear to give voice to both of these views in the *Remarks*. Whether or not this conflict can be resolved, what is of interest in the clash is the picture it presents of two different types of philosophizing by Wittgenstein. When stressing the Nietzschean side of the contrast, Wittgenstein appears as iconoclast, destroying mythical idols by uncovering their confusions (witness his critique of the scapegoat ritual). It is this destructive intention which is generally attributed to Wittgenstein.[5] Yet the other side of the picture is of the mythological aspects of our language evidencing its depth: we are urged not to destroy these but to respect them. On *this* view, the myths embedded in language constitute the precious *Weltanschauung* of a culture (cf. Spengler 1926: 302). This second view suggests a greater sympathy on Wittgenstein's part with the ancient beliefs, along with the perception that with their decline something of great value is lost. It is with this thought that the final section of this book shall begin.

9.4 CONCLUSION: 'I AM NOT A RELIGIOUS MAN ... '

There is a fundamental disagreement between Wittgenstein and Frazer over the reasons for the decline of religious belief and practice, coupled with an equally strong division over whether this decline is a cause for optimism. A brief analysis of their respective positions on these issues will lead us into consideration of Wittgenstein's view of the modern world. This excursion is not superfluous to the needs of a concluding chapter, since it is precisely Wittgenstein's rejection of the values and concerns of the culture in which he found himself which provides the context for the *Remarks on Frazer* and, indeed, for his own attitude to religion. As Gordon Graham has illustrated, the philosophical presumption which underlies the secularization thesis lies in a broadly Hegelian conception of history as the progressive development of human culture, in which better social forms emerge from inferior ones. Graham understands the secularization thesis as a special application of this framework, bringing with it two significant features entailed by such a progressive vision of history:

> First, the decline of religion is inevitable – it is a phase through which human beings have passed and which they have outgrown. Secondly, the decline of religion is desirable – in leaving religion behind we discard more primitive beliefs and practices and move to more enlightened ones. (Graham 1992: 185)

Such a schema can indeed be found in many discussions of the decline of religion, and is undoubtedly present in the final chapter of *The Golden Bough*, where Frazer's optimism is not disguised. There he describes science as 'a golden key' which can lead man out of the dark labyrinth in which he has been groping for countless ages (Frazer 1922: 712).

The view of the decline of religion held, on the other hand, by Wittgenstein does not fit into the progressive schema and reflects, rather, a vision of history diametrically at odds with Hegel's. Spengler, rejecting 'that empty figment of *one* linear history', saw instead:

> the drama of *a number* of mighty Cultures ... each having *its own* idea, *its own* passions, *its own* life, will and feeling, *its own* death ... Each Culture has its own new possibilities of self-expression which arise, ripen, decay, and never return. (Spengler 1926: 21)

In the stage of decay, 'the Culture suddenly hardens, it mortifies, its blood congeals, its force breaks down and it becomes *Civilization*' (Spengler 1926: 106), characterized by materialism and a tendency toward atheism. In the materialistic winter of a culture (such as, Spengler contends, we are in) the media through which value is expressed become faddish and passionless: 'We go through all the exhibitions, the concerts, the theatres, and find only industrious cobblers and noisy fools, who delight to produce something for the market, something that will "catch on" with a public for whom art and music and drama have long ceased to be spiritual necessities' (Spengler 1926: 293).

The tracing of links between Spengler and Wittgenstein is well-trodden ground which I shall not here traverse.[6] What does need to be noted is the cultural pessimism which we find in Wittgenstein's writings and in which he was so profoundly influenced by *The Decline of the West*. Although rejecting a strict historical determinism (cf. Wittgenstein 1980a: 60), many of the remarks in *Culture and Value* are broadly Spenglerian, and Wittgenstein's description of 'the truly apocalyptic view of the world' reveals just how contemptuous he was of the idea of 'progress':

> It isn't absurd, e.g., to believe that the age of science and technology is the beginning of the end for humanity; that the idea of great progress is a delusion, along with the idea that the truth will ultimately be known; that there is nothing good or desirable about scientific knowledge and that mankind, in seeking it, is falling into a trap. It is by no means obvious that this is not how things are. (Wittgenstein 1980a: 56)

The contrast here between Frazer's view of science as a 'golden key' and Wittgenstein's judgement that it is 'a trap', could not be more stark.

Wittgenstein's contribution to the secularization debate is thus that of turning the secularist conception on its head. The decline of religion may indeed be inevitable, but this is by no means an occasion for rejoicing, for it signifies the collapse of a once-vibrant culture into a materialistic civilization. Religion, for Wittgenstein, declines *not* because its adherents recognize it to be intellectually unsatisfactory or in any other way erroneous. Rather, it declines because the values to which it gives expression are largely absent in an age of decay. To this extent the religion of a culture, like its architecture, acts as a barometer for its values, and as Wittgenstein writes:

> Architecture immortalizes and glorifies something. Hence there can be no architecture where there is nothing to glorify. (Wittgenstein 1980a: 69)

This is an explicit statement of the expression-media thesis, and applied to the question of secularization it provides a radical challenge to the secularist, intellectualist account of the decline of religion.

Moreover, it is Wittgenstein's perception of our culture in decline, and not progressing in an ever-upward movement, which provides us with the key to understanding his personal attitude toward religion. Wittgenstein had a great admiration for religion, yet fell short of embracing the religious life. Famously, he proclaimed: 'I am not a religious man but I cannot help seeing every problem from a religious point of view' (Drury 1984: 79). This enigmatic remark encapsulates two important aspects of Wittgenstein's personal world-view: his awe of religion and ritual, and his feeling that it is in our age impossible to partake in the religious life. We can flesh this out further by once again appealing to Spengler, and to a passage which appears to have profoundly influenced Wittgenstein.

Early on in *The Decline of the West*, Spengler addresses the consequences of living in a period of decline, in which all artistic and architectural possibilities have been exhausted. Should artistically minded individuals appalled by bland civilization fight against the decay surrounding them? Spengler responds in the negative, for 'we have to reckon with the hard cold facts of a *late* life' (Spengler 1926: 40). All that can be pointed out to those individuals is to show them 'what is possible – and therefore necessary – and what is excluded from the inward potentialities of their time' (Spengler 1926: 40). This involves turning away from art to technics and from philosophy to politics.[7] As Heller dramatically summarizes: 'Don't waste your life in the futile agony of trying to realize what you have left of a soul' (Heller 1961: 161). Spengler's lesson was certainly not lost on Wittgenstein, and it was undoubtedly one of the reasons why he continually tried to disengage himself from philosophy. He even described his subject as 'one of the heirs of the subject which used to be called "philosophy"' (Wittgenstein 1969: 28), and his lectures in the early 1930s are evidently informed by the same concern which led Spengler to appeal to the men of his generation to become 'civilized engineers':

The nimbus of philosophy has been lost. For we now have a method of doing philosophy, and can speak of *skilful* philosophers ... But once a method has been found the opportunities for the expression of personality are correspondingly restricted. The tendency of our age is to restrict such opportunities; this is characteristic of an age of declining culture or without culture. (Wittgenstein 1980b: 21)

Reflection on this should lead us to suggest that although his followers tend to speak of the production of a new philosophical method as Wittgenstein's great triumph, Wittgenstein himself saw this creation as being only another necessity entailed by the decline of a culture. As Bouveresse says, far from being rabidly anti-metaphysical, 'everything leads to the belief that he would have preferred to live in an age where philosophy was able to produce something more grandiose and more exalting' (Bouveresse 1991: 14). Wittgenstein, then, was convinced, as Spengler was, that someone living in 'an age of declining culture' could not endeavour to produce anything which exceeded the possibilities of the time.

Just as this was held to be true of art, architecture and philosophy, Wittgenstein held it to be true of religious belief and practice. Thus he wrote that certain religious feelings were incompatible with the scientific spirit of the age (cf. Wittgenstein 1980a: 5). Just as one must temper one's artistic impulses to suit the exhausted possibilities of our time, so one's religious impulses must be curtailed, for they can be nothing other than fraudulent. Spengler writes:

The megalopolitan *is* irreligious; this is part of his being, a mark of his historical position. Bitterly as he may feel the inner emptiness and poverty, earnestly as he may long to be religious, it is out of his power to be so. All religiousness in the Megalopolis rests upon self-deception. (Spengler 1926: 409–10)

If Spengler's reasoning was accepted by Wittgenstein, then we are able to construct a plausible interpretation of the 'religious point of view' remark. Wittgenstein, with his passionate feeling for religion and, perhaps, longing for salvation, could not but view every problem confronting him from a religious perspective. Yet an acceptance of Spengler's thesis (which informed his views of music, art and architecture, as well as dictating the limits of his philosophical programme), would have made him unable to embrace religious dogmas and rites.

In addition to enabling us to understand Wittgenstein's personal religious stance, a grasp of the extent to which his reflections were permeated by the thought of *decline* also helps to frame the context of the *Remarks on Frazer*. For if anything was to arouse Wittgenstein's contempt for a twentieth-century thinker (and a scientifically minded one at that) it would be the contention that the civilized West stood at the apex of human development. It is Frazer's unbridled optimism at the end of *The Golden Bough* which contrasts so sharply with the vision which Wittgenstein culled from Spengler.[8] Frazer too often speaks of the ancient rituals as a monstrous farrago of error and suffering, the waning of which can be only of benefit to mankind. These attitudes contrast sharply with those of Wittgenstein, who sees in the loss of religious practice a terrible tragedy. This encapsulates the contention, not just that with the loss of a religious perspective goes one way of viewing the world, but also that this loss is symptomatic of a corresponding lack of *passion* in the culture, that atheism signifies a 'decline into the inorganic' (Spengler 1926: 408). True, the passionate expressions we find in religion often cause great suffering, but, Wittgenstein contends, there is something marvellous in the intensity of such actions.[9]

Regardless of the acceptability of Wittgenstein's views on this matter, this is certainly what lies at the root of his criticisms of Frazer. Faith, said Wittgenstein, is a *passion* (Wittgenstein 1980a: 53), and such a pre-reflective and passionate activity as he perceives religion to be is truly difficult to understand in an age which is essentially passionless and rationalistic. In Frazer, Wittgenstein discerns a figure fully representative of the modern age, lacking in passion and spirituality, and intent upon understanding everything in terms of the dominant fad of the culture: scientific progress. For 'in the darkness of this time', where science dominates, it would be only too likely that an account of the religious life of human beings would be drawn in terms of purported utility; an account which would see it as the early, but now outdated and bankrupt, exercise of instrumental reason. The concept of natural piety stands full square against this presumption of intellectualism. Ritual actions are not the result of a long process of hypothesizing, but are the spontaneous expressions of a passionate and ceremonial animal. Wittgenstein saw the intellectualist account as a radical misunderstanding of the nature of ritual actions: to say that they are based on opinions or theories is to be in thrall to the debilitating rationalism typical of our age.

In attacking Frazer, then, Wittgenstein was launching a broadside against the presumptions of a declining yet conceited culture, characterized by Ernst as 'today's banal world' (Ernst 1910: 272). The triumph of the *Remarks on Frazer* is that this attack emerges from a deeply profound meditation on the nature of rites which an enlightened Westerner will tend to see as barbaric. Wittgenstein approaches such practices, not with scorn, but with wonderment, stressing the strange and awesome aspect of human life which we in the modern world are in peril of losing, or have already lost. In a conversation with Bouwsma, Wittgenstein said:

> In the city, streets are nicely laid out. And you drive on the right and you have traffic lights, etc. There are rules. When you leave the city, there are still roads, but no traffic lights. And when you get far off there are no roads, no lights, no rules, nothing to guide you. It's all woods. And when you return to the city you may feel that the rules are wrong, that there should be no rules, etc. (Bouwsma 1986: 35)

And it is this kind of view which informs Wittgenstein's critique of Frazer. Although the *Remarks on Frazer's Golden Bough* are of significance for the philosophy of religion and the study of religion in general, this is perhaps not their predominant worth. What Wittgenstein is elucidating is a vision of human nature and of human culture radically distinct from the rationalist glosses of our time. In place of the 'city', Wittgenstein recommends the 'woods'; that wilderness of passionate ritual action which contrasts so sharply with the cheaply wrapped vapidity of a megalopolitan existence.

Notes

1 Wittgenstein, Frazer and Religion

1. Barrett's book is nearly three hundred pages long, and yet only ten pages are devoted to the *Remarks on Frazer* – the same amount which is given to a discussion of the rather more marginal matter of predestination. For an evaluation of *Wittgenstein on Ethics and Religious Belief* involving further discussion of these matters, see Clack 1992: 577–9.
2. The third edition ran to eleven volumes by 1915. Including the volume incorporating an extensive bibliography and index, and *Aftermath*, added in 1936, we have a total of thirteen.
3. Much of *The Golden Bough* can be read as a veiled attack on Christianity, with Christ's death and resurrection implicitly linked with other dying and rising gods of the ancient near-east, and with the pagan veneration of the death and subsequent rebirth of the corn. In the second edition, this attack becomes explicit, and Jesus is characterized as having been killed as part of a barbaric Semitic custom performed at Purim (cf. Frazer 1900 : iii 138–200). 'The sceptic', says Frazer, 'will reduce Jesus of Nazareth to the level of a multitude of other victims of a barbarous superstition' (1900: iii 198).
4. Frazer's distinction between magic and religion is not rigidly followed in this book and, except in obvious cases, 'religion' is generally employed to refer to the whole field of ritual phenomena. The principal reason for this is that Wittgenstein himself does not seek to distinguish the two. (Though see also Tambiah 1990: 18–24 for an account of why the magic/religion distinction cannot be thought to possess universal applicability.)
5. It is very unlikely that they did ever meet. When Wittgenstein first came to Cambridge he was simply an affiliated student, and there would have been little occasion for Frazer to meet him, while on Wittgenstein's return in the late 1920s, Frazer would have been largely absent, for in 1914 he moved to London and never lived permanently in Cambridge again. Neither man was by nature gregarious, and so a meeting could only have come about through a formal introduction. The obvious candidate to perform this duty would have been Russell, but relations between him and Frazer must have been frosty. As Frazer's biographer, Robert Ackermann, informs me, one of the times Frazer did return to Cambridge was in 1916, when he voted to strip Russell of his lectureship following the latter's conscientious objection to the Great War. Hence, 'if Frazer associated Wittgenstein

in any way with Russell, that definitely would have dissuaded him from meeting Wittgenstein after the War if the occasion ever presented itself' (private correspondence 6.7.93). (I am grateful to Robert Fraser for further information regarding this; information which, again, points to the improbability of an encounter.)

6. Wittgenstein maintained that while a very clever man may be shallow, only a deep thinker can be a true philosopher (cf. Drury 1984: 80).

2 Wittgenstein's 'Expressivism'

1. Wittgenstein is adamant that primitive peoples do not believe that rain-makers can alter the course of the weather, or that magicians have any special powers whatsoever. The sentiments of his remark on the African rain-king are repeated in another comment, which functions as a criticism of Frazer's statement that: 'At a certain stage of early society the king or priest is often thought to be endowed with supernatural powers or to be an incarnation of a deity, and consistently with this belief the course of nature is supposed to be more or less under his control, and he is held responsible for bad weather, failure of the crops, and similar calamities' (Frazer 1922: 168). Wittgenstein's response runs as follows:

    > It is, of course, not so that the people believe that the ruler has these powers, and the ruler knows very well that he doesn't have them, or can only fail to know it if he is an imbecile or a fool. (1979c: 73)

    It is remarkable that Wittgenstein does not think for one moment that people could believe that a ruler has supernatural powers. Within our own isles it was firmly believed that the king could cure scrofula (the 'king's evil'). Keith Thomas, who records how popular 'touching for the evil' was (between May 1682 and April 1683, 8577 sufferers were touched by Charles II), notes how 'Charles I's sacred touch made Royalist propaganda during the aftermath of the Civil War' (Thomas 1978: 231). People do often seem to believe that kings have remarkable powers (this is, perhaps, one of the many ideas which surround our notion of kingship), and if Wittgenstein really thinks that people are 'too sensible' to think such things, then he is even more of a rationalist than Frazer himself. Even now, some people hold television weather forecasters responsible for bad weather, and such tendencies are far more widespread than Wittgenstein seems to credit.

2. Wittgenstein's idea of metaphor, as expressed in this comment, is too narrow. It is not so that *all* metaphors are translatable, and Janet Martin Soskice (1987: 93–6) has described certain ways in which some metaphors may be said to be 'irreducible'. The force of Wittgenstein's point remains unchanged.

3 The Possibility of Expressivism

1. The distinction between 'beliefs' and 'attitudes' is drawn by Stevenson in his reflections on what is involved in ethical disagreement, the issue being whether such disagreement 'involves an opposition of beliefs, both of which cannot be true', or whether it 'involves an opposition of attitudes, both of which cannot be satisfied' (Stevenson 1963: 2).

2. Consider a sentence such as 'I am in pain'. In certain circumstances (such as a calm report to a doctor or a dentist), this sentence would undoubtedly function as a description. Yet, Wittgenstein contends, as with all first-person psychological utterances, and particularly avowals (*Äusserungen*) of pain, its origin lies not in a description of a subjective experience, but as a spontaneous *manifestation* of pain. The picture of such utterances presented in the *Investigations* is that an expression such as 'I am in pain' *replaces*, rather than *describes*, the primitive expressions of the sensation of pain, which are, for example, crying and moaning. And as Wittgenstein is quick to remind us, 'You couldn't call moaning a description!' (Wittgenstein 1971: 258). What emerges from this is that although the sentence 'I am in pain', when uttered by an individual, may be true or may be false, it is misleading to say that it functions straightforwardly as a description. As with his remarks on the statement 'I am afraid' (cf. Wittgenstein 1958: 187–8), Wittgenstein would have no difficulty in calling certain uses of 'I am in pain' descriptive, but it is nevertheless important to note that even in these instances the sentence differs greatly from what we may call a 'paradigm case' of description: namely, 'giving a word-picture of perceptible states of affairs' (Hacker 1990: 189). Wittgenstein, in other words, is denying that a description of a pain-sensation is analogous to a description of a room: 'I am in pain' is not read off from an (internal) state of affairs.

3. That Banner's desire to use 'belief' as a category with which to categorize interpretations of religion has certain difficulties can be illustrated further by noting a feature of Rodney Needham's argument in his *Belief, Language, and Experience*. In this Wittgenstein-influenced work, Needham argues against the conception that 'belief' is a universal faculty 'given in human experience' (Needham 1972: 38), one which shares 'a common definitive characteristic' (1972: 111). Consequently, he is sceptical toward the widespread view that 'belief' is a useful tool in ethnological description or conceptual analysis. Needham shows how the English concept of belief (itself 'complex, highly ambiguous, and unstable' (1972: 44)), which is taken to be capable of universal applicability, has been 'formed by a Christian tradition' (1972: 44), and hence has a particular history which entails that it is unsuitable for the general analysis to which it has been employed. Needham also engages in an examination of the polythetic nature of the concept of 'belief', noting that Wittgenstein's investigations 'give us sound reason to think that belief is not a concept in the sense of a class of phenomena defined by

a common feature' (Needham 1972: 119). The import of all this is that if we come to recognize the fundamentally polythetic and historically conditioned character of the concept 'belief' (and, we might add, 'description', 'truth', etc.) we will cease to be tempted to frame hard and fast categories such as those employed by Banner. This is, of course, not to say that such words are not to be used, for they are crucially important. However, they are what Wittgenstein calls 'odd-job' words (Waismann (1968: 59) calls them 'peg-words') and: 'What causes most trouble in philosophy is that we are tempted to describe the use of important "odd-job" words as though they were words with regular functions' (Wittgenstein 1969: 44). We might then say: the descriptive/non-descriptive dichotomy relies on the employment of odd-job words but attributes to them such regular functions as they do not possess.

4 Perspicuous Representation

1. In the 'Big Typescript', Wittgenstein writes: 'As I do philosophy, its entire task consists in expressing myself in such a way that certain troubles //problems// disappear. ((Hertz.))' (Wittgenstein 1993: 181).
2. Hence Wittgenstein's words in *Culture and Value*: 'it is as though [thought] flies above the world and leaves it as it is – observing it from above, in flight' (Wittgenstein 1980a: 5). Two things are worthy of comment here. First, Wittgenstein is in this passage talking about the view of the world *sub specie aeterni*, and the connection between the concept of an *Übersicht* and this mystical view has not gone unremarked (cf. Hallet 1977: 217). Secondly, one could certainly place this explicit statement of the bird's-eye view ideal alongside Roland Barthes' depiction of the structuralist ideal of understanding, occasioned by a view of Paris from the Eiffel Tower. This vision is not purely perceptual, for it adds 'the incomparable power of *intellection*: the bird's-eye view, which each visitor to the Tower can assume in an instant for his own, gives us the world to *read* and not only to perceive' (Barthes 1982: 243; see also the chapter of Hugo's *Notre-Dame de Paris*, significantly entitled 'A Bird's-Eye View of Paris').
3. This may have affinities with the method adopted by Mircea Eliade in *Patterns in Comparative Religion*, where material is accumulated on a great many 'hierophanies', indicating similarities, differences and relations, but without classifying historically (cf. Eliade 1987: 461–2).

6 The Frontiers of the *Remarks*

1. Wittgenstein's stress on the idea of ritual as a 'gesture-language' is found also, and perhaps surprisingly, in the work of the intellectualist anthropologist and formative influence on Frazer, E. B. Tylor. In *Primitive Culture*, Tylor contends that rituals are, in part, 'expressive and symbolic performances, the dramatic utterance of religious thought, the gesture-language of theology' (Tylor 1891: ii 362; cf.

Tylor 1865: 14–82).
2. 'A vow could be called a ceremony' (Wittgenstein 1980d: §581).
3. Iris Murdoch (1992: 338–9) adopts a somewhat similar interpretation when she compares Wittgenstein's attitude in the *Remarks* with that of Socrates, who disregards the issue of whether such-and-such a mythical event actually occurred, for: 'I can't as yet "know myself"...; and so long as that ignorance remains it seems to me ridiculous to inquire into extraneous matters' (Plato 1952: 24). The analogy is not quite correct. Socrates sees reflection on mythical events as a frivolous distraction from the task of self-understanding, whereas Wittgenstein, on Cioffi's view, reflects on rituals *in order* to understand his own nature, Typhonic or otherwise.
4. I owe the distinction between We- and They-discourse to Cioffi. Private correspondence, 24.2.93.

7 'Metaphysics as a Kind of Magic'

1. Chesterton's point might be better stated by substituting for 'irrational' the term 'non-rational' or 'a-rational'.
2. Compare Wittgenstein's thoughts with a remark made by Ernst: '*Eine grandiose Mythologie ist etwa Darwinsche Theorie*' (Ernst 1910: 310). ['Darwinian theory is a grandiose mythology'.]
3. Nietzsche's thought really has only a superficial resemblance to Wittgenstein's as it is explicitly stated in the *Remarks*. Consider both statements in the original German. Nietzsche's idea is expressed thus: '*Es liegt eine philosophische Mythologie in der Sprache versteckt*' (Nietzsche 1967: 185). The important word here is *versteckt*, and as comes over clearly in Hollingdale's translation, this means 'hidden' or 'concealed'. Hence, Nietzsche's remark ascribes to the mythology in language a rather conspiratorial function, hiding in order to mislead us. Wittgenstein's remark, on the other hand, suggests a rather different notion. He writes: '*In unserer Sprache ist eine ganze Mythologie niedergelegt*' (Wittgenstein 1967: 242). Here the important word is *niedergelegt*. A. C. Miles translates this as 'deposited', but John Beversluis' 'stored' is probably better. Seen in this way the difference between the two remarks is quite marked, for Wittgenstein seems to be referring to a feature of language which gives witness to its great age. It is almost a geological metaphor. There are features of the *Remarks* which undoubtedly manifest the Nietzschean insight, yet this *particular* comment is worthy of a separate – and different – interpretation. This will be offered in the concluding chapter.
4. The Big Typescript (TS 213 in the von Wright catalogue) was constructed by Wittgenstein in 1933. He draws on a number of earlier manuscripts, including MS 110, in which the first set of notes on Frazer are found. In the (Ernstian) section on 'The Mythology in the Forms of our Language', Wittgenstein culls a number of passages from the *Remarks*. These are: his comments on the gesture language; on the scapegoat; on our kinship with Frazer's savages; on 'Carrying

out Death'; and the *niedergelegt* remark. It is significant that in this typescript Wittgenstein distinguishes between the mythology in our language and what he calls the 'traps of language' (Wittgenstein 1993: 183). Nietzsche makes no such distinction: for him 'traps' and 'mythology' seem to be equivalent.

5.   In the form in which it appears in the Big Typescript, Wittgenstein ends this remark in the following manner: '(Plato.)' (Wittgenstein 1993: 199).

6.   For examples of name-magic, see Clodd 1898: 79–113; Clodd 1920: *passim*; Frazer 1922: 244–62.

8 Frazerian Reflections

1.   Wittgenstein is alluding to the tale of 'Clever Else', collected by Jacob and Wilhelm Grimm. The eponymous heroine of this story, sent to collect beer from her father's cellar, forgets her task, for, spying a pickaxe suspended above the beer-barrel, she laments: 'If I marry Hans, and we have a child, and it grows big, and we send it here to draw beer, that pickaxe might fall on its head and kill it' (Grimm 1993: 526). Else's worries are forward-looking; those of the person contentiously piecing together the sinister history of a physiognomically harmless practice are backward-looking.

2.   This episode does not occur in the *Nibelungenlied*. What Wittgenstein is (presumably) thinking of is the moment in Wagner's *Der Ring des Nibelungen* where Siegfried's parents, Siegmund and Sieglinde, first encounter one another and experience the feeling of having previously met. Hence the words of Sieglinde: 'A marvel stirs in my memory: although you came but today, I've seen your face before' (Wagner 1976: 92; cf. Coveos 1990: 518–21).

3.   Dylan: 'You don't need a weatherman to know which way the wind blows'.

9 'The Collapse into the Inorganic'

1.   Holiday (1985: 137) is over-hasty in claiming that Wittgenstein is here employing the form of life conceit. When Wittgenstein refers to the 'community of life' in which man and the oak were united, he uses the word *Lebensgemeinschaft* and not *Lebensform*.

2.   'I do not mean that it is especially *fire* that must make an impression on anyone. Fire no more than any other phenomenon, and one will impress this person and another that. For no phenomenon is particularly mysterious in itself, but any of them can become so to us, and it is precisely the characteristic feature of the awakening human spirit that a phenomenon has meaning for it' (Wittgenstein 1979b: 7).

3.   Significantly, an earlier variant of the thought that 'to imagine a language is to imagine a form of life' (Wittgenstein 1958: §19) reads:

'Imagine a language (and that means again a culture) ...' (Wittgenstein 1969: 134).

4. 'A language which had not "grown organically" seemed to [Wittgenstein] not only useless but despicable' (Carnap 1967a: 35).

5. Wittgenstein himself concedes that his enterprise 'seems only to destroy everything interesting, that is, all that is great and important' (Wittgenstein 1958: §118). Even more starkly: 'I destroy, I destroy, I destroy' (Wittgenstein 1980a: 21).

6. On these affinities see: Bloor 1983: 162–7; Bouveresse 1991: 20–5; Haller 1988: 74–89; Hilmy 1987: 83–6, 260–3, 299–301; Wright 1982b: 115–18.

7. Wittgenstein's remark that 'in times like these, genuine strong characters simply leave the arts aside and turn to other things' (1980a: 6) is evidently inspired by Spengler.

8. Frazer's optimism is comparable to that expressed by Carnap in the preface to *The Logical Structure of the World*. There Carnap expounds the 'basic scientific attitude' of the Vienna Circle, saying that the work of the group is 'carried by the faith that this attitude will win the future' (Carnap 1967b: xviii). It is precisely this preface (written in 1928) which was before Wittgenstein's mind when he drafted *his* foreword to the *Philosophical Remarks*. There, repugnance at the scientific attitude is expressed (cf. Hilmy 1987: 213–14; Wittgenstein 1980a: 6–7).

9. Wittgenstein's admiration for such intensity is shown in the following remark, related by Drury:

> The Cathedral of St Basil in the Kremlin is one of the most beautiful buildings I have ever seen. There is a story – I don't know whether it is true but I hope it is – that when Ivan the Terrible saw the completed cathedral he had the architect blinded so that he would never design anything more beautiful. (Drury 1984: 165)

'What a *wonderful* way of showing his admiration!' he added (Rhees 1984: 224). Illuminatingly, Rhees compares this example of Wittgenstein's respect for passionate expression with his treatment of the Beltane festival.

Bibliography

Ackerman, R. (1990) *J. G. Frazer: His Life and Work*, Cambridge: Cambridge University Press.

Anderson, R. J., J. A. Hughes and W. W. Sharrock (1984) 'Wittgenstein and Comparative Sociology', *Inquiry* vol. 27 no. 3, pp. 268–76.

Anon (1905) *Gesta Romanorum*, London: George Bell & Sons.

Aubrey, J. (1972) *The Remaines of Gentilisme and Judaisme*, in *Three Prose Works*, Fontwell: Centaur Press.

Ayer, A. J. (1971) *Language, Truth and Logic*, Harmondsworth: Penguin.

—— (1986) *Ludwig Wittgenstein*, Harmondsworth: Penguin.

Baker, G. P. (1986) 'Philosophy: Simulacram and Form', in S. G. Shanker (ed.), *Philosophy in Britain Today*, Albany: State University of New York Press, pp. 1–57.

—— (1991) '*Philosophical Investigations* section 122: neglected aspects', in R. L. Arrington and H. Glock (eds.), *Wittgenstein's Philosophical Investigations*, London: Routledge, pp. 35–68.

Baker, G. P. and P. M. S. Hacker (1984a) *An Analytical Commentary on Wittgenstein's Philosophical Investigations*, Oxford: Basil Blackwell.

—— (1984b) *Wittgenstein: Meaning and Understanding*, Oxford: Basil Blackwell.

—— (1985) *Language, Sense and Nonsense*, Oxford: Basil Blackwell.

—— (1988) *Wittgenstein: Rules, Grammar and Necessity*, Oxford: Basil Blackwell.

Banner, M. C. (1990) *The Justification of Science and the Rationality of Religious Belief*, Oxford: Clarendon Press.

Barrett, C. (1991) *Wittgenstein on Ethics and Religious Belief*, Oxford: Basil Blackwell.

Barthes, R. (1982) 'The Eiffel Tower', in S. Sontag (ed.), *A Barthes Reader*, London: Jonathan Cape, pp. 236–50.

Bartley, W. W. (1977) *Wittgenstein*, London: Quartet.

Bastian, A. (1895) *Ethnische Elementargedanken in der Lehre vom Menschen*, Berlin: Weidmann.

Baum, W. (1980) 'Ludwig Wittgenstein's World View', *Ratio* vol. 22 no. 1, pp. 64–74.

Beattie, J. H. M. (1966) *Other Cultures*, London: Routledge & Kegan Paul.

—— (1970) 'On Understanding Ritual', in B. R. Wilson (ed.), *Rationality*, Oxford: Basil Blackwell, pp. 240–68.

Bell, R. H. (1978) 'Understanding the Fire-Festivals: Wittgenstein and Theories in Religion', *Religious Studies* vol. 14 no. 1, pp. 113–24.

—— (1984) 'Wittgenstein's Anthropology: Self-understanding and Understanding Other Cultures', *Philosophical Investigations*, vol. 7 no. 4, pp. 295–312.

Bloor, D. (1983) *Wittgenstein: A Social Theory of Knowledge*, London: Macmillan.

Boltzmann, L. (1974) *Theoretical Physics and Philosophical Problems*, Boston: Reidel.

Borges, J. L. (1985) *Doctor Brodie's Report*, Harmondsworth: Penguin.

Bouveresse, J. (1991) '"The Darkness of this Time": Wittgenstein and the Modern World', in A. P. Griffiths (ed.), *Wittgenstein Centenary Essays*, Cambridge: Cambridge University Press, pp. 11–39.

Bouwsma, O. K. (1986) *Wittgenstein: Conversations 1949–1951*, Indianapolis: Hackett Publishing Company.

Braithwaite, R. B. (1971) 'An Empiricist's View of the Nature of Religious Belief', in B. Mitchell (ed.), *The Philosophy of Religion*, Oxford: Oxford University Press, pp. 72–91.

Brand, J. (1848) *Observations on the Popular Antiquities of Great Britain* (3 vols.), London: Henry Bohn.

Branston, B. (1974) *The Lost Gods of England*, London: Thames & Hudson.

Browne, T. (1927) *Religio Medici*, Edinburgh: John Grant.

Buchan, J. (1916) *The Power House*, London: Blackwood.

Burkert, W. (1979) *Structure and History in Greek Mythology and Ritual*, Berkeley: University of California Press.

Byrne, P. A. (1989) *Natural Religion and the Nature of Religion*, London: Routledge.

Carnap, R. (1935) *Philosophy and Logical Syntax*, London: Routledge & Kegan Paul.

—— (1967a) 'From his "Autobiography"', in K. T. Fann (ed.), *Ludwig Wittgenstein: The Man and his Philosophy*, Sussex: Harvester Press.

—— (1967b) *The Logical Structure of the World*, London: Routledge & Kegan Paul.

Cassirer, E. (1953) *Language and Myth*, New York: Dover.

Cherry, C. (1976) 'Explanation and Explanation by Hypothesis', *Synthese* vol. 33 no. 4, pp. 315–39.

Cherry, C. (1984) 'Knowing the Past', *Philosophical Investigations* vol. 7 no. 4, pp. 265–80.
—— (1985) 'Meaning and the Idol of Origins', *Philosophical Quarterly* vol. 35 no. 138, pp. 58–69.
Chesterton, G. K. (1905) *Heretics*, London: John Lane.
—— (1930) *The Everlasting Man*, London: Hodder & Stoughton.
—— (1939) 'The Priest of Spring', in *Selected Essays*, London: Collins, pp. 199–204.
—— (1961) *Orthodoxy*, London: Fontana.
Churchill, J. (1984) 'Wittgenstein on the Phenomena of Belief', *International Journal for Philosophy of Religion* vol. 16 no. 2, pp. 139–52.
—— (1992) 'Something Deep and Sinister', *Modern Theology* vol. 8 no. 1, pp. 15–37.
Cioffi, F. (1969) 'Wittgenstein's Freud', in P. Winch (ed.), *Studies in the Philosophy of Wittgenstein*, London: Routledge & Kegan Paul, pp. 184—210.
—— (1981) 'Wittgenstein and the Fire-Festivals', in I. Block (ed.), *Perspectives on the Philosophy of Wittgenstein*, Oxford: Basil Blackwell, pp. 212–37.
—— (1984) 'When Do Empirical Methods Bypass "The Problems Which Trouble Us"?', in A. P. Griffiths (ed.), *Philosophy and Literature*, Cambridge: Cambridge University Press, pp. 155–72.
—— (1988) 'Explanation, Understanding, and Solace', *New Literary History* vol. 19, pp. 337–60.
—— (1990a) 'Wittgenstein and Obscurantism', *Proceedings of the Aristotelian Society*, Supplementary Volume 64, pp. 1–23.
—— (1990b) 'Wittgenstein on Making Homeopathic Magic Clear', in R. Gaita (ed.), *Value and Understanding*, London: Routledge & Kegan Paul, pp. 42–71.
Clack, B. R. (1992) 'Review of *Wittgenstein on Ethics and Religious Belief* by C. Barrett', *Religious Studies* vol. 28 no. 4, pp. 577–9.
—— (1995) 'D. Z. Phillips, Wittgenstein and Religion', *Religious Studies* vol. 31 no. 1, pp. 111–20.
—— (1996) 'Wittgenstein and Expressive Theories of Religion', *International Journal for Philosophy of Religion* vol. 40 no. 1, pp. 47–61.
Clodd, E. (1898) *Tom Tit Tot*, London: Duckworth.
—— (1920) *Magic in Names*, London: Duckworth.
Collingwood, R. G. (1946) *The Idea of History*, Oxford: Clarendon Press.
—— (1958) *The Principles of Art*, Oxford: Oxford University Press.

Conrad, J. (1983) *Heart of Darkness*, Harmondsworth: Penguin.
—— (1992) *The Rover*, Oxford: Oxford University Press.
Cook, J. W. (1983) 'Magic, Witchcraft, and Science', *Philosophical Investigations* vol. 6 no. 1, pp. 2–36.
Coveos, C. M. (1990) 'Wittgenstein on Frazer's *Golden Bough*', *Philosophy* vol. 65 no. 254, pp. 518–21.
Davies, P. (1983) 'Remarks on Wittgenstein's "Remarks on Frazer's *The Golden Bough*"', *King's Theological Review* vol. 6 no. 1, pp. 10–14.
Dilman, I. (1974) 'Wittgenstein on the Soul' in G. Vesey (ed.), *Understanding Wittgenstein*, London: Macmillan, pp. 162–92.
—— (1987) *Love and Human Separateness*, Oxford: Basil Blackwell.
Douglas, M. (1978) 'Judgments on James Frazer', *Daedalus* vol. 107, pp. 151–64.
Drury, M. O'C. (1973) *The Danger of Words*, London: Routledge & Kegan Paul.
—— (1984) 'Some Notes on Conversations with Wittgenstein' and 'Conversations with Wittgenstein', in R. Rhees (ed.), *Recollections of Wittgenstein*, Oxford: Oxford University Press, pp. 76–171.
Eldridge, R. (1987) 'Hypotheses, Criterial Claims, and Perspicuous Representations: Wittgenstein's "Remarks on Frazer's *The Golden Bough*"', *Philosophical Investigations* vol. 10 no. 3, pp. 226–45.
Eliade, M. (1987) *Patterns in Comparative Religion*, London: Sheed & Ward.
Engelmann, P. (1968) *Letters from Ludwig Wittgenstein with a Memoir*, New York: Horizon Press.
Ernst, P. (1910) 'Nachwort', in J. and W. Grimm, *Kinder-und Hausmärchen* (vol. 3), Berlin: Propyläen Verlag, pp. 271–314.
Evans-Pritchard, E. E. (1965) *Theories of Primitive Religion*, Oxford: Oxford University Press.
—— (1976) *Witchcraft, Oracles and Magic among the Azande*, Oxford: Oxford University Press.
Flaherty, R. P. (1992) '"Todaustragen": The Ritual Expulsion of Death at Mid-Lent – History and Scholarship', *Folklore* vol. 103 no. 1, pp. 40–55.
Fraser, R. (1990) *The Making of The Golden Bough*, London: Macmillan.
Frazer, J. G. (1900) *The Golden Bough* (2nd edition, 3 vols.), London: Macmillan.
—— (1909) *Psyche's Task*, London: Macmillan.
—— (1922) *The Golden Bough* (abridged edition), London: Macmillan.

—— (1923) *Folk-lore in the Old Testament*, London: Macmillan.
—— (1936) *The Golden Bough* (3rd edition, 13 vols.), London: Macmillan. Consisting of:
—— (1936a) *The Magic Art and the Evolution of Kings* (vol. 1).
—— (1936b) *The Magic Art and the Evolution of Kings* (vol. 2).
—— (1936c) *Taboo and the Perils of the Soul.*
—— (1936d) *The Dying God.*
—— (1936e) *Adonis Attis Osiris* (vol. 1).
—— (1936f) *Adonis Attis Osiris* (vol. 2).
—— (1936g) *Spirits of the Corn and of the Wild* (vol. 1).
—— (1936h) *Spirits of the Corn and of the Wild* (vol. 2).
—— (1936i) *The Scapegoat.*
—— (1936j) *Balder the Beautiful* (vol. 1).
—— (1936k) *Balder the Beautiful* (vol. 2).
—— (1936l) *Bibliography and General Index.*
—— (1936m) *Aftermath: A Supplement to The Golden Bough.*
Fustel de Coulanges, N. (1979) *The Ancient City*, Gloucester: Peter Smith.
Ginzburg, C. (1990) *Ecstasies*, London: Hutchinson Radius.
Girard, R. (1977) *Violence and the Sacred*, Baltimore: Johns Hopkins University Press.
Glebe-Møller, J. (1988) 'Two Views of Religion in Wittgenstein', in R. H. Bell (ed.), *The Grammar of the Heart*, San Francisco: Harper & Row, pp. 98–111.
Goethe, J. W. (1970) *Italian Journey*, Harmondsworth: Penguin.
—— (1986) *Selected Verse*, Harmondsworth: Penguin.
Graham, G. (1992) 'Religion, Secularization and Modernity', *Philosophy* vol. 67 no. 260, pp. 183–97.
Grimm, J. and W. (1993) *Complete Fairy Tales*, New York: Barnes & Noble.
Hacker, P. M. S. (1986) *Insight and Illusion*, Oxford: Oxford University Press.
—— (1990) *Wittgenstein: Meaning and Mind*, Oxford: Basil Blackwell.
—— (1992) 'Developmental Hypotheses and Perspicuous Representations: Wittgenstein on Frazer's *Golden Bough*', *Iyyun* vol. 41 no. 3, pp. 277–99.
Haller, R. (1988) *Questions on Wittgenstein*, London: Routledge & Kegan Paul.
Hallet, G. (1977) *A Companion to Wittgenstein's 'Philosophical Investigations'*, Ithaca: Cornell University Press.

Hallpike, C. R. (1979) *The Foundations of Primitive Thought*, Oxford: Clarendon Press.

Hegel, G. W. F. (1956) *The Philosophy of History*, New York: Dover.

—— (1991) *Elements of the Philosophy of Right*, Cambridge: Cambridge University Press.

Heller, E. (1961) *The Disinherited Mind*, Harmondsworth: Penguin.

Herder, J. G. (1969) 'Essay on the Origin of Language', in F. M. Barnard (ed.), *J. G. Herder on Social and Political Culture*, Cambridge: Cambridge University Press, pp. 115–77.

Hertz, H. (1956) *The Principles of Mechanics*, New York: Dover.

High, D. M. (1990) 'Wittgenstein: On Seeing Problems from a Religious Point of View', *International Journal for Philosophy of Religion* vol. 28 no. 2, pp. 105–17.

Hilmy, S. S. (1987) *The Later Wittgenstein*, Oxford: Basil Blackwell.

Hogg, G. (1958) *Cannibalism and Human Sacrifice*, London: Robert Hale.

Hole, C. (1940) *English Folklore*, London: Batsford.

Holiday, A. (1985) 'Wittgenstein's Silence: Philosophy, Ritual and the Limits of Language', *Language and Communication* vol. 5 no. 2, pp. 133–42.

Hone, W. (1826) *The Everyday Book and Table Book*, London: William Tegg.

Horton, R. (1970) 'African Traditional Thought and Western Science', in B. R. Wilson (ed.), *Rationality*, Oxford: Basil Blackwell, pp. 131–71.

Hudson, W. D. (1968) *Ludwig Wittgenstein: The Bearing of his Philosophy upon Religious Belief*, London: Lutterworth Press.

—— (1975) *Wittgenstein and Religious Belief*, London: Macmillan.

Hugo, V. (1987) *Notre-Dame of Paris*, Harmondsworth: Penguin.

Hume, D. (1987) *A Treatise of Human Nature*, Harmondsworth: Penguin.

Hunter, J. F. M. (1971) 'Forms of Life in Wittgenstein's *Philosophical Investigations*', in E. D. Klemke (ed.), *Essays on Wittgenstein*, Chicago: University of Illinois Press, pp. 273–97.

Hutton, R. (1996) *The Stations of the Sun*, Oxford: Oxford University Press.

Jahoda, G. (1970) *The Psychology of Superstition*, Harmondsworth: Penguin.

Janik, A. (1979) 'Wittgenstein, Ficker, and Der Brenner', in C. G. Luckhardt (ed.), *Wittgenstein: Sources and Perspectives*, Hassocks: Harvester Press, pp. 161–89.

Janik, A. and S. Toulmin (1973) *Wittgenstein's Vienna*, New York: Simon & Schuster.

Johnston, P. (1989) *Wittgenstein and Moral Philosophy*, London: Routledge & Kegan Paul.

Kamenka, E. (1970) *The Philosophy of Ludwig Feuerbach*, London: Routledge & Kegan Paul.

Keightley, A. (1976) *Wittgenstein, Grammar and God*, London: Epworth Press.

Kenny, A. (1982) 'Wittgenstein on the Nature of Philosophy', in B. McGuinness (ed.), *Wittgenstein and his Times*, Oxford: Basil Blackwell, pp. 1–26.

Kerr, F. (1986) *Theology after Wittgenstein*, Oxford: Basil Blackwell.

Leach, E. R. (1961) 'Golden Bough or Gilded Twig?', *Daedalus* vol. 90, pp. 371–87.

—— (1985) 'The Anthropology of Religion: British and French Schools', in N. Smart *et al.* (eds.), *Nineteenth Century Religious Thought in the West*, vol. 3, Cambridge: Cambridge University Press, pp. 215–62.

Lewis, C. S. (1961) *An Experiment in Criticism*, Cambridge: Cambridge University Press.

Lewis, W. (1967) *Blasting and Bombardiering*, London: Eyre & Spottiswoode.

Lorenz, K. (1967) *On Aggression*, London: Methuen.

Lukes, S. (1973) *Emile Durkheim*, London: Allen Lane.

McGuinness, B. (1982) 'Freud and Wittgenstein', in B. McGuinness (ed.), *Wittgenstein and his Times*, Oxford: Basil Blackwell, pp. 27–43.

—— (1988) *Wittgenstein: A Life*, London: Duckworth.

Malcolm, N. (1964a) 'Anselm's Ontological Arguments', in *Knowledge and Certainty*, Englewood Cliffs: Prentice-Hall, pp. 141–62.

—— (1964b) 'Is it a Religious Belief that "God Exists"?', in J. Hick (ed.), *Faith and the Philosophers*, London: Macmillan, pp. 103–10.

—— (1977) 'The Groundlessness of Belief', in *Thought and Knowledge*, Ithaca: Cornell University Press, pp. 199–216.

—— (1981) 'Wittgenstein: The Relation of Language to Instinctive Behaviour', Swansea: University College of Swansea.

—— (1984) *Ludwig Wittgenstein: A Memoir*, Oxford: Oxford University Press.

—— (1986) *Wittgenstein: Nothing is Hidden*, Oxford: Basil Blackwell.

Malcolm, N. (1993) *Wittgenstein: A Religious Point of View?*, London: Routledge & Kegan Paul.

Malinowski, B. (1948) *Magic, Science, and Religion*, New York: Doubleday.

Marett, R. R. (1914) *The Threshold of Religion*, London: Methuen.

—— (1920) *Psychology and Folk-Lore*, London: Methuen.

—— (1928) *Man in the Making*, London: Ernest Benn.

—— (1933) *Sacraments of Simple Folk*, Oxford: Clarendon Press.

Margalit, A. (1992) 'Sense and Sensibility: Wittgenstein on *The Golden Bough*', *Iyyun* vol. 41 no. 3, pp. 301–18.

Monk, R. (1991) *Ludwig Wittgenstein: The Duty of Genius*, London: Vintage.

Moore, G. E. (1959a) 'A Defence of Common Sense', in *Philosophical Papers*, London: George Allen & Unwin, pp. 32–59.

—— (1959b) 'Wittgenstein's Lectures in 1930–33', in *Philosophical Papers*, London: George Allen & Unwin, pp. 252–324.

Morris, B. (1987) *Anthropological Studies of Religion*, Cambridge: Cambridge University Press.

Mounce, H. O. (1973) 'Understanding a Primitive Society', *Philosophy* vol. 48 no. 186, pp. 347–62.

Müller, F. M. (1893) *Introduction to the Science of Religion*, London: Longmans, Green & Co.

—— (1968) 'Comparative Mythology', in R. M. Dorson (ed.), *Peasant Customs and Savage Myths* (vol. 1), Chicago: University of Chicago Press, pp. 67–119.

Murdoch, I. (1992) *Metaphysics as a Guide to Morals*, London: Chatto & Windus.

Needham, R. (1972) *Belief, Language, and Experience*, Oxford: Basil Blackwell.

—— (1985) *Exemplars*, Berkeley: University of California Press.

Nietzsche, F. (1967) *Der Wanderer und sein Schatten*, *Werke* IV 3, Berlin: Walter de Gruyter & Co.

—— (1986) 'The Wanderer and his Shadow', in *Human, All Too Human*, Cambridge: Cambridge University Press, pp. 301–95.

Nyíri, J. C. (1982) 'Wittgenstein's Later Work in Relation to Conservatism', in B. McGuinness (ed.), *Wittgenstein and his Times*, Oxford: Basil Blackwell, pp. 44–68.

Oakeshott, M. J. (1991) *On Human Conduct*, Oxford: Clarendon Press.

O'Hear, A. (1984) *Experience, Explanation and Faith*, London: Routledge & Kegan Paul.

Palmer, A. S. (1882) *Folk-Etymology*, London: George Bell & Sons.

Pascal, F. (1984) 'Wittgenstein: A Personal Memoir', in R. Rhees (ed.), *Recollections of Wittgenstein*, Oxford: Oxford University Press, pp. 12–49.

Phillips, D. Z. (1976) *Religion Without Explanation*, Oxford: Basil Blackwell.

—— (1981) 'Wittgenstein's Full Stop', in I. Block (ed.), *Perspectives on the Philosophy of Wittgenstein*, Oxford: Basil Blackwell, pp. 179–200.

—— (1988) *Faith after Foundationalism*, London: Routledge & Kegan Paul.

Pitkin, H. F. (1972) *Wittgenstein and Justice*, Berkeley: University of California Press.

Plato (1952) *Phaedrus*, Cambridge: Cambridge University Press.

Radcliffe-Brown, A. R. (1952) *Structure and Function in Primitive Society*, London: Routledge & Kegan Paul.

Ray, R. J. (1990) 'Crossed Fingers and Praying Hands: Remarks on Religious Belief and Superstition', *Religious Studies* vol. 26 no.4, pp. 471–82.

Redding, P. (1987) 'Anthropology as Ritual: Wittgenstein's Reading of Frazer's *Golden Bough*', *Metaphilosophy* vol. 18 nos. 3 & 4, pp. 253–69.

Rhees, R. (1971) 'Introductory Note to Remarks on Frazer's *Golden Bough*', *The Human World* no. 3, pp. 18–28.

—— (1979) 'Introductory Note to *Remarks on Frazer's Golden Bough*', Doncaster: Brynmill Press, pp. v–vi.

—— (1982) 'Wittgenstein on Language and Ritual', in B. McGuinness (ed.), *Wittgenstein and his Times*, Oxford: Basil Blackwell, pp. 69–107.

—— (1984) 'Postscript', in R. Rhees (ed.), *Recollections of Wittgenstein*, Oxford: Oxford University Press, pp. 172–209.

—— (1990) '"Ethical Reward and Punishment"', in R. Gaita (ed.), *Value and Understanding*, London: Routledge & Kegan Paul, pp. 179–193.

Ross, A. (1990) *The Folklore of the Scottish Highlands*, London: Batsford.

Rowe, M. W. (1991) 'Goethe and Wittgenstein', *Philosophy* vol. 66 no. 257, pp. 283–303.

Rudich, N. and M. Stassen (1971) 'Wittgenstein's Implied Anthropology: Remarks on Wittgenstein's Notes on Frazer', *History and Theory* vol. 10 no. 2, pp. 84–9.

Russell, B. (1920) Contribution to 'The Meaning of "Meaning"' Symposium, *Mind* vol. 29 no. 116, pp. 398–404.

—— (1986) 'On Scientific Method in Philosophy', in *Collected Papers* vol. 8, London: George Allen & Unwin, pp. 55–73.

Sachs, D. (1988) 'On Wittgenstein's *Remarks on Frazer's Golden Bough'*, *Philosophical Investigations* vol. 11 no. 2, pp. 147–50.

Santayana,G. (1905) *Reason in Religion*, London: Constable.

Schatzki, T. R. (1991) 'Elements of a Wittgensteinian Philosophy of the Human Sciences', *Synthese* vol. 87 no. 2, pp. 311–29.

Schopenhauer, A. (1897) *On Human Nature*, London: Swan Sonnenschein.

Scott, W. (1902) *Minstrelsy of the Scottish Border* (4 vols.), Edinburgh: William Blackwood & Sons.

Sharp, M. (1989) *A Land of Gods and Giants*, Gloucester: Alan Sutton.

Sharpe, E. J. (1986) *Comparative Religion*, London: Duckworth.

Shields, P. R. (1993) *Logic and Sin in the Writings of Ludwig Wittgenstein*, Chicago: University of Chicago Press.

Skorupski, J. M. (1976) *Symbol and Theory*, Cambridge: Cambridge University Press.

Smith, J. Z. (1973) 'When the Bough Breaks', *History of Religions* vol. 12 no. 4, pp. 342–71.

Sontag, F. (1995) *Wittgenstein and the Mystical*, Atlanta: Scholars Press.

Soskice, J. M. (1987) *Metaphor and Religious Language*, Oxford: Clarendon Press.

Spengler, O. (1926) *The Decline of the West: Form and Actuality*, London: George Allen & Unwin.

—— (1928) *The Decline of the West: Perspectives of World-History*, London: George Allen & Unwin.

Stevenson, C. L. (1944) *Ethics and Language*, New Haven: Yale University Press.

—— (1963) *Facts and Values*, New Haven: Yale University Press.

Stewart, W. G. (1823) *The Popular Superstitions and Festive Amusements of the Highlanders of Scotland*, Edinburgh: Archibald Constable.

Swinburne, R. G. (1986) *The Coherence of Theism*, Oxford: Clarendon Press.

Tambiah, S. J. (1990) *Magic, Science, Religion and the Scope of Rationality*, Cambridge: Cambridge University Press.

Thomas, K. (1978) *Religion and the Decline of Magic*, Harmondsworth: Penguin.

Trilling, L. (1966) *Beyond Culture*, London: Secker & Warburg.

Tylor, E. B. (1865) *Researches into the Early History of Mankind*, London: John Murray.

—— (1891) *Primitive Culture* (2 vols.), London: John Murray.

Vickery, J. B. (1973) *The Literary Impact of The Golden Bough*, Princeton: Princeton University Press.

Wagner, R. (1976) *The Ring of the Nibelung*, London: Faber & Faber.

Waismann, F. (1965) *The Principles of Linguistic Philosophy*, London: Macmillan.

—— (1968) *How I See Philosophy*, London: Macmillan.

—— (1979) *Ludwig Wittgenstein and the Vienna Circle*, New York: Barnes & Noble.

Walsh, W. H. (1967) *An Introduction to Philosophy of History*, London: Hutchinson.

Westermarck, E. (1906) *The Origin and Development of the Moral Ideas* (vol. 1), London: Macmillan.

—— (1908) *The Origin and Development of the Moral Ideas* (vol. 2), London: Macmillan.

Winch, P. (1958) *The Idea of a Social Science*, London: Routledge & Kegan Paul.

—— (1967) 'Understanding a Primitive Society', in D. Z. Phillips (ed.), *Religion and Understanding*, Oxford: Basil Blackwell, pp. 9–42.

—— (1987) *Trying to Make Sense*, Oxford: Basil Blackwell.

Wisdo, D. (1993) *The Life of Irony and the Ethics of Belief*, Albany: SUNY.

Wittgenstein, L. (1922) *Tractatus Logico-Philosophicus* (trans. C. K. Ogden), London: Routledge & Kegan Paul.

—— (1956) *Remarks on the Foundations of Mathematics* (first edition), Oxford: Basil Blackwell.

—— (1958) *Philosophical Investigations*, Oxford: Basil Blackwell.

—— (1961a) *Notebooks 1914–1916*, Oxford: Basil Blackwell.

—— (1961b) *Tractatus Logico-Philosophicus* (trans. D. Pears and B. McGuinness), London: Routledge & Kegan Paul.

—— (1965) 'A Lecture on Ethics', *Philosophical Review* vol. 74 no. 1, pp. 3–12.

—— (1966) *Lectures and Conversations on Aesthetics, Psychology and Religious Belief*, Oxford: Basil Blackwell.

—— (1967) '*Bemerkungen über Frazers The Golden Bough*', *Synthese* vol. 17 no. 3, pp. 233–53.

—— (1969) *The Blue and Brown Books*, Oxford: Basil Blackwell.

—— (1971) 'Notes for Lectures on "Private Experience" and "Sense Data"' in O. R. Jones (ed.), *The Private Language Argument*, London: Macmillan, pp. 232–75.

—— (1973) *Letters to C. K. Ogden*, London: Routledge & Kegan Paul.

—— (1974a) *Letters to Russell, Keynes and Moore*, Oxford: Basil Blackwell.

—— (1974b) *Philosophical Grammar*, Oxford: Basil Blackwell.

—— (1975) *Philosophical Remarks*, Oxford: Basil Blackwell.

—— (1976) 'Cause and Effect: Intuitive Awareness', *Philosophia* vol. 6 nos. 3–4, pp. 409–45.

—— (1977a) *On Certainty*, Oxford: Basil Blackwell.

—— (1977b) *Remarks on Colour*, Oxford: Basil Blackwell.

—— (1978) *Remarks on the Foundations of Mathematics* (third edition), Oxford: Basil Blackwell.

—— (1979a) 'Letters to Ludwig von Ficker', in C. G.Luckhardt (ed.), *Wittgenstein: Sources and Perspectives*, Hassocks: Harvester Press, pp. 82–98.

—— (1979b) *Remarks on Frazer's Golden Bough* (trans. A. C. Miles), Doncaster: Brynmill Press.

—— (1979c) 'Remarks on Frazer's Golden Bough' (trans. John Beversluis), in C. G. Luckhardt (ed.), *Wittgenstein: Sources and Perspectives*, Hassocks: Harvester Press, pp. 61–81.

—— (1980a) *Culture and Value*, Oxford: Basil Blackwell.

—— (1980b) *Wittgenstein's Lectures: Cambridge 1930–1932* (ed. Desmond Lee), Oxford: Basil Blackwell.

—— (1980c) *Remarks on the Philosophy of Psychology* (vol. 1), Oxford: Basil Blackwell.

—— (1980d) *Remarks on the Philosophy of Psychology* (vol. 2), Oxford: Basil Blackwell.

—— (1981) *Zettel*, Oxford: Basil Blackwell.

—— (1982a) *Last Writings on the Philosophy of Psychology* (vol. 1), Oxford: Basil Blackwell.

—— (1982b) *Wittgenstein's Lectures: Cambridge 1932–1935* (ed. Alice Ambrose), Oxford: Basil Blackwell.

—— (1989) *Wittgenstein's Lectures on the Foundations of Mathematics* (ed. Cora Diamond), Chicago: Chicago University Press.

—— (1992) *Last Writings on the Philosophy of Psychology* (vol. 2), Oxford: Basil Blackwell.

—— (1993) 'Philosophy (sections 86–93 of the "Big Typescript")', in *Philosophical Occasions 1912–1951*, Indianapolis: Hackett, pp. 158–99.

Woolley, L. (1954) *Excavations at Ur*, London: Ernest Benn.

Wright, G. H. von (1982a) 'The Wittgenstein Papers', in *Wittgenstein*, Oxford: Basil Blackwell, pp. 35–62.

—— (1982b) 'Wittgenstein in Relation to his Times', in B. McGuinness (ed.), *Wittgenstein and his Times*, Oxford: Basil Blackwell, pp. 108–20.

Index

197